The Daily Telegraph

BOOK OF LETTERS

The Daily Telegraph

BOOK OF LETTERS

Edited by

DAVID TWISTON DAVIES

ROBINSON
London

Robinson Publishing Ltd
7 Kensington Church Court
London W8 4SP

First published in the UK by Robinson Publishing Ltd 1998

A copy of the British Library Cataloguing in Publication data
is available from the British Library

ISBN 1–85487–580–9

Printed and bound in the UK

10 9 8 7 6 5 4 3 2 1

CONTENTS

INTRODUCTION

SIR—Sitting down to write an introduction to this selection of letters published in *The Daily Telegraph* between January 1987 and December 1998, I am conscious of the rare opportunity for a Letters Editor to enjoy that much-heralded modern liberty, a right of reply. Letters Editors are properly an anonymous group. They are little known to each other and totally unknown to readers, except for the few who receive a personal phone call to check a detail in an offering being prepared for publication. Any success they enjoy lies in their necessarily anonymous skill of choosing, cutting and co-ordinating the items of the daily column. Not without consciousness of my presumption, I take this opportunity to salute the readers and explain certain aspects of the task.

Choosing the eleven to twenty letters to appear next day always seems a daunting task in the morning. But the sounds of envelopes from the two daily deliveries of post being slit open, the rasping slide of fresh faxes arriving and the eerie silence of e-mails, with their texts all too often draped in mind-boggling codes, mean that we receive more than 350 letters most days; by lunchtime spirits are usually rising. Each offering is examined and allotted to one of three categories. First, there are those which *must* be printed because of the importance of their ideas and information and, perhaps in some measure, because of who their authors are. Second, there are those which *must not* be run, either because they are clearly erroneous or libellous or perhaps their points could have been made better or earlier by others. They could simply be dull, obscure, too long or irrelevant. Thirdly, there are those which *might* be run. While these are chosen for their undoubted merits, their chance of being printed from the thirty or more put into the computer system by our copytakers depends as much on the way they would fit alongside others, providing variety and appropriateness for the next day's column, as on their individual virtues.

The rule for the public, of course, is that the Letters Editor's decision is final and all but an occasional, foolhardy minority accept this. They realise that their chances of being published can be no more certain than the outcome of a sporting fixture. Nevertheless, it must be said that in the office this rule is stretched. The Editor sends round items which, in his view, must be included. Department heads explain why they think others should be used; and the writers for the paper instinctively *feel* that the column should be filled up with paeans of praise beginning 'May I congratulate—' for his/her accurate/perceptive/brilliant—.

Such a flow of interruptions may not make the work of a single Letters Editor easy; but this is as it should be. The Letters column must be the heart of any newspaper: the point where the minds of readers and staff meet, often with a ringing clash. Special polls can be conducted to elicit public opinion on a particular issue at a certain time, but correspondence is a continuous and public monitor.

However, a Letters column is much more than simply a record of reactions to the news contained in yesterday's paper. Even a desultory skim through this volume will reveal not only reactions to certain events but a central core of belief about the fundamentals of British life. In choosing the letters included here I have had to exclude many fine examples because they were part of a debate which would have to be given in full to show their particular value. Even so, I have been aware in going through the columns of these eleven years that several books could be compiled from those left out. I have also become conscious in a fresh way of the deep concerns of the readers. The first set of letters, which deal with the monarchy, reflect the struggle between the desire to see the royal family retain and deserve their traditional position of respect and the public's belief that it has an inalienable right to be informed about their most intimate secrets. Edward Bishop's account of obtaining a scoop about Princess Elizabeth and her fiancé Prince Philip with the co-operation of Lord Louis Mountbatten makes a chilling contrast to the appalled reactions to the later doings and death of the Princess of Wales.

The fall of Margaret Thatcher provoked a shock wave across the world which prompted Mrs P. E. Sullivan, a true-blue Royalist Tory, to wonder if she should throw herself off Beachy Head, and John Howard, the future Prime Minister of Australia, to make a perceptive assessment of the lady's achievement. It was also a warning of what has emerged as the most important political question of our age: how should the British people be reacting to the creation of a European superstate and its corollary, devolution? Part of the problem is that we still retain close links—historical, political, economic, cultural and personal—with the peoples of the old Empire. That relationship is fundamentally bound up with the concepts of Britishness and the British way of doing things. One reason for this is that the past provides an attractive, admirable and extremely useful yardstick by which to measure the present.

Closely linked to the story of Empire, the Armed Forces provide a good example of an efficient machine, dedicated to maintaining national security. Their members represent standards of decency, demonstrate exemplary selflessness and show how to concentrate on clear goals. They are a source of rich and varied anecdote, such as Colonel Maurice Willoughby's tale of his watch being stolen from a Khartoum housetop and John Ward's memories of using mules in the Mau Mau emergency. Lieutenant-Colonel Jeffery Williams, the Canadian historian, recalls attacks on Allied troops by 'friendly fire' in Normandy while a frothy discussion is conducted on the question of whether servicemen who have been in action father more girls than boys. The half concealed manoeuvres of Brussels bureaucrats will never be able to match these in British hearts, one suspects.

While nobody could deny the vital importance of these issues, it must not be forgotten that most of us are personally concerned with more mundane yet no less absorbing matters in the course of our daily lives. A sprinkling of serious subjects are included. Lord Denning's denunciation of the conviction of an Ohio car worker for crimes supposedly committed as a wartime prison guard sparked off widespread unease about the staging of trials fifty years after the events concerned took place. Fr Ian Ker's answer to the question of what Cardinal Newman would have thought about the General Synod's decision to sanction the ordination of women priests in 1992 helped Anglo-Catholics to identify the direction on which they should focus. However, I have generally concentrated on the lighter aspects of life demonstrated in the Letters column. Literature, language, manners, differences between the sexes as well as country life, dogs, pubs and humour are all strongly represented.

Who are the *Telegraph*'s letter-writers, it is often asked. The ill-informed, traditional view is that our correspondents consist entirely of retired colonels living in Cheltenham. The assertion contains some truth, of course; but those who served under arms in the Second World War are now passing from the scene, and their replacements are far fewer thanks to governments' determination to cash in 'the peace dividend' created by the fall of communism no matter what threats to our security remain. The proper answer is that the typical *Telegraph* letter-writer is anyone who feels that he, or she, has something to add to national debate on issues of interest to the readership. They range from Brian Clifton, proudly declaring that he wears an anorak, to the Duke of Wellington, who enjoys the right to sign himself Prince of Waterloo. Since a letter to a newspaper offers the freedom to write exactly what you like, as you like it, this is an attraction for the professional author as much as for the amateur. Both have only to satisfy the criteria of the Letters Editor who, despite a widely held assumption, is constantly on the look out for fresh subjects, fresh views and fresh writers.

While people like to see distinguished names at the bottom of letters—and it is true that the views of eminent figures deserve respect—no Letters Editor ever satisfied his master for long by putting in worthy yet predictable letters for the sake of their signatures. Inevitably, such letters play some part in the daily column, but they are not included here for those reasons. The former prime minister Sir Edward Heath was not chosen for one of his unflinching pronouncements on the inevitability of our destiny in the European Union but for a protest at the paper's failure to include him in a list of speakers who had drawn MPs into the chamber of the House during the 1980s. Whether they are internationally famed or known only in their own offices, villages or families, all who are published here write with an authority born of knowledge, experience or common sense, though a flash of wit can sometimes command a place in the column with a single obvious or outrageous sentence. On education Nirad Chaudhuri, the Greatest Living Indian, surveys the ill-effects of neglecting the classics, but confident schoolchildren pass clear-sighted judgment on the value of discipline, boarding and mixed-sex establishments. *Telegraph* letter-writers can demonstrate the widest and, sometimes, the oddest views on any subject. Who would have imagined, for instance, that a chance remark by the Libyan leader Colonel Gaddafi would have prompted a long exchange on the burning issue of whether Shakespeare might have been an Arab.

Clearly those who write to us are only a small proportion of the readership at any one time. A few claim to be doing so for the first time since they switched from the *Morning Post* to *The Daily Telegraph* in 1937; some write half a dozen times a year or more on one particular subject; others write every day on every conceivable topic, clearly as part of their post-breakfast routine. All are welcome, though one inevitable rule is that the more you write the higher your chances are of not being published.

Many deserve my special thanks for their support and tolerance. Charles Moore, the Editor, has been an encouraging leader who was responsible for expanding the size of the column and moving it to a more prominent position on the Leader page after his appointment in 1995. His predecessor Max Hastings should be mentioned for dispatching me to the column in the first place, and then having sufficient trust to leave me largely alone to find my feet. Susannah Charlton, the *Telegraph*'s publishing manager, has been an unfailing support with this book, not least in finding me two excellent editorial assistants Jonny Feinberg and Beth Vaughan. I must also pay tribute to my stalwart secretary over the years, the incomparable Dorothy Brown. Last and most important, the biggest thank you must go to the readers: more than one million buyers of the paper every day, who after reading it share their copy with more than the same number within their families and circle of friends. There are also the subscribers of *The Weekly Telegraph*, the Electronic Telegraph and our syndication service to more than forty newspapers in the Commonwealth and beyond. In addition, there are those, often thousands of miles away, whose reaction to an event, such as the attempt to assassinate the Prince of Wales in Sydney or the explosion in the Mall of a bomb, was to send a fax to us in London.

Without all your contributions, loyalty and unflagging interest there would be no Letters column, and probably no *Daily Telegraph* either.

DAVID TWISTON DAVIES
Letters Editor
The Daily Telegraph
London E14

PALACE UNDER SIEGE

Gentlemanly scoop

SIR—Palace dismay at the hounding of the Princess of Wales reminds me of a royal photographic scoop obtained without today's intrusive techniques.

Despatched to Malta as a young foreign correspondent by Ian Fleming, foreign manager of the Kemsley Newspapers Group, to cover a story about the courtship of Princess Elizabeth and Prince Philip 40 years ago, I telephoned Adml Lord Louis Mountbatten, C-in-C Mediterranean Fleet, at his villa. I explained that I needed photographs to satisfy my boss, Cdr Fleming, formerly of Naval Intelligence.

'Difficult,' said Lord Louis, 'but station yourself in Capt Caruana's bar in Valletta at 11 a.m. tomorrow. When you hear somebody whistling. "The Londonderry Air", pop out and have a word with my wife.' I confessed I was not very musical, and Lord Louis kindly gave a rendering on the phone.

In the morning, Lady Louis briefed me to appear with the photographer at the villa the next day.

The result was a magnificent set of pictures of the happy couple dallying by an orange tree in the garden—and then a cable from Fleming saying: 'Chairman delighted. Sending £100 bonus. Take much deserved holiday in Mediterranean.'

EDWARD BISHOP

November 18, 1988   St Leonards-on-Sea, E. Sussex

～

When the Queen Mother gave an interview . . .

SIR—Hugh Montgomery-Massingberd (article, June 29) suggests that Queen Elizabeth the Queen Mother, after nearly 70 years as a member of the Royal Family, is shrewd enough 'to know to whom she is talking and to calculate the risks involved'. Such knowledge was not acquired without experience.

In January 1923, after the announcement of her engagement to the Duke of York, the then Lady Elizabeth Bowes-Lyon agreed to talk to some of the reporters who had been queuing outside her parents' house in Mayfair.

'How kind of you to come,' the *Star* reported her as saying. 'And I am so happy—as you can see for yourself. You ask where is the Duke? Well, Bertie—you know everybody calls him Prince Bertie— has gone out hunting and he won't be back until this evening, when I've no doubt [with a smile] I shall see him.'

Doubtless hardly able to believe their luck, the representatives of the popular press then asked Lady Elizabeth if she was fond of hunting too.

'Oh yes,' she replied, 'but I have done little lately. I play golf— badly—and I am fond of lawn tennis.'

'And so many people know what a beautiful dancer you are.'

'That *is* kind of you to say that . . .'

And so it went innocently on, though some eyebrows were raised by Lady Elizabeth's quoted statement that 'the story he proposed or had to propose three times—well it amused me, and it was news to me'.

The *Daily Sketch* observed that Lady Elizabeth's interviews ('for which . . . both press and public are duly grateful') were 'surely without precedent'. Never before had 'the bride-to-be of a prince of the blood royal established such a link between the teeming millions and the private affairs of the exalted few.'

But, the *Sketch* writer continued, he 'shouldn't be at all surprised to find a complete cessation of these interviews in the very near future'.

So indeed it proved. Down at Sandringham King George V and Queen Mary were not amused. Lady Elizabeth, whether as Duchess of York, Queen Elizabeth or the Queen Mother, never gave another, unscripted, interview.

THOMAS BYRNE
Dublin

July 2, 1990

A nasty, niggling campaign

SIR—A nasty, niggling campaign is under way against the Queen. It is a campaign whipped up by the third-rate tabloid press and by politicians with a ready eye to publicity and self-promotion.

Some are unashamed republicans like the Australian billionaire newspaper tycoon Rupert Murdoch, while others would like to see the British monarchy reduced to the levels of other so-called 'bicycling' monarchies. At a time of recession when everyone is feeling the pinch, they are seeking to ride the wave of the politics of envy and to court cheap popularity by calling on the Queen to pay tax like any other citizen.

What they deliberately and deviously fail to put before the public is the fact that the Royal Family, by assigning revenue from the Crown Estates to Parliament, is currently contributing no less than £60 million a year to the Exchequer, which in addition receives one quarter of the net revenues of the Duchy of Cornwall.

The fact is that the British public and taxpayer get incredible value for money from the Queen, both in her capacity as Head of State and as Head of the Commonwealth. Let no one imagine that a presidency would be any cheaper—indeed, most presidencies are far more expensive. Does anyone believe that a visit to America or Africa by a President Benn, President Steel or President Thatcher—or indeed their children—would inspire the level of interest, acclaim and affection which is showered upon the Queen and members of the Royal Family, who work so tirelessly to promote Britain abroad?

Thanks to our constitutional monarchy and our parliamentary democracy, the British nation has for over 300 years been spared the horrors and bloodshed of revolution, civil war, invasion and dictatorship.

How easy it is to forget the debt we owe our Royal Family. The truth is that the monarchy is a very special institution in which the overwhelming majority of British people take great pride. Let us not take away the mystique by bringing them down to the level of being just 'one of us'.

WINSTON S. CHURCHILL MP (Con)

July 5, 1991   London SW1

Royal Family miss our prayers

SIR—While congratulating you on your leader (June 6) I would like to point out that there is another aspect to the difficulties of the Queen and her family.

Until the past 20 years or so, the church-going section of the nation prayed collectively for the Queen, the Prince of Wales, and all the Royal Family every week at Matins, Evensong or Holy Communion. Now, almost invariably, these prayers are omitted from the traditional services, and some of the new services such as the Rite A Communion service do not include an appropriate prayer at all.

As someone who believes in the power of prayer, I am sure this omission has made much more difficult the Royal Family's task of creating successful relationships and setting a moral example.

That section of the nation who are practising Christians have a duty to pray for all our leaders. If that duty is disregarded, we cannot reasonably expect the Royal Family, with the pressures they face today, to be able to set the example they once did.

(Mrs) VANLA OXLEY
Queen Camel, Som

Monarchy not laid low

SIR—The attack on the Prince of Wales (report, Jan. 26) is not the first made on a member of the Royal Family in Sydney.

In 1868 the first royal visitor to Australia, Prince Alfred, Queen Victoria's second son, was shot by an Irishman while walking in a beachside park. The wound was serious, but Prince Alfred, who had a naval background like the Prince of Wales, survived.

The attack on Prince Charles, which happened beside another of Sydney harbour's little inlets, was by an Australian of Cambodian origin. He wanted to publicise the sufferings of Cambodian refugees in Australian concentration camps, just as the Irishman O'Farrell, in his way, was protesting about Irish grievances.

Apologies reached fever-pitch in 1868, as many Irish Australians hurried to prove their own loyalty to the Crown. A few thought that 'it served the Prince right, he had no business in this country'. But, on the whole, Australians gathered in vast numbers throughout the country to demonstrate their old allegiance.

In 1994 the picture is very different. There is now a very large republican movement, although it has lately lost some of its appeal. Prince Charles is no help to the republican cause. Coming alone, without his wife, has made him look good, like the Prince Charles who came here on his own many times before his marriage. It gives him a substance which he lacked while she was with him.

The attack must help, too. Today there may be no great demonstrations of loyalty. But sudden danger has given an immediacy to monarchy which it often lacks, especially in Australia. Prince Charles was not laid low in any sense, and it seems less and less likely that the monarchy will be laid low either.

Prof ALAN ATKINSON
January 28, 1994   Armidale, New South Wales

~

Wodehouse backed a royal couple

SIR—The Press Complaints Commission's criticism of the tabloids for photographing Prince Edward and his girlfriend (report, May 26) brings to mind a 1906 poem by P. G. Wodehouse which demonstrates that the problem is not new.

Thoughts on a Recent Wooing was prompted by the engagement of Queen Victoria's granddaughter Princess Victoria-Eugenie to King Alphonso XIII of Spain. Its last verse runs:

> *But when a royal couple woo,*
> *It can't be done in private:*
> *For thousands rally round to view*
> *If they can but contrive it.*
> *With cameras behind the trees*
> *Reporters cut their capers.*
> *He gives her hand a tender squeeze—*
> *Next day it's in the papers.*

What a pity that Princess Ena did not have the chance then to seek redress from a sympathetic Press Complaints Commission.

JAMIE ELSTON
May 28, 1994   London SW18

~

The Prince of Wales gave a television interview on ITV in connection with his biography by Jonathan Dimbleby.

Dimbleby should have known

SIR—Jonathan Dimbleby's complaint that the tabloid press 'piranhas' distorted extracts from his biography of the Prince of Wales 'to the point where they became lies' (report, Oct. 31) comes oddly from a journalist.

As an experienced member of our rough trade, he must have known that the price of the worldwide publicity he sought by selling syndication rights to the *Sunday Times* for more than £200,000 would be the degutting of the juicier bits by the lower end of the market, which depends on 'scandal', above all royal scandal, particularly with sexual connotations, true or untrue, in the fierce circulation war.

After all, the Prince's alleged extra-marital adventures have been staple for newspapers at all editorial levels since the notorious 'Camilla-gate' tapes reached the public prints.

He may be naïve and badly advised by amateur courtiers in his attempts to recover some credibility as heir to the throne, but one must ask if Mr Dimbleby warned him strongly enough that public frankness is a risky commodity to be handed on a plate to Fleet Street sleaze specialists.

Whether the 'hot' revelations were volunteered or came from probing questioning, the immediate PR attempts by Mr Dimbleby and royal 'sources' to fudge the impact on public opinion suggest the Prince realised too late that, with Mr Dimbleby's aid, he had blown it.

Perhaps one should add that the press watchdogs have much more serious ethical problems to deal with than the flesh wound of a biographer who shoots both himself and his royal subject in the foot with one barrel.

TOM BAISTOW
November 1, 1994   Petts Wood, Kent

Insulting tradition

SIR—Look where this petty, piddling, gawping interest and interference in the private lives of the Royal Family has got us. This must stop!

It is not just a pity that the Royal Family are driven to co-operating with manipulative authors keen on a quick buck. One imagines all this is motivated by those intent on emasculating the British Isles by absorption into Europe.

The 'Crown' belongs to many millions of people who live outside the British Isles, who are loyal and true to Her Majesty the Queen and the Prince of Wales.

In the Queen's Silver Jubilee Year, 400,000 out of a population of 500,000 Newfoundlanders signed a Declaration reaffirming their fidelity to the Queen. Recently, the loyalty of the people of the North West Territories was very evident: loyalty to the Crown, not Canada.

It is difficult for residents of the British Isles to realise just what the Crown means to the rest of us; it is the 'law', a guarantee of freedom, the foundation of government. When you insult the Crown, you insult all of us.

Lady BARLOW
St John's, Newfoundland

SIR—There is no doubt that the Royal Family is under the microscope. Advice floods in from all sides. Alan Clark tells the Queen she should abdicate. Other commentators hope that she will live for a very long time, so that the Prince of Wales can never ascend to the Throne. The likelihood of a royal divorce is debated endlessly.

We live in an age of technology, of telephoto lenses, bugged telephones and tape recorders, of instant books, so that the emphasis on the unseemlier aspects of the Royal Family's life appears unavoidable.

There is nothing new in all this. A brief inspection of the activities of the Queen's predecessors produces a far greater amount of scandal and sleaze. George I was implicated in the murder of his wife's lover, had his wife incarcerated for the last 32 years of her life, and when he arrived in England brought with him what Thackeray called two 'ugly, elderly German favourites', and created one a duchess and the other a countess.

George II quarrelled publicly and bitterly with his eldest son. George III, his 'madness' we now know to have been the symptoms of porphyria, was nevertheless thought at the time to be crazed, given as he was to somewhat unconventional conversations with the historian Gibbon, Fanny Burney and the trees in Windsor Great Park.

George IV kept a plethora of mistresses, and ordered his wife to be turned from the doors of Westminster Abbey at his coronation. His brothers behaved little better. Even Queen Victoria, supposedly a model of rectitude, did not escape the wrath of the editor of the *Times*, nor innuendoes concerning John Brown and the *munshi*.

The eighteenth century was, in addition, even more savage than the late twentieth century in its assault on the Royal Family. Cartoons by Gillray and Rowlandson, public speeches and diaries, all portrayed their victims in the most unflattering, indeed malicious manner. Even the pen of Gerald Scarfe and the typewriter of Anna Pasternak seem kinder in comparison.

Perhaps we should blame the impeccable home life of George V and George VI. The media had a thin time of it for many decades, enlivened only by the abdication crisis. They are certainly making up for it now, but we should still think occasionally of the first four Georges.

CHRISTOPHER SINCLAIR-STEVENSON

October 19, 1994   London SW3

The Princess of Wales retaliated by being interviewed on BBC's *Panorama* by Martin Bashir.

After the interview: sympathy and despair

SIR—The Princess was very frank about her life, and came across as very caring. I would liken her to Lady Jane Grey, the nine-day Queen. She has a common touch unlike other members of the Royal Family. God bless her.

BILL JACQUES
London, N7

SIR—The Princess stated in her interview that she had once remarked that she was as thick as a plank. As a former executive director of Mensa, the high IQ society, I can assure you that, if she is as thick as a plank, I am a Martian.

HAROLD GALE
Lilleshall, Shrops

SIR—Am I the only person to be perplexed by the Princess of Wales's ambition to be some sort of peripatetic British ambassador at large? I was under the impression that we had quite enough of those already.

If, however, their numbers are to be increased should we not be looking for experience: professional old birds with a strong sense of duty (Queen Mother, Duke of Edinburgh) rather than a loose-cannon royal princess of no very obvious qualifications?

In any case, how can you be an effective ambassador when you are at such public loggerheads with what previous monarchs used to refer to, with reason, as 'the family firm'?

Part of the present problem with the Royal Family is that most members of the older generation are serious pros whereas the new ones all too obviously aren't. Apart from the fact that she is extremely decorative, I simply don't see what qualifications the Princess possesses for representing Great Britain abroad.

TIM HEALD
November 22, 1995   Polruan, Cornwall

Princess's feminism

SIR—Yvonne Roberts may be gleeful that the Princess of Wales has found a 'feminist version of the happy ending' for the Royal marriage (article, Nov. 22), but I suspect that millions of women will disagree.

The whole of the Princess's jargon was ego-centred, the results of a currently ubiquitous form of therapy that says you must first 'put a value on yourself' and then have 'a clear idea of what is acceptable and unacceptable behaviour on the part of others' (Yvonne Roberts again).

This provides the user with a whole package of phrases, all highly media-friendly and very valuable socially. It is, however, wholly contrary to that fundamental turning away from self and out towards others which is at the core of true peace of mind. It leads almost inevitably to a sense of unreality and puts up a big barrier between the user and ordinary folk who are still talking normal English.

I listened to the Princess on the radio rather than watching her on television, and found that at several points I was able to prompt her by calling out the next appropriate piece of jargon in response to the carefully posed questions. It was by no means difficult: all the bits about self-worth and inner pain and being a strong woman and needing space and time to adapt were text-book stuff.

To suggest that this has anything to do with her true discovery of herself is delusion. A really strong woman, for instance, will never refer to herself as such, and a woman with a coherent set of beliefs and ideas will not need to resort to the jargon of others in order to discuss personal topics.

The real sadness is that neither the Princess nor her husband appears to have looked to a more helpful source of strength and encouragement in getting to grips with the tensions and temptations of life—the Christian faith into which both were baptised. Among its many healthy aspects, this belief-system discourages the blaming of others and suggests instead that repentance for misbehaviour starts with an acknowledgement of personal responsibility. Incidentally, the privacy of the confessional seems to me infinitely more attractive than the publicity of the television studio when discussing personal sins.

JOANNA BOGLE
November 23, 1995 New Malden, Surrey

The view from Dynasty land
SIR—Out here where the tumble-weeds tumble and the oil wells gush, the womenfolk no longer seem to cotton to the Princess of Wales. When the Prince admitted his adultery, women generally were furious for that poor sweet young *thang*. The very idea!

Even in Texas, the anti-man mood of the United States is prevalent. Television commercials still market their products on the theme of intelligent-practical-sensible-woman shows inept-help-less-stupid-man how to change the tyre of his pick-up truck.

But surprisingly, a poll of the ladies in my office after the extensive reporting of the Princess's television interview, in advance of its showing here, has produced about as much sympathy for Princess Diana as a coiled rattlesnake on the back seat of a Cadillac.

'I thought these people were supposed to have class!?' spluttered one matron. 'Why, even a girl working in a dime store would have had sense enough not to tell some reporter what she did or didn't do. It's the trashiest thing I ever heard.' A young woman remarked: 'It lowers the Royal Family to the level of a *Dynasty* episode.'

Another young woman, something of a royalty fan, said: 'I realise Diana had to be a virgin and all that, but they should have taken her to a shrink before they took her to the gynaecologist. Did she consider her son at school before agreeing to this interview?'

Another woman declared the whole thing 'very sly'. 'I think it was "a gotcha"—a retaliation thing against Charles—but it did not need to be aired in public.' The youngest woman of the group, applying her college psychology course, believes the Princess '. . . is succumbing to her own neuroses by constantly having to seek attention. She needs psychiatric help.'

Unfortunately, the Princess's admission of adultery with her riding instructor, Captain James Hewitt, led to the popular TV talk show host Jay Leno coming up with a series of quips with obvious jocular references to 'mounting'.

BILL LEADER
November 24, 1995   Euless, Texas

Crown strengthened in Canada

SIR—Despite the suggestion that Winnipeg residents were more interested in hockey than in the recent visit of the Prince of Wales (report, April 26), the Prince's homecoming to Canada was a triumph. It is one of three developments that have enormously strengthened the Monarchist position in Canada over recent weeks.

The Prince's trip taking in Manitoba, Ontario and New Brunswick was a working tour: long on substantive events, short on ceremony. His itinerary focused on his work with the environment, youth and business and needed support for our scandal demoralised Armed Forces.

Yet his public appearances were met with enthusiastic crowds of all ages. He showed a keen interest in meeting individuals—and so invariably extended the time scheduled for walkabouts. This adroit public touch met its greatest response in his spectacular welcome by 17,000 in Hamilton, Ontario.

On that occasion, the Deputy Prime Minister Sheila Copps led the crowds in cheers for the Prince and the Queen, and the Prince felt able to express the wish—to loud applause—that one of his sons would be present for the bicentennial 50 years on. Media commentators routinely referred to the Prince as 'Canada's future King', a phrase not often heard here of late.

A poll released on Accession Day by the respected Southam/Angus Reid organisation revealed support for the Maple Crown has significantly increased in every part of Canada, save Alberta. Two of the dramatic surges in monarchical strength negated popular wisdom: that recorded in British Columbia which over the last decade has seen a much greater Asian immigration; and data revealing that the highest level of support is among younger Canadians, aged 18 to 35.

It was a 21-year-old Monarchist student at the University of Toronto, Gordan Rennie, who took on the Liberal MP Alex Shepherd at the Liberal Party's Ontario policy convention last weekend. Mr Shepherd's resolutions calling for a republic and the Queen's removal from currency and postage stamps were defeated 2–1. The upshot of these happy events is that loyalists here now confidently expect to live under Charles III and William V.

JOHN AIMERS

May 1, 1996   Monarchist League of Canada, Oakville, Ontario

King William V?

SIR—There is an intriguing aspect to Andrew Gimson's report (Dec. 19) on the Berlin exhibition on the close ties between the British and German royal families. Had Lord Archer's Bill been law in 1901, Queen Victoria would have been succeeded by her eldest child, of the same name. Princess Victoria died only a few months later, and *her* heir was Kaiser Wilhelm II, who would have been King of England as well as of Germany. The 1914–18 War, had it been fought at all, would have been very different from the Allies v Germany—with what consequences?

V. E. THOMPSON
December 28, 1996   Birkdale, Shrops

Lord Archer of Weston-Super-Mare, the 'blockbuster' novelist Jeffrey Archer, introduced a Bill into the Lords to enable a daughter of the sovereign to succeed to the throne if she is the eldest child.

Ritual ruined

SIR—I became increasingly irritated with David Dimbleby's commentary on the State Opening of Parliament on BBCI yesterday.

The reason for televising the ceremony is to hear the Queen announcing the Government's plans to Parliament. But it is also a colourful occasion, steeped in symbolic ritual, and viewers expect the minutiae to be explained to them.

I lost patience with Mr Dimbleby when he judged it 'flummery and flammery'. The implication is that the ceremony was so much stuff and nonsense. Neither the admirable Speaker nor Peter Mandelson took this line.

But it was significant, I felt, that Mr Dimbleby drew our attention to the 'tradition' of Dennis Skinner insulting Black Rod in the House of Commons and refusing to go to the Upper House, while dismissing the Queen's procession as full of figures whose roles were, apparently, meaningless and of no importance.

The camera lingered for about a minute on the entry into the Chamber of the Duke and Duchess of Gloucester and Princess Margaret. I spotted that the Duke was wearing the collar of the Order of the Garter, given to him on Tuesday, the kind of elegant detail that would not have escaped Mr Dimbleby's much missed father. All right, it is not of vital interest, but during that part of the proceedings David Dimbleby told us nothing.

Enthusiasm for what you are describing is infectious. If Mr Dimbleby finds it all such a bore, could we not have a better-informed guide?

HUGO VICKERS
May 15, 1997   Ramsdell, Hants

Hounded to the end

SIR—I cannot be alone in feeling both outrage and shame at the Princess's tragic death. Every person who has chosen to read the media's voyeuristic soap-opera treatment of her private life must bear some responsibility for the circumstances of her death.

These circumstances are simply the logical conclusion of this cankerous cultural discourse to which we have all contributed. If this tragedy does not bring about a fundamental sea-change in our attitudes towards other people's private lives, nothing will.

RICHARD HOUSE
Norwich

SIR—During visits to five Asian-owned shops in the Bradford area yesterday morning, I experienced first-hand how deeply affected the Asian community is by this tragedy.

As a sign of respect, Sunrise, the local Asian radio station, was playing music all day, with very short breaks on the hour for news. There is a lesson there.

JAMES HALL

September 1, 1997　　　　　　　　　　　Shipley, W. Yorks

~

Time to address responsibility of the media

SIR—Your leading article (Sept. 1) was humane and magnificent. But while agreeing with almost every word of Earl Spencer's forthright condemnation of the press, I found Stephen Glover's article placing all the blame on the paparazzi and the 'tabloids' appallingly smug.

Surely the long-term responsibility for the Princess's death lies far deeper, and wider. Can any editor of a so-called 'quality' newspaper—even you, Sir—really put hand on heart and say he never 'hounded' the Princess or other members of the Royal Family?

Sometimes on travels abroad one really does get the feeling that Britain has—in their obsession with trivia, sex and violence—the world's most destructive media, as foreigners often claim.

But we all bear a heavy charge: proprietors, editors, contributors (like myself) and the consumer who presents the appetite for offal.

Before the shock begins to recede, now must be the time, not just to introduce a privacy Bill, but to re-examine fundamentally what kind of media we truly want.

ALISTAIR HORNE
Henley-on-Thames, Oxon

SIR—The only consolation I can find in this awful tragedy is that Diana and Dodi died together while they were happy and in love.

Mrs PEGGY WINSTON
Lower Broadheath, Worcs

SIR—The death of Diana, Princess of Wales in a car crash echoes not only that of Princess Grace of Monaco in September 1982, when her car went off the road, but also that of an equally fascinating royal figure: the 29-year-old Queen Astrid of Belgium in 1935.

Like the Princess of Wales and Princess Grace, Queen Astrid was beautiful and elegant with a refreshing naturalness and a great warmth of heart. Her husband, King Leopold III, once explained that her secret was that 'she likes everybody so much, and is so pleased to see them, that she takes it for granted they are glad to see her, too'. She enjoyed immense popularity.

In the summer of 1935, the royal couple spent a few days in their villa on Lake Lucerne. On the morning of August 29, having decided to go climbing, the royal party left the villa in two cars headed for the little town of Küssnacht.

Leopold, with Astrid by his side and the chauffeur in the dicky behind, was driving the first car. At about 10 a.m. the king turned to the queen to answer a question and lost control of the car. It mounted the kerb, skidded sharply right, shot down a steep embankment and hit a tree. The queen was flung against the tree, and the car careened on. When it hit a second tree, the king was thrown clear and the car, rolling on, plunged into the lake. The chauffeur emerged from the water with a badly cut face.

Leopold, with his head and right arm injured, hurried to his wife's side. In spite of a fractured skull, she was still alive. A member of the royal party in a car behind hurried to fetch help, but the doctors could do nothing. The village curé was just able to administer the last sacraments before Queen Astrid died in her husband's arms.

THEO ARONSON

September 2, 1997
Frome, Som

~

Callous tabloids shame us all

SIR—In these past few bitter days full of shock and grief, it is reassuring to see that the *Sun* and other tabloids remain fixed points amidst the tumult. The hypocrisy, the spite, the accusing finger, the conspicuous lack of guilt are in evidence still.

Do not mistake silence for callousness. We would all now profit from a little silence and reflection.

CHRISTOPHER PINCHER
London SE1

SIR—The Princess's death has become a public circus. May God help those who think the Royal Family is not grieving in a manner that meets with their approval.

Mercifully the press for once has not been able to intrude upon Her Majesty's privacy at Balmoral.

Viscountess WEIR
Mauchline, Ayrshire

SIR—Would we have the Royal Family beat their breasts and wail in public just to satisfy the whim of the small minority of voyeurs?

When my son was killed in a road accident, I cried all the time—inside; but to the world, I presented a calm and accepting front. Maybe people thought I was hard and unfeeling, but probably no one noticed as I was not royal.

(MRS) PAMELA MURPHY
Sevenoaks, Kent

SIR—I am astonished that there should be any suggestion that the Prince of Wales should not have gone to church with his sons.

The church is not a place one goes to for show. It is God's house, provided so that the congregation can meet in fellowship and pray together, in the knowledge that their prayers are heard. They find a spiritual strength within its walls.

Surely, if any question is asked, it should be: how could the Prince possibly presume to keep his sons *away* from the place where they should find help and comfort?

AMANDA FORSYTH
September 5, 1997   Edinburgh

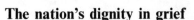

The nation's dignity in grief

SIR—I went to Kensington Palace at about nine o'clock on Thursday night. The vast majority of the crowd was not emotional. A subdued holiday outing atmosphere prevailed. People came with their flowers, queued, talked with their friends, placed their flowers and walked off chatting.

In about an hour in the crowd I saw two people in tears. One young woman who was being photographed at the time was genuinely distraught, and a young child was overtired. The pictures in the popular press of individuals weeping beside fields of flowers do not give a true picture of the nation's state of mind.

If anything, more people were behaving with the sort of dignity which the tabloids have criticised the Royal Family for showing.

NICHOLAS BOYS SMITH
London SW1

SIR—Talking to my pupils at school on the first day of term, I was surprised that, almost without exception, they felt that the reaction to the death of the Princess was excessive and that the funeral arrangements were almost hysterical.

The consensus was that, yes, they were sorry she was dead, yes, she could be given a funeral somewhat out of the ordinary, but that if you took away her title and looks, what had she really done to merit this extraordinary world reaction?

They put forward the name of the Princess Royal, whose death by comparison will receive none of the present outpourings, but whose charitable works far outweigh in practical terms those of Diana.

ALLAN FRISWELL
Leighton Buzzard, Beds

SIR—The monumental disrespect and lack of manners shown to the

Royal Family at this most difficult of times does not in any way reflect the 'exquisite manners' of the Princess, to which a friend of hers referred recently.

Such outbursts reflect, rather, the unlovely age in which we live and which the Princess, through her courtesy and compassion, tried to alleviate.

Rev. PETER LYNESS
London, W6

SIR—God save the Queen!

CALUM McNICOL
September 6, 1997   Kincardine, Fife

~

Earl and Blair acted out of turn

SIR—After the mass hysteria and malice of early last week, I was soothed by the television coverage of the funeral—until Earl Spencer's unseemly retaliatory words.

I fear that the fires of anger directed at our beloved Royal Family, thankfully reduced to embers by the Queen's broadcast to the nation, will again have been fanned into flame by a bereaved but vengeful young man. Using this sacred occasion to express such bitterness was unseemly in the extreme.

(Mrs) HAZEL McMANUS
Kinmel Bay, Clwyd

SIR—Earl Spencer spoke for us all.

LES KUYPERS
Hoddesdon, Herts

SIR—The past week has shown the true nastiness behind the pseudo-intellectual façade of the republican movement. To dispute the validity of the monarchy on constitutional grounds is one thing; to use a week of mourning to sneer and jeer at a group of people already grief-stricken, and who cannot answer back, demonstrates that paparazzi mercenaries are not the only weevils to find a snug home in our media.

FREDERICK FORSYTH
Hertford

SIR—Tony Blair's opportunism in muscling in on the funeral was misplaced and distasteful. It was unsuitable to have a politician taking part in the service.

Mr Blair made matters worse by his delivery, which was in the manner of an amateur theatrical society. If it is true that he personally demanded that Elton John sing at the concert, then this was another misjudgment. The lyrics, which stressed that the Princess was 'English', must have caused inevitable disquiet among Scots and Welsh, particularly as we approach the devolution referendums.

WILLIAM NEIL
London E3

SIR—The Prime Minister's substitution of 'love' for 'charity' in his reading from the King James Bible is, I fear, characteristic of a modern tendency—obvious in his attitudes to abortion and homosexuality—to pick and choose from Scripture.

Holy Writ ought not to be rewritten for political purposes; nor the New Covenant identified with New Labour.

JOHN STEWART
Glasgow

SIR—How dare Mrs Blair appear in Westminster Abbey without a hat?

ANGELA ELLIS
September 8, 1997　　Murcott, Oxon

A prince for our time

SIR—As a tutor who helped the Prince of Wales prepare to read history at Cambridge more than 30 years ago, I would like to correct the current dismal perception of him.

He suffered greatly when his marriage broke up before the media's unrelenting gaze, and the death of Diana, Princess of Wales can only have made this hurt so much worse. He must have passed in the past three weeks through the valley of the shadow of death as many of his critics never will.

His goodness, talents and achievements are of a kind that are all too easy to misinterpret. He has the historian's and the romantic's fascination with the past, which some dismiss as a stultifying straitjacket; they do not understand that it can be used to adapt the institutions of the past, reinterpret tradition and promote fresh growth.

The Prince has a spirituality, an awareness of the metaphysical world that can be easily dismissed as vague and ineffectual. He is a great defender of much that is under threat—from the simplicity of life enjoyed by primitive peoples and the beauty of the English countryside, through medieval crafts and the dignity of traditional Anglican worship to the glories of Elizabethan literature and Georgian architecture. His common sense makes him a vital champion in opposing shallowness of thought, mediocrity of taste and mere iconoclasm.

His services to the unemployed, the sick and suffering are substantial. He has made his own the causes of ethnic minorities and those on the margins of society. He has defended faith in general, and his own Anglican faith in particular.

He has been courageously, some would say dangerously, open about his own shortcomings, thereby endearing himself to the kindly and those prepared to say: 'There but for the grace of God go I.' The range of his public duties and commitments is extremely wide. In a single year he normally raises for his charities, notably by the Prince's Trust, several times his income, and he loves, not least, Australia.

All this—and more—amounts to something rare and precious. We have in him a remarkable human being, a true prince for our time who is a monarch in waiting with rare qualities of mind and heart. He needs, and deserves strong support.

MICHAEL COLLINS PERSSE
September 20, 1997   Geelong Grammar School, Corio, Victoria

Delusions in Brighton

SIR—I was interested to read that Barbara Follett believes the hysterical reaction of one section of the public to the death of Diana,

Princess of Wales constituted a 'sea-change in the British people' (report, Oct. 1).

If this socialite MP can so easily mistake the week-long frenzy of emotional excess that followed the Princess's untimely death for genuine 'compassion and caring', it is small wonder that she and the other shiny, happy Blairites were prepared to swallow the vacuous, theatrical rantings of their party leader at the Brighton conference.

Mrs Follett should beware the dangers of believing in the hype that she and others like her helped to create, lest her political career prove a great disappointment to her.

ROBERT SHARR

October 2, 1997   Hornchurch, Essex

We other people

SIR—I am one of the other people, referred to by Robert Hardman in his cautionary article on changes in the Monarchy who 'have not spoken yet' (Nov. 25).

Well, I am speaking now. We see little need for changes. We like the ceremony, the pageantry, the colour and the necessary formality, including the uniforms of the Lord Lieutenants.

We want a new royal yacht, and beg Her Majesty to take little notice of giving the people an unquenchable appetite for change. For the people, as opposed to the other people, are representative of little more than an area round the metropolis led by the media, particularly the BBC and the Labour/Lib Dem consensus.

RUSSELL CLARKE

December 3, 1997   Nottingham

PARLIAMENTARY CHANGE

Seeking headroom?

SIR—Under the headline 'MPs rush to join TV charm school' (June 1), you inform us of the activities of the latest PR spivs to invade the House of Commons. Leaving aside my secretary's request to nominate suitable candidates, I am intrigued by the quotation from the company's representative, Miss France-Hayhurst that 'we teach them to prop their head up by their hand, which looks intelligent and thoughtful'.

As the television cameras will be on Members who are actually speaking, and it is the normal custom to address the House while standing up, one can only contemplate how intelligent and thoughtful a Member will look standing with his head propped up by his hand. It is lucky that we don't all take ourselves that seriously, although I suppose it is fortunate for PR companies that some do.

ROBERT ADLEY, MP (Con)

June 9, 1989   London SW1

Sir Robert Adley (1935–93) was a Conservative MP with a passion for railways.

Plenty to see in televised Commons

SIR—As someone who has served in the Canadian House of Commons for 16 years, much of that time with television cameras following proceedings, I awaited the televising of the British House with great interest. Predictions that the coverage would be so restrictive as to provide a distorted view of the workings of Parliament had whetted my appetite.

Now, after two weeks of viewing, my observation is that the British public is well served by the coverage. Thanks to the long shots of the Chamber, viewers get the feeling of the whole House rather than, as in Canada, simply watching a talking head.

Because of the difference in the seating arrangements of the two Houses, the television audience here has been spared the worst agony that beset the early days of Canadian coverage. In the Canadian House, MPs are assigned specific seats with school-like desks. The reactions of Members to a good exchange or a rousing speech had been to pound one's desktop but, with the introduction of television, sensitive microphones had to be installed in the desktops. The pounding continued, the microphones vibrated, the audio coverage became ear-shattering and viewers by their thousands phoned in to protest. A time-honoured tradition was quickly abandoned.

I've noticed that a number of British MPs when they step up to the dispatch box seem to be looking downwards as if too reliant on their notes. They seldom look up or glance around the chamber or speak directly to the Opposition benches. This denies them the opportunity to look into the camera from time to time— to the larger audience outside. The desks in the Canadian House of Commons are too low to allow a Member to read notes from that level with any ease—the practice being to hold the notes in one hand and to be seen using them as an aid rather than an anchor.

One of the advantages of having continuous coverage on a separate Parliamentary channel, as is the case in Canada, is that the programme can then have its own presenter who provides background information to the day's debate, explains procedures in the House and generally helps viewers to become more familiar with the working of their parliament. But behaviour in the Canadian House of Commons has changed since the introduction of the cameras—not, in my opinion, for the better. This may be due to the use on national newscasts of short sallies from the daily proceedings in the House. The items selected must be lively, but pressure has pushed the selection from the merely lively to virulent or raucous exchanges. At times there seems to be a competition to see who can make the most outrageous contribution.

This may not happen in the British House—that's what we thought in Canada.

FLORA MacDONALD

December 8, 1989 Kingston, Ontario

Flora MacDonald was the first woman to become Canada's Secretary of State for External Affairs in 1979.

I packed in the MPs, too

SIR—Yet again I suspect that it is no mere accident that your newspaper happens to distort the facts by being economical with the truth.

Your editorial (Sept. 2) said: 'During the 1980s only three MPs could routinely empty Westminster's bars and corridors and fill the benches of the House of Commons whenever they rose to speak: Mrs Margaret Thatcher, Mr Enoch Powell and Dr Owen.'

I will refrain from commenting on them. However, in November 1988, *The Spectator* (from your own stable) appointed an independent group of journalists—Noel Malcolm (*Spectator*), Alan Watkins (*Observer*), Colin Welch (*Daily Mail*), Ian Aitken (*Guardian*) and Peter Riddell (*Financial Times*)—to judge the Parliamentarian of the Year. I was awarded the prize.

They declared, 'One of the best tests of a Parliamentarian is whether the chamber fills when his name appears on the screen. Mr Heath comes top in this test . . . they (the speeches) are the eloquent performances of a Statesman. Delivered with considered wit and without the rancour that some have detected in extra parliamentary utterances, Mr Heath's speeches are major contributions to public argument.'

As the present Deputy Editor of *The Daily Telegraph* was Editor of *The Spectator* at the time, I am sure that he would not mind me pointing out this typical factual inaccuracy from your leader column.

Nor will he mind me adding that your Political Editor displayed equal ignorance on June 27 when he reported that I spoke to a half-empty chamber during a debate on the European Community. It was, I assure him, quite full. Perhaps he had only managed to catch the start of the debate on television?

EDWARD HEATH, MP (Con)

September 5, 1991 London SW1

Sir Edward Heath was Prime Minister, 1970–74, and has graced the House since 1950.

Sisterly tips for the Speaker

SIR—Since Mr Conrad Black's purchase of the John Fairfax organisation has made you a (sort of) member of the Australian family, would you kindly pass on this letter to the new Speaker of the House of Commons.

Dear Speaker Boothroyd—Warmest congratulations on your election to the loneliest job in Parliament. So glad you're not going to wear a wig.

I wonder how your Members will address you. I prefer Speaker Boothroyd. When I was elected Speaker of the House of Representatives (a predominantly male House—aren't they all?) I was mainly 'Madam Speaker'.

During my three-and-a-half years in the Chair, from 1986 to 1989, some persevered with Speaker Child, which I preferred. One Member insisted on calling me Madam, until one of the House wags called his attention to the fact that that was applicable to a different house altogether.

Every Speaker is confounded by the existing standing orders under which the House is run. I hope your standing orders are better than ours. Some of them are ambiguous, some are contradictory and some downright useless. We have an earnest committee which frequently considers the standing orders, but it seems loath to make any changes, and I guess it is easier to whinge about them than try to improve them.

It's usually at Question Time, or Theatre Time as I call it, that the Speaker is called on to rule upon innumerable points of order. There is one standing order I hope you share with us. Shorn of its formal language, it simply says: when the Speaker rises everyone else will sit down and shut up. Speakers don't have many weapons, but that one is very powerful and ensures silence almost immediately. Mind you, it can't be used too often.

Do you have a gavel? We don't. Judiciously used, a gavel can also be quite powerful, because men have such loud voices. As Speaker you will never please all the Members all the time—it will be a miracle if you please some of them some of the time.

I have found that former Speakers become saints, and their infinitely superior rulings are constantly quoted back to you. It is a lonely job, with all the decisions yours and yours alone—rather like the referee of a football match. You don't make the rules, you just interpret them, usually against a background of constant interruptions and interjections.

As you well know, it is sometimes impossible to hear what is said, and sometimes impossible to identify who said it. Perhaps we should all consider a sinbin. It would be a little less drastic than the Tower.

The office of Speaker does not demand rare qualities; rather, it demands common qualities in a rare degree. Well done, and good luck.

(Mrs) JOAN CHILD

April 29, 1992 Carnegie, Victoria, Australia

Joan Child, who was congratulating Betty Boothroyd on becoming the first woman to be elected Speaker at Westminster, was the first woman Speaker in the Australian House of Representatives.

RIGHT FOR THE JOB?

Loves of a bachelor Liberal candidate

SIR—Your story 'Is a single man an electoral liability?' (March 13) strikes a chord. I was adopted in the early Sixties as the Liberal party's prospective parliamentary candidate for Falmouth and Camborne, and soon sensed that a wife would be an electoral and social asset.

On the advice of Jeremy Thorpe, then member for North Devon, I said in my address at the next fund-raising garden fête: 'I feel you would like to have a married man as your candidate, and who knows but that I will find her here today . . .'

The press reaction was overwhelming. The headlines ranged from the *Cornish Guardian*'s sober 'Liberal candidate seeks a Cornish wife' to the *Daily Herald*'s 'Liberal Romeo at large'. There was also an avalanche of letters from Cornish girls living at home and abroad. One letter from Toronto, in which a suitor introduced herself as 'a Canadian Cornish girl who wishes to return home', was particularly appealing.

In the event I married a Danish girl, honeymooned in Jutland, and did not fight the election.

EDWARD BISHOP
St Leonards-on-Sea, Sussex

March 14, 1992

~

Decline in quality of MPs

SIR—You hit the nail on the head (editorial, Jan. 10). The character of MPs has changed dramatically in my 30 years in the Commons, to some extent drastically. As a result Parliament, though much harder working than its predecessors, is less effective than it has ever been and held in lower esteem.

When I was made responsible for Conservative parliamentary candidates in 1974, I considered that Parliament should be a microcosm of the people—tall ones, short ones, rich ones, poor ones—yet, at the same time, just a cut above most of those represented. I believed that it should be tough to get on the candidates' list.

But in the course of the following two years, in the light of the Heath Government's defeat, we had entered 'the age of the common man'. I was accused (wrongly) of favouring public school men, Guards officers and other grandees. I was 'elitist' and 'snobbish'.

In the period since I ceased to be party vice-chairman in charge of candidates, the egalitarian fervour has encouraged the growth of the so-called 'professional politician', the 'identikit' candidate, obsessed with party dogma and with the sole desire to be 'the next Prime Minister but three'.

At the same time, the work of an MP has changed in a way unrecognisable to earlier generations. Seventy-five per cent of MPs' time is taken up with local matters properly the preserve of councillors.

This has come about through the 'community politics' of Mr Peter Hain's Young Liberals (before he switched to the Labour Party). Lighter has become Parliament's 'weight'; narrower its vision.

The ship of state has become top heavy through too many pushing upwards. It is in danger of capsizing and more heavyweight ballast is needed in the hold. In short, we need more *gravitas* in Parliament. If only constituencies would choose older candidates who have achieved something in their lives instead of 'high fliers' with an eye to the main chance, the better we would be.

Sir ANTHONY GRANT, MP (Con)

January 13, 1994   London SW1

~

Honourable path for an MP

SIR—In the light of the current concern being voiced about the quality of the MPs we have today. I enclose the following 'Old Man's Advice to a Young Member of Parliament', which appeared in *The Naval Chronicle* of 1818:

'Enter the House of Commons as the temple of liberty: do not dishonour that temple: preserve your freedom as the pledge of your integrity. Read, inquire, hear, debate and then determine.

'Do not without enquiry approve of, nor without good cause oppose, the measures of the court. The true patriot will lend his assistance to enable the King to administer justice, to protect the subject, to aggrandise the nation. Avoid bitter speeches: you meet not to revile, but to reason. The best man may err, and therefore be not ashamed to be convinced yourself, nor be ready to reproach others. Remember, that your electors did not send you to make your own fortune, but to take care of theirs.

'When you do speak, take special care that it is to the purpose, and rather study to confine yourself to the subject with brevity and perspicuity, than to indulge yourself in the unnecessary display of a flowery imagination.

'If you feel all right within, you will scorn to look round the House for support; for be assured, that God, your conscience, and your country, will support you.'

LANCE ELVY
January 24, 1994   Mayfield, Sussex

Consultancies help MPs to talk sense

SIR—I hold no brief for MPs who enjoy consultancies, and I do not have one myself (although I should declare an interest: I was once invited to advise a company manufacturing police speed cameras. I declined the offer as I felt sure I would inevitably become one of the product's victims).

But I fear the public may be persuaded by adverse media coverage that consultancies can be equated with a form of social corruption.

The reality is that anyone speaking with a detailed knowledge of any subject in the House of Commons is treated with some respect (perhaps because there is something approaching a novelty value in politicians manifesting such a quality). The fact that an MP has accepted (and declared) a consultancy on any particular issue does not automatically devalue the weight of his views.

Indeed, it invariably demonstrates that there is a real likelihood he may have undertaken some research into the topic about which he is speaking, and that his statistics may be authentic.

RUPERT ALLASON, MP (Con)
October 27, 1994   London SW1

IN THE OTHER HOUSE

Minister peer's other records

SIR—While Peterborough reports that the young new Transport Minister, Viscount Goschen, likes to challenge speed records (Aug. 5), the peer has been breaking a number of other political records.

Goschen is not just the youngest member of the Government; when he was appointed a whip after the 1992 election at the age of 26, he joined Lord Melchett, who was a Labour whip in 1974 at the same age, as the youngest Government member since the Second World War.

Between 1986, when he first took his seat in the House of Lords, and 1992, he was also the youngest member of the House of Lords.

As a result, he is the first Government minister to be born during Harold Wilson's premiership and Edward Heath's Conservative leadership.

Furthermore, while some of Viscount Goschen's colleagues can point to relatives who have also been in government, only Nicholas Soames can also say that his father, grandfather and great-grandfather were all government ministers; the Goschens, however, can go one better, as they all held office within this century.

Who says the hereditary principle is dead?

MATTHEW SEWARD

August 9, 1994   Ringwood, Hants

Duke preferable to Jack Straw

SIR—Jack Straw, shadow home secretary, asks how the Duke of Buccleuch and Queensberry, who is Britain's largest private land-lord, can represent the common man in Parliament when he owes his title to an ancestor's royal but illegitimate parentage (report, Dec. 31).

Equally, how is a duke to be criticised either for his ancestry, which he can do nothing to alter, or for belonging to a family who have managed their affairs so competently as to preserve their lands and titles for centuries?

Were the Duke a bad landlord, then presumably Mr Straw would have attacked him on that score. Were he a Scrooge, indifferent to the needs of his inferiors, then surely Mr Straw would have said so.

Or is it the case that the Duke happens to come from a family who have demonstrated that they can run their own affairs and so might have something to contribute to the affairs of the nation?

Claiming my rights as a 'common man', I believe I would as soon have the Duke to represent me as Mr Straw. But happily that choice need not arise. If Labour wins the election and leaves the House of Lords as it is, this common man will look both to the Duke and Mr Straw to represent him in Parliament; a perfect example of a mixed blessing!

KEITH TOPLEY
January 1, 1997   Cowes, Isle of Wight

Labour shown up

SIR—The Duke of Buccleuch, who was an MP for many years and has been confined to a wheelchair since he had a riding accident, has a keen sense of humour.

When asked to comment on his paralysis some years ago, he remarked that it was 'what happens to a politician who tries to take a fence rather than to sit on it'.

The envious bile flowing from Mr Straw's pen illustrates that 'New Labour' is a myth.

R. A. FITZPATRICK
Belton in Rutland, Rutland

SIR—Your suggestion that 'Labour's hostility to the House of Lords has reached a new pitch' (leading article, Jan. 1) may be flawed.

Luckily, the new, New Labour generation do not feel that the House of Lords is all wicked. Lady Blackstone took her grand-daughter there recently for a Christmas tea treat.

She introduced her to me and Baroness Parke of Monmouth. The conversation went as follows:

Lady Blackstone: 'My grand-daughter thinks this is a castle filled with fairies.'

Lady Parke of Monmouth: 'Really, and have you seen any dragons?'

Lady Blackstone: 'No, no, she says they are all fairies here.'

Lady Rawlings: 'What a shame Granny and her party want to get rid of it.'

Lady RAWLINGS

January 2, 1997   London SW1

Computers v peers

SIR—My husband and I have been in receipt of mail addressed in various amusing ways (letter, May 2) due to the inability of any computer to recognise any title other than Mrs, Mr, Miss or Ms.

My husband is the 11th Earl of Coventry, and a high-street bank computer sent him a letter with the salutation 'Dear Mr Eleventh'. When contracting mail order companies, any hint of a title is met with confused silence.

The goods usually arrive addressed to Mr Coventry, or Earl O Coventry (presupposing an American christian name).

Tony Blair needs to make no effort to reform the House of Lords. Computer programmers have for some time been making an excellent job of it.

Countess of COVENTRY

May 5, 1997   Earls Croome, Worcs

THE LADY
VANQUISHED

Why we Irish love your Margaret

SIR—It would be disconcerting if anyone were to express surprise at Mrs Thatcher's showing in Ireland's popularity polls (report, April 26). We have truly 'grappled her to our hearts with hoops of steel' and why not? 'Margaret', as the man or woman in the street refers to her here, is a big favourite with all of us.

Surely that can be little surprise when you consider that despite evidence to the contrary, Ireland is a matriarchal society. Victoria Regina was quite an item here. It may not be that overt but we have more than a few Victorians knocking about the place even today.

We Paddies love the Mammy and Margaret is one of the greatest of them all, as a friend of mine from Harlem recently proclaimed above the strains of the pop group Run DMC. Charles Haughey's gift to her in 1980 was a silver teapot. By which of course he was saying . . . 'You be mother'.

This country has been badly shaken by moving statues in recent times. No wonder then, that elements here should turn to someone rather more immovable. One has to ask how long it will be before the Madonna is discreetly spirited away from the grottos that may be found around this country to be replaced by a likeness—which will be fashioned not in plaster, nor yet in bronze but appropriately in iron—of our Lady of Whitehall.

One has little doubt that like Zola Budd she will continue to run no matter what the world may say. Who can argue that she brings 'harmony where once there was discord'? She is music to our ears. It somehow comforts us, and all sensible Europeans, to know that God is in Her heaven and Denis is down the pub.

DERMOT MORGAN
April 27, 1988   Dublin

Dermot Morgan (1952–98) was a writer and comedian best known for his television series *Father Ted*.

~

She who is the one

SIR—Mrs Thatcher has surely achieved something quite remarkable when the pronoun 'she' indicates immediately whom the speaker is talking about, without any reference to her actual name.

I have been in the company of a variety of people and on quite separate occasions when suddenly someone will say out of the blue 'Oh she's quite right on that,' or 'If she wants to continue she'll have to stop that,' or 'I think she had to do something for the nurses, don't you?' I can't think of any previous Prime Minister who became known as 'he'.

PAULINE KAVANAGH
June 10, 1988   Sutton, Surrey

~

Out of the mouth . . .

SIR—W. F. Deedes (Sixth Column, April 19) need not worry about the general knowledge and perception of all the younger generation. I was listening to *Yesterday in Parliament* with my son, then aged 2½ years.

'Who is that speaking?' I asked. 'That is Mrs Thatcher,' he replied correctly. 'What does she do?' 'She is Prime Minister and she shouts,' he responded.

NIGEL DUDLEY
April 23, 1990   Dubai

~

Toppled by a squalid conspiracy . . .

SIR—So the greatest peace time prime minister of this century has been toppled by a squalid conspiracy, led by a light-weight political opportunist backed by the rottenest lot of so-called Tory MPs to have disgraced the Conservative parliamentary party in my experience.

It is some small consolation that many of them will deservedly lose their seats at the next election. I hope that their fate will act as a salutary lesson to those who misguidedly selected them as candidates.

Is it too much to hope that the party will now unite—if only for the sake of self-preservation—and get on with the not unimportant business of governing the country?

Lord MAUDE OF STRATFORD-UPON-AVON
South Newington, Oxon

Angus Maude (1912–93) was director of the Conservative Political Centre, 1951–5, and Paymaster-General, 1979–81.

SIR—As the longest-serving party leader in Britain I am sorry to see off my fourth Tory leader since I began in politics in 1963.

Although the Official Monster Raving Loony party was fundamentally opposed to Mrs Thatcher and what she stood for, she did at least share our objective of bringing some colour into politics. However, her departure proves only one thing—Thatcherism may come and go, but Loonyism, which we believe represents the true spirit of the British people, will go on for ever.

'SCREAMING "LORD" SUTCH'
November 23, 1990   London W8

'Screaming "Lord" Sutch' is a perennial general election candidate who started out life as a pop singer.

Inspired a worldwide movement

SIR—If the true measure of great leadership is whether a leader has changed the direction of the nation he or she has led, then Margaret Thatcher has met and passed that test.

As the former leader of a conservative party which draws inspiration from her philosophy, I would argue that the only leaders since the 1939–45 War who had such a marked effect on the direction of their nations have been Charles de Gaulle and Mikhail Gorbachev. However, Mrs Thatcher achieved something which neither of them did. She inspired a worldwide political movement.

As Prime Minister, she was the boldest and foremost exponent of the spirit of the Eighties—a belief in popular capitalism, market solutions and dramatically less government intervention. Ronald Reagan told Americans what they *wanted* to hear; Margaret Thatcher told Britons what they *needed* to hear. That she never enjoyed the ephemeral adulation so craved by some politicians was in fact one of her enormous strengths.

I well remember her meeting a group of ministers in the former coalition government in Australia not long after her election in 1979, when she paid a brief visit to our country. She gave the meeting a brief outline of her plans. Afterwards one of my then colleagues said that Mrs Thatcher would need to go more softly, 'otherwise she won't last'.

This remark not only misread the person, it totally misread the nature of the task about to be undertaken. When I saw her again in 1988, there was no sign of her slowing up.

Although the circumstances were very different, my own removal from the Australian Liberal party leadership in favour of an allegedly more charismatic leader (who then failed to win the subsequent election) gives me some sense of *déjà vu* about opinion polls in Britain which now show Heseltine, Hurd and Major as all more popular than Thatcher.

Such polls are virtually meaningless; they are the product of an ad hoc response from the electorate which sees any change at the top as offering some miracle cure.

I will be fascinated to see the opinion polls in three months' time. My fear is that they will reflect a continuation of the trend which has been apparent in recent months. I hope I am wrong.

JOHN HOWARD, MP (Lib)
November 24, 1990   Sydney

John Howard, Prime Minister of Australia, first led the Liberal Party, 1985–89.

Long-healing Tory split of 1903
SIR—I fear that if Conservatives are hoping for a united party under a new leader, their experience from 1903 to 1913 suggests reason for doubt.

In September 1903 the party split over Imperial Preference, then an issue as explosive as Thatcherism: Joseph Chamberlain, the most uncompromising British leader of the radical Right before Mrs Thatcher, left the Cabinet to conduct the last of his great campaigns.

Joe, the Brummagem screw manufacturer, resembles Mrs Thatcher in that he was an 'outsider' who was disliked and feared by the Etonian and Harrovian crowd who have ruled the Conservative party most of our century. Like her, he could humiliate and destroy enemies, and he showed the same kind of driving energy and single-minded certainty about a cause which attracted into the party voters who were not necessarily traditional Tories.

Chamberlain was passionately committed to British greatness. He saw tariff reform and imperial union as the country's only chance to remain a great power.

In the years that followed, the hapless Arthur Balfour tried to keep the party together, as the slick Heseltine, the sombre Hurd or the smug Major—more flexible if infinitely less interesting than Mrs Thatcher—will attempt to do. The party went down to colossal defeat in 1906 by a united, though also far more talented, Liberal team than that fielded by Mr Kinnock.

In the subsequent bitter skirmishing that rent the party all but one of the Conservative free traders were purged from the Commons by January 1910. The solitary survivor was Lord Hugh Cecil, who remained barricaded within the walls of Oxford University, which, it is worth recalling, has not proved entirely sympathetic to Mrs Thatcher.

It can be expected that Mrs Thatcher will not take any active and personal part in directing the battle for the party's soul after her departure in the way that Chamberlain did, conducting operations even when he was confined by a stroke to a wheelchair from 1906.

But battles cannot be fought without willing armies. The two created out of one by this week's ejection of the Prime Minister can only feed fears for the worst.

Prof RICHARD REMPEL
November 24, 1990   Hamilton, Ontario

A breaker of records

SIR—Mrs Thatcher became Britain's first woman Prime Minister, went on to break all records as the longest-serving Prime Minister this century. She won a war and three elections in a row, helped to set Eastern Europe free, and has become a major figure giving her name to an era. All this from a lady who has gone on record as saying that she owes nothing to feminism.

Certainly her accounts of her childhood show it to be markedly different from the sort decreed by the feminists with their code of non-sexist books, non-sexist attitudes and non-traditional views of family relationships. Mrs T got standard 1930s, middle England ideological fare, including home-cooked meals, church every Sunday and a father whom she recalls with gratitude and affection.

She was evidently taught to believe, not in an Equal Opportunities Commission which would smooth her path to the top, but in herself and her own ability to work hard for the things that mattered.

In public life, always attractively dressed, she has made the dungarees school of feminism look idiotic.

She saw off the GLC and its women's committee, and has clipped the wings of other local authorities similarly wasting our money. Her courage, dignity and integrity have not only served the nation well; they are impressive examples for other women to emulate.

I am glad that we have had her in these years as a foil to the liberationists. And I suspect that we have not seen the last of her yet for her qualities are of the enduring kind and she still has a great contribution to make.

(Mrs) JOANNA BOGLE
New Malden, Surrey

SIR—Mrs Thatcher is suffering the same fate as many working females who try to realise their full working potential in a male-dominated world.

M. CARTER
Lympsham, Som

SIR—Mrs Thatcher will be seen by history as the last truly great Prime Minister of Great Britain. With her departure she takes with her our Sovereignty and the Great from Britain once and for all time. She was a first class Prime Minister in what has become a second class country.

(Mrs) GEORGINA BUTCHER
Pinner, Middx

SIR—The conduct of the parliamentary party in its challenge to the leadership without consideration of the consequences to Britain's international standing on both political and economic issues, has brought shame upon the British people, irrespective of their party allegiance. What has become of public service?

G. H. COURTIER
Cairo

SIR—All my life I have been that character beloved by satirists: a True-Blue Tory, a Royalist, a member of the Church of England, and a believer in Man the Head of the Household.

Now, in my late sixties, due to the shenanigans of all these groups, I find myself an ex-Tory, ex-Royalist, ex-member of the Church of England, and a feminist. As the Communist party seems a thing of the past, can anyone suggest what I should now do, apart from throwing myself off Beachy Head?

(Mrs) P. E. SULLIVAN
November 26, 1990   Hastings, E. Sussex

~

A Roman parallel

SIR—I wonder if anyone else has noticed an interesting parallel between Mrs Thatcher and Shakespeare's Coriolanus? Like him, she was elected by public acclaim at a time of crisis and saved the country from disaster. Like Coriolanus, she was incapable of pandering to public popularity, but simply told the truth as she saw it, regardless of electoral acceptability. Like him, she found that the Tribunes of the People—in our case self-elected journalists of radio and television—had contrived to arouse the mob against her once the crisis was past, and that the Senators—Geoffrey Howe as Menenius?—were not prepared to back her.

Clearly, a poll tax whereby everyone in the country paid about £5 per week for all local services—with, possibly, rebates for the genuinely impoverished—made a lot of sense.

And, clearly, a property tax based on capital values whereby estate agents set the value of a house in which a widow, a son or daughter may have lived for 30 years but are now unreasonably penalised by an influx of yuppies is grossly unjust. A dwelling house is just that, and bears no relation to the values of those property developers who buy and sell for profit.

Mrs Thatcher understood that. Does Mr Heseltine? Does Mr Major?

I think Mrs Thatcher might well say to the mob whose will has triumphed, and the many Conservative voters among them:

> *I banish you*
> *And here remain with your uncertainty.*
> *Let every feeble rumour shake your hearts*
> *Your enemies with nodding of their plumes*
> *Fan you into despair. Have the power still*
> *To banish your defenders, till at length*
> *Your ignorance, which finds not till it feels*
> *Making but reservation of yourselves,*
> *Still your own foes, deliver you, as most*
> *Abated captives, to some nation*
> *That won you without blows.*

ROSEMARY ANNE SISSON
March 29, 1991   London SW6

MAJOR ROAD
TO BLAIR

Sounds right?
SIR—Is Majorism Thatcherism in a Minor key?

MARY LACEY
June 14, 1991   Chesham, Bucks

~

Lines of a familiar Tory dilemma
SIR—Listening to the satisfaction being expressed on the radio by pro- and anti-federalists after Mr Major's Guildhall speech (report, Nov. 11) made me think of a verse celebrating Arthur James Balfour's attempt to hold a Tory party together early this century.

The split then was between Imperial Protectionists and Free Traders. It was duly recorded by the Liberal MP Sir Wilfrid Lawson, Bt, and published in 1904 with a sketch by F. Carruthers Gould:

> *I'm not for Free Trade, and I'm not for Protection;*
> *I approve of them both, and to both have objection.*
> *In going through life, I continually find*
> *It's a terrible business to make up one's mind.*
> *And it's always the best in political fray*
> *To take up the line of the Vicar of Bray.*
> *So, in spite of all comments, reproaches, and predictions,*
> *I firmly adhere to Unsettled Convictions.*

It is perhaps worth adding that Lawson was first elected to the House in 1859 and was returned in the 1905–6 general election which saw the greatest Tory defeat this century. One wonders what he would make of the Tories' present dilemma of trying to square a circle.

WILLIAM WILSON
November 13, 1991   London W5

~

Was Aristotle a proud Tory?

SIR—I was interested to see that Mr Kenneth Baker thinks that Aristotle, were he alive now, would be a John Major man (Peterborough, March 16). If this is a sample of Mr Baker's forthcoming book on the history of Conservatism, it will make fascinating reading. For Aristotle seems a little unsound on several of Mr Major's cherished beliefs.

Back in the fourth century BC, Aristotle taught that some people were slaves by nature. He wrote that a slave is simply an article of property, an 'animate instrument' of his master who has 'no life or being' other than as his master's property. I feel that this does not chime in perfectly with Mr Major's vision of a classless society.

Aristotle's understanding of family life was also a little remote from current Tory ideas. He wrote that a father rules his children in the way a king rules over his subjects; and that a husband governs his wife as a statesman rules over his fellow citizens.

He also taught that a man who was only as brave as a brave woman would be a coward. Indeed, he believed that 'both the temperance and the courage of a man differ from those of a woman in much the same sort of way as the same virtues in a ruler differ from those in a subject'.

Aristotle delineated an ideal human type whom he called the *magalopsychos*, or Proud Man. The Proud Man claims the greatest honours from others because he knows himself to be superior. He uses irony when speaking to folk humbler than himself. He likes to own beautiful and useless things rather than useful ones. He has a deep voice and moves slowly.

By the way, the Proud Man also likes to remember benefits he has conferred on others, but hates to remember any he has received from a benefactor—for that would make him feel inferior. If what

Mr Baker says is right, then the forthcoming Conservative election manifesto should make everyone sit up.

Dr JOHN CASEY
Cambridge

SIR—Kenneth Baker thinks he knows how Aristotle would vote on April 9. So do I.

Aristotle believed the Athenians ought to make their own laws in their own democratic assembly. He would not, I believe, vote for anybody who thinks the laws of the United Kingdom should be made, its taxes levied and its policies settled otherwise than by Parliament.

ENOCH POWELL
March 17, 1992   London SW1

Enoch Powell (1912–1998) was a Minister in the late 1950s and early 1960s and the most powerful influence on Tory policy afterwards.

～

Kinnock unsound on God

SIR—I cannot understand why the Church is saying nothing during this election campaign. Before the last election, Mr Kinnock declared: 'My wife and I do not believe in God and we have not had our children baptised.'

Since then they have both affirmed that this was true. Mrs Kinnock the other day said: 'I do not believe in God, and when I get to 10 Downing Street I am going to go on teaching children.'

It seems to me appalling that in a so-called Christian country we might have a man ruling over us and our children who is an avowed agnostic.

I, alone, with the help of only a tabloid newspaper, brought prayers back into the state schools in 1988. They had been cancelled for eight years without any reproach or regret expressed by the Church.

Are the Archbishop of Canterbury and all the bishops going to stay silent while the people vote for a man who is against God and has no understanding how much, at this time, children need the guidance and the prayers which can come only from religion?

My election call to all wavering Conservatives is: if you vote for Kinnock, you are voting against Christ who said 'Suffer the little children to come unto me'.

Dame BARBARA CARTLAND
March 19, 1992   Hatfield, Herts

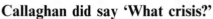

Callaghan did say 'What crisis?'

SIR—Maurice Weaver is wrong to suggest that James Callaghan's phrase 'Crisis, what crisis?', which did so much to bring down Labour in 1979, was simply a misleading paraphrase by the tabloids (April 6).

When the 10th anniversary came round, it was claimed that the incident was invented by the nasty Tory press. But I remember having a day off from teaching at the time, probably because of the various strikes, and watching the lunchtime television.

I saw Mr Callaghan come down the steps of his plane, stop at the foot and greet the throng of journalists waiting on the tarmac to question him about the current discontents. Perhaps unwisely, he was still in an avuncular mood after his trip abroad, and duly uttered those fatal words.

I immediately rang my sister-in-law, another teacher stranded at home, and she had seen it. We agreed that the prime minister had now definitely lost the coming election.

But, by the six o'clock news, that tarmac scene had been replaced by a news conference in the airport lounge with the usual polished platitudes.

Has that early bit of film or tape been lost, I wonder.

GEORGE BICKERSTAFFE
April 10, 1992   Oldham, Lancs

Can't fight back

SIR—Mr Major tells us: 'When your back's to the wall, it's time to turn round and fight.' Why pick on the wall?

FRANK PETERS
May 6, 1995 Latchley Halt, Cornwall

~

Winning case

SIR—Tony Blair says that he is personally against abortion, but he believes in a woman's right to choose. Either this is a contradiction or 'personally' is to be interpreted in a very narrow way. If it is contradictory, it is an affront to both logic and the electorate. If, on the other hand, 'personally' means in Mr Blair's own case, then it is meaningless because it is uttered by a man. In fact, in saying this he takes the traditional socialist passion for dialectic into the realm of the absurd.

Imagine the howls of derision that would have greeted 'I'm personally against slavery, but I believe in the slave-owner's right to choose'; or more topically, 'I'm personally opposed to child sex abuse, but believe in a paedophile's right to choose'. It is Mr Blair's statement, not Cardinal Winning's repudiation of it, which is ridiculous. This sophistry disfranchises pro-life members of the Labour Party and jeopardises a Labour victory.

PETER GARRETT
October 28, 1996 Leamington Spa, Warks

~

Waking up to the change of government

SIR—Stranded in Washington during the election, I have been unable to buy an English newspaper. The famous Willard and Marriott hotels and the news-stands at the National Press Centre all say they no longer carry them. Almost the only detail I have learned from television is that Cherie Blair answered the door to take in flowers in her nightie. What does this attitude in the capital of the world's superpower say about Britain?

REGINALD TURNILL
Washington, DC

SIR—How refreshing that we have a public school-educated prime minister back in Downing Street.

MARTYN HOLLAND
May 5, 1997   Marlow, Bucks

Election lessons

SIR—Next Tuesday's stamp issue, the first under the new Labour administration, is called 'Tales of Terror'. How apt.

NICK RUSSELL
May 6, 1997   Evenley, Northants

Tudor doubles

SIR—The Lord Chancellor's recent identification of himself with Cardinal Wolsey suggests to me a new Christmas game—'fitting the Tudor cap'—which can be played by all ages in mixed company. It consists of pairing members of the 'New Labour' Government with well-known Tudor figures.

Thus we can pair off the Chancellor, Gordon Brown, with Henry VII's Chancellor, Cardinal Morton. The latter's taxation device of 'Morton's fork' could well have been invented by Gordon Brown.

Harriet Harman seems a natural Anne Boleyn—certain to get the chop! Whereas Margaret Beckett is more likely to follow the destiny of Catherine of Aragon. Peter Mandelson could find his role model in Thomas Cromwell—'spin doctor' first to Cardinal Wolsey and then to Henry VIII. John Prescott could fill the role of Henry VIII's court jester, Will Somers, or possibly that of the royal wrestler.

Those of us who see Henry VIII through the medium of Holbein's great portrait might find some difficulty in pairing off Tony Blair with Henry VIII. But if we go back to the young Prince Henry, who succeeded his father in April 1509 and who was reported to have 'commanded the stage with an easy authority', then the pairing becomes credible.

Indeed, the forthcoming six months' presidency of the European Union by Tony Blair could well be compared to Henry VIII's much publicised summit conference with the French in June 1520—the Field of the Cloth of Gold—the results of which were definitely negative.

There remains the open question of who is destined to wear the cap of Thomas More? Any suggestions?

Sir DAVID PRICE
December 26, 1997 Beaulieu, Hants

~

'Rebranded' Britain a poor project

SIR—Tony Blair's intention to 'rebrand' Britain at the Commonwealth Summit in Edinburgh (report, Oct. 20) is all too typical of the Government's slavish devotion to short-sighted trends. To shun tartan, bagpipes and pageantry, in favour of video footage of frock designers and a four-man percussion band, will do nothing to make Britain 'dynamic'; it will merely discard the very elements which appeal to foreigners.

Visitors do not crowd into Princes Street in search of technology—which usually means computer games and hi-fi—that they can as easily find in Seattle or Sydney, nor for clothes they might pick up in Milan or Toronto. Of course, Silicone Glen and clothing manufacture are as 'vibrant' and 'modern' in Scotland as similar enterprises throughout the developed world, as the fundamental principle of marketing is the 'unique' selling proposition. For even the hardest nosed businessman, that means trips to Edinburgh Castle, whisky distilleries and kilt shops.

Many of these features—so appealing to visitors, a source of pride for Scots, and roundly condemned as 'outmoded' by Mr Blair—were invented by Sir Walter Scott for George IV's visit to the city. But, if sometimes artificial, they sprang from a genuine attempt to retrieve and revive a culture nearly forgotten since the Battle of Culloden in 1746.

By contrast with this reverence for tradition, the Government is following the dismal examples set by the BBC and BA. A witless pursuit of the latest trend leads only to a succession of excruciatingly modish logos and revamps, each more quickly outdated and outmoded than the last. The only way to avoid becoming trapped by fashion is to stick to what is already timeless (or as Mr Blair would have it, out of date).

The destruction of institutions and traditions, whether as seemingly trivial as a white tie at Guildhall banquets or as important as the hereditary principle in the House of Lords, is an article of faith for this government. But it is as myopic as the vandalism of cities such as Glasgow and Birmingham by 1960s planners.

Mr Blair says his generation has 'moved on' from ceremony. Edinburgh has moved on from Sir Walter Scott to *Trainspotting*. It is when we in Britain guard our unique place in the world that others most readily turn towards us.

THOMAS CORRIE
October 22, 1997   Edinburgh

SCOTLAND ARISING

A tonic for the Scots

SIR—Perhaps the most touching part of Richard Ehrman's complacent and sentimental defence of the Union (article, Sept. 4) is his assumption that England without Scotland, despite having a population more than three times as large as that of the Netherlands, could not hold her own in Europe.

As for his belief that, having been married so long, the two nations cannot possibly divorce, I can only think of the modern examples of Austria and Hungary, or Norway and Sweden, or the Czech Republic and Slovakia—let alone Serbia and Croatia—to disprove the point.

As an Englishman in Glasgow, now conscious of the deep and patronising arrogance towards and ignorance of Scotland displayed by most of my compatriots, I have become acutely aware that the Union needs at least radical reform. It is true that many in Scotland benefited from the Union of 1707—although no modern historian would describe a shotgun marriage achieved by threats and bribery to be one of 'mutual convenience'; it is also true that the Scots played a prominent part in the Empire—indeed, one might say they ran it.

But the British Empire has gone, and there seems little point in the Scots now running a mere United Kingdom in severe decline and tortured by the trauma of loss of that Empire. Mr Ehrman thinks it would be a risk for Scotland to strike out 'as a small country on the north-west fringe of Europe', though this is a fate analogous to that enjoyed by decent nations of comparable population size such as Norway and Finland. Perhaps he forgets that nationalism can be a vital and creative force.

I have come to the conclusion that devolution or independence could only reinvigorate the ancient but demoralised kingdom of Scotland. I also think it would be good for poor, sad England, for it might make this blinkered and disillusioned nation rediscover her own true character and identity.

GAVIN STAMP
September 6, 1995   Glasgow

Monumental joke

SIR—The story of how the Stone of Destiny was patched up after it split in two (report, July 4) was one of the favourite party stories of Bertie Gray, the sculptor and Glasgow magistrate. Gray liked to recall how he mended it in his monumental mason's yard in Sauchiehall Street.

I remember him saying on several occasions in the bar of his club that he had hidden a message in the original stone before repairing it. The contents of this message would be revealed only in his will.

When Gray eventually died, about 20 years ago, the contents of his will were eagerly awaited by those in the know. Alas, there was nothing—he was a joker to the end.

However, Gray was perfectly serious when he said he made two exact copies of the stone which were so good that he got quite mixed up as to which was which, and he could not be sure that the right one had gone back to London.

HUGH FERGUSON
July 5, 1996   Glasgow

Northern wrong

SIR—Now that the Prime Minister has offered to return the 'Stone of Destiny' to Scotland (report, July 4), will he also seek compensation for the sheep taken from the innocent farmers of Cumbria and Northumbria by our northern neighbours?

D. W. NAYLOR
July 6, 1996   Maryport, Cumbria

England has fake Stone of Scone

SIR—It is an interesting coincidence that the Rosetta Stone, the black basalt rock that the Egyptians want to recover in the light of John Major's generous gesture to the Scots (report, July 8), is made of the same material as the rock said to be the real Stone of Scone.

According to tradition, the lump of sandstone that has rested at Westminster Abbey for the past 700 years was quarried for King Edward I by the Abbot of Scone when he heard that Edward was coming to take away the symbolic stone. The abbot had the real stone, the *Lia Fail*, hidden.

Edward almost certainly learnt later that he had been duped, for he came up again two years later and all but pulled Scone Abbey apart in a futile effort to find the genuine stone. When he did not succeed, he had a wooden coronation chair at Westminster Abbey to go over the fake stone, instead of the bronze one he had originally ordered.

All this is vouched for by the ancient chroniclers. The true stone was, in fact, of seat height, as is shown by the seals of the early monarchs sitting thereon. The Westminster stone is only 11in high—and an undignified seat it would have made for all but a dwarf.

In 1951 Dr James S. Richardson, former HM Chief Inspector of Ancient Monuments for Scotland, wrote an authoritative booklet on this subject, which was approved by the renowned Professor W. Croft Dickinson of Edinburgh.

As well as being of seat height, the stone was chair-like (it was known as Scotland's Merble Chair) and decorated with carvings. It had rounded handles at the sides for lifting and the top was hollowed somewhat, according to Hemingborough and Fordoun and other chroniclers.

Possibly, it was originally a Roman altar. It may well have been utilised by St Columba when he came to convert the Picts and Scots in 563, for he was apt to use symbols of pagan worship in his successful efforts to promote the true faith.

At any rate, the stone came to his Iona and remained there until Kenneth Macalpine removed it to save it from the raiding Vikings; so, Robert the Bruce was able to be crowned sitting on the true stone.

On his deathbed, the Bruce gave it to the keeping of Angus Og of Islay, Lord of the Isles, to keep it secure until such time as a worthy successor sat on his throne. Where is it now? Descendants of the Lords of the Isles should know.

I have recounted all this in my trilogy about Robert the Bruce.

NIGEL TRANTER

July 9, 1996   Aberlady, East Lothian

~

Learning to live with Scots' referendum vote

SIR—The Scots have voted and the Welsh are to vote. But the English have not been offered the chance to have their say—on their wish for an English parliament or assembly; on how they feel about Wales and Scotland becoming devolved (it will have a significant impact on England); or on whether they think it acceptable for Scottish and Welsh MPs to have a say in what happens in England, but not for English MPs to have a say in what happens in Scotland and Wales.

This is blatant racial discrimination, and I suggest that the Commission for Racial Equality be asked to investigate the whole matter. At the very least, the two referendums should be declared null and void.

Prof. J. C. DEARDEN

Helsby, Ches

SIR—Let the hairy-kneed men in skirts take their porridge, haggis and Satanic pipes away to the God-forsaken wastes of the heathen North and be heard of no more. May their taxes rise rampant, their new Parliament do them as little good as the Mother of Parliaments has done us, and may Donald Dewar visit them frequently. Our Caledonian brethren deserve all they get.

MICHAEL CARRIGAN

East Grinstead, W. Sussex

SIR—Perhaps Tony Blair would now instruct Peter Mandelson to cancel his Millennium Dome and transfer some of the funds set aside for that temporary structure to Edinburgh for a fitting and permanent building for our Scottish Parliament.

PETER FITCH

Lhanbryde by Elgin, Morayshire

SIR—Congratulations to the Scottish people on laying the foundations for the latest quango. Responsibility for the export of jobs and businesses away from higher taxes will lie with this talking shop. Wales, be warned!

RICHARD DAVIES
September 13, 1997 Sudbury, Suffolk

~

Whose nation?

SIR—G. O. Paton asks: 'What is a Scot?' (letter, Nov. 23). It was early 1989. He was in his sixties and of Polish origin. Like many others in a town near Inverness, he had moved to Scotland during the war. I was the medical registrar at the regional hospital. His problem was chest pains from heart disease. He said, perhaps rightly, that it was all stress.

'You know, doctor, it has been very difficult. The café that my daughter has been working in all these years has been bought by an English couple; and they don't need any extra hands.

'I am retired and we may have to move. I don't know where. It is terrible—these bloody English with all their money moving up from down south and buying up businesses and property here. It shouldn't be allowed.'

Here was a Polish immigrant complaining to me, an Asian who had then lived in Britain for 18 months, that the English should be banned from buying property in Scotland. Can someone explain nationalism to me, please?

Dr M. K. SRIDHAR
November 27, 1996 Stafford

~

Beware the tartan tide

SIR—I watch with wonder the English electorate falling for the shiny image of New Labour, with its policy of promising anything for a vote. Don't they realise that, if Labour wins, they will be ruled by a cabinet dominated by the tartan element—Blair (Prime Minister, Scots by parentage and education), Gordon Brown

(Chancellor), Robin Cook (Foreign Secretary), Gavin Strang (Agriculture) and Alistair Darling (Treasury).

To crown it, Labour proposes a Scottish parliament, with taxing powers, while Scottish MPs will still be able to vote on English affairs. As a staunch Unionist Scot, I say to all our friends south of the Border: 'You are being conned.'

W. B. TEVENDALE
March 17, 1997   Dalbeattie, Dumfries & Galloway

WALES FOLLOWING

England should have its say

SIR—As a British citizen, born and resident in Wales, I am astounded at the way the devolution ballot has been treated so lightly.

I received only one leaflet telling me to 'Vote Yes' but not really explaining why. The other piece of literature I received was something entitled 'The Rose' which informed the electorate 'Giggsy says Vote Yes'.

Can Tony Blair really justify setting up an assembly when only one in four Welsh residents voted 'Yes'?

(Mrs) JILL MAULE
Chepstow, Monmouthshire

SIR—As a Welshman who lives in England, I was ineligible to vote in the referendum. I would, however, have voted 'No', purely on the basis that with no Bill yet being placed before Parliament, there can be no certainty, despite the vague words of New Labour, about what form of assembly we would have been voting for.

Could it be that this was not so much a referendum as New Labour carefully testing the water to find out what would be popular with 'the people', that marvellous group we hear so much about?

DAVID LEWIS
Luton, Beds

SIR—Major constitutional change is being forced upon my country with the support of 45 per cent of the Scottish electorate and 25 per cent of the Welsh.

I begin to feel like Old Labour—ruthlessly sidelined, resentful and waiting for revenge.

GERALD JAMES
Newcastle upon Tyne

SIR—May the English please now vote for their own assembly?

Mrs J. D. RADCLIFFE

September 20, 1997   Winchester, Hants

Party power

SIR—One of the oddities of the Welsh Devolution White Paper is the suggested treatment of by-elections. When an elected constituency member of the Welsh Assembly dies, there is a normal by-election.

But when an additional member taken from the party list under the additional member system passes on, no by-election will take place. Instead, the party holding the seat simply nominates another member, regardless of public opinion.

This makes no allowance for huge swings in public opinion, such as we have recently seen. Once a party holds a nominated seat, it holds it until the next general election—and by-elections on vacancies are a thing of the past. Seats will belong to parties, no matter what the people actually want. Is this modernisation?

Prof. JOHN VINCENT

October 2, 1997   Bristol

One-way

SIR—Randall Enoch (letter, Nov. 29) suggests Machynlleth as the seat of the Welsh assembly. Whatever town is chosen will present a problem—because the best roads run west to east, into England, Wales's gateway to the world. Will one of the assembly's first acts be to order the construction of a north—south super highway to enable all its members to get there expeditiously?

HAROLD ATKINS

December 1, 1997   Wrexham, Clwyd

IRISH HOME TRUTHS

Soldier was right: 'Go home, Congressman'

SIR—The soldier in Northern Ireland was right (report, April 6): Congressman Joseph Kennedy should go back to his own country. He should tell his fellow Irish American Catholics that if it was not for people like them who contribute to Noraid then the IRA would not be so easily financed and perhaps the death and destruction we have seen over the years would be much diminished.

On his vote-grabbing public relations gesture the Congressman visited the Divis Flats and said: 'There is something terribly wrong in Northern Ireland when children have to live in these conditions.'

But, Congressman Kennedy, what about the blacks in your own country who live in equally appalling if not worse conditions. Of all the disasters of public sector housing, the Divis Flats must be the worst; but will Congressman Kennedy tell any of his fellow Irish Americans that the Flats are in the process of being decanted and demolished? I doubt it.

The soldier's anger was easy to understand. Interference from the likes of Congressman Kennedy does much to keep alive the hatred and the violence. If he really cared he would mind his own business.

BARBARA REID
April 7, 1988   Hounslow, Middlesex

No 'Great Man' tradition

SIR—In his review of Neil Jordan's film *Michael Collins* (Nov. 8), Quentin Curtis points out several serious flaws, but adds one of his own.

Collins may or may not have been a great man. On that point

contributions to the debate from historians which you have recently printed established, at the very least, the case for scepticism.

He certainly did not see himself as 'part of a Great Man tradition of history' which included Parnell and O'Connell. Indeed, there is no such tradition. To Collins and his IRA henchmen—and to all those disposed to the use of violence—Irish leaders who sought to remedy Irish grievances by strictly constitutional means were mere lackeys of the British.

Yet, ironically, what Collins secured from Lloyd George in 1921 was not very different from the kind of self-government that the derided nineteenth-century constitutional leaders sought.

ALISTAIR COOKE
November 13, 1996   London SW1

~

The Commonwealth beckons

SIR—If there is an IRA ceasefire (report, Aug. 30), the Irish Republic could give worried Ulster Protestants no greater reassurance than by showing a willingness to consider returning to the Commonwealth, the United Kingdom and allegiance to the Crown.

For long, people in the South have been afraid to speak out about their uneasiness over the broken marriage with the rest of the British Isles. But there are some indications of a shift now that an older generation of leaders has passed from the political scene.

The young middle classes are unhappy about the way Ireland's matchless Georgian architecture has been destroyed or allowed to rot, with the excuse that it represented an alien inheritance. They see that the Irish language has fared far worse under republican government than Welsh and Gaelic have done on the mainland.

Already two members of the ruling Fianna Fail party, Eamon O'Cuiv, a grandson of former president Eamon de Valera, and James McDaid, have spoken out in favour of rejoining the Commonwealth. The way forward has been shown by President Mandela of South Africa and Benazir Bhutto of Pakistan, who both made return to the Commonwealth a priority on coming to power.

The Irish Republic's re-entry would help to bring North and South closer together and pave the way for a united Ireland. For instance, young men and women from both North and South would be eligible to participate in the Commonwealth Games, which could be held in Dublin.

However, that should be only a start. After applying to re-enter the Commonwealth, the Irish government should take steps to abolish the present Constitution with its controversial articles II and III and scrap the Anglo-Irish Agreement. Henry Grattan's Constitution of 1782—which contains the doctrine that no power but the King (or Queen), Lords and Commons of the Kingdom of Ireland can make its laws—should become the basis for a substitute.

A united Ireland should have a federal link with the United Kingdom and a Bill of Rights to reassure the Unionists. The tricolour should be replaced by the white ensign with the cross of St Patrick. And the Prince of Wales could perhaps be made regent.

FRANK MEEHAN
August 31, 1994 Portlaoise, Co. Leix

Unity on the Somme

SIR—Your drama critic Charles Spencer feels a certain sense of dismay about Frank McGuinness's play *Observe the Sons of Ulster Marching Towards the Somme* (Aug. 22); it 'reinforces one's despair that a lasting peace will never be achieved'.

Mr Spencer should not take the play as a factual, historic statement. It is drama, and packs a powerful punch, but it is *fiction*, not history. In portraying the Sons of Ulster as being irredeemably locked into their tribal myths, obsessed with the love for King Billy and a loathing for Papists, it may well represent the writer's comments on the depths of partisan loyalties, but there is no evidence that it portrays what actually happened among Irish Protestants and Catholics on the Somme.

On the contrary, there is good evidence that, in the trenches of the First World War, Irishmen of both persuasions, politically and religiously, fought together as comrades and put aside their differences. In Michael MacDonagh's reports, published as *The Irish at the Front* and *The Irish on the Somme* (in the 1916–17 period), it is claimed that Catholic and Protestant Irishmen prayed together, and that Ulster Protestants even joined in with the Rosary.

He also quotes a Father Plater of the Westminster Catholic Federation, who 'met in the train some soldiers of the Ulster Division, all Orangemen, and instead of consigning the holy father to other realms, as they probably would have done in other times, they actually asked him to bless their miraculous medals'.

Nuns said that Ulster Protestant soldiers accepted medals and Sacred Heart badges warmly—possibly as 'lucky amulets' but in any case, without animosity.

The letters of Willie Redmond, the Irish Home Rule MP for East Clare (a devout Catholic), also described a touching sense of comradeship between the southern Irish Catholics and the Ulster Protestants in the 1914–18 War. In his last letter to his friend J.J. Horgan, he wrote: 'I wish I had time to write you all I have seen here. My men are splendid and we are pulling famously with the Ulstermen . . . I shall never regret I have been out here.' He was killed shortly afterwards, in 1917, and his body was carried to burial by his Ulster comrades. Among his last wishes were that the Irishmen who had fought together would 'bring that spirit back with us to Ireland'.

In the present peace process, perhaps Willie Redmond's prayer *will* be granted at last.

MARY KENNY

August 24, 1995   London W11

~

A peek behind the curtains

SIR—Recent reports that Mrs Jean Kennedy Smith, the American Ambassador to the Irish Republic, has spent over £60,000 of public funds on redecorating her residence in Dublin prompt me to wonder what she spent the money on.

Mrs Kennedy Smith's predominant Irish passion seems to be Anglophobia and the support of Sinn Fein, not the promotion of Irish arts or architecture. Not long ago she appealed to American companies represented in Ireland for money to buy new 'drapes' (curtains) for her embassy in Phoenix Park, a nobly proportioned building which was once the residence of the Chief Secretary, the head of the British civil service in Ireland.

The original curtains were of superbly pleated Irish linen, created by Sybil Connolly, doyenne of Irish fashion designers. Curious about their replacements, I asked a recent visitor to the Kennedy Smith menage about the new curtains and was told they were 'sort of run-of-the-mill Laura Ashley'.

So much for Mrs Kennedy Smith's interest in the extrinsic value of Irish crafts or culture. Further, thirsty visitors to the embassy have remarked that she sometimes serves an undistinguished Californian wine—more evidence of curious taste.

The earliest Chief Secretary and occupant of this house, Colonel John Blaquiere, boasted a cellar which in 1772 was worth £2,000. It was noted that the militia were staying longer in Ireland than hitherto, and that this was due, not to political necessity, but to the lavish hospitality of the good colonel. His illustrious successor, Sir Robert Peel, also boasted a groaning board and a cellar inventory, in 1813, of French wines worth more than £2,300.

This great house, whose distinguished occupants have included Arthur Wellesley (later Duke of Wellington) and the young Winston Churchill, has always been an uneasy berth for its colonial visitors.

One of the first American envoys to the Irish Free State, William Wallace McDowell, evidently overcome by the weight of history surrounding him, dropped dead at a banquet on the evening he presented his credentials in 1934. Another ambassador, an octogenarian called Fitzgerald, made a speech expressing his delight at 'having arrived in London'.

It is to be hoped that when the State Department's lease expires in 2048 this building will be put to better use by the government of the Irish Republic, perhaps as a museum of the house's own distinguished past, which ended in 1922.

HORACE WOOLINGTON

January 1, 1997 Castleknock, Co. Dublin

Quakers deserve apology

SIR—Mr Blair's apology to the Irish for the famine (report, June 2) smacks of political hypocrisy. Nevertheless, now that the new Government is prepared to apologise for the behaviour of former governments to minority groups, I hope that the same sort of apology that was extended to the Irish Catholics will also be given to the Quakers who died for their faith in the seventeenth century.

Thomas Stordy, who died in Carlisle jail, is my direct ancestor and I would like his name to be specifically mentioned as a victim of a British government that 'failed their people', in England, by their cruelty and persecution of a gentle people known as Quakers.

It might also be of interest to Tony Blair and his Government that Quakers were prominent in alleviating the suffering of the Irish people in the nineteenth century. On the other hand, Irish immigrants to America were soon persecuting the indigenous people of that continent in order to acquire their lands!

Quakers driven out of England by government persecution to that same continent showed the world how people of all races could live in peace, by establishing friendship and trust with the Indians of Pennsylvania.

H. G. STORDY
Carlisle

June 6, 1997

Send RUC to Israel

SIR—I am a Palestinian post-graduate student, and watched with considerable interest the events leading up to the recent Drumcree march and the violence that spilt over.

I could not help noticing how the RUC handled these very violent demonstrations; the police managed to control the situation without resort to extreme measures, despite the fact that they were fired on. No demonstrators lost their lives. I discovered later that there had been up to 700 bombings and several attacks with automatic weapons.

I can see the irony when comparing this with the way the Israeli security services manifestly seek to resort to extreme measures of violence against young Palestinians throwing stones in protest.

I wish the RUC could come to Hebron, or any other of our troubled cities, to instruct the Israeli security services in humanitarian behaviour. It is clear to me that human life has a much higher value in Northern Ireland than it has in Israel.

RANIA HAMMAD

July 18, 1997   London E4

Lost art of cursin'

SIR—There is most certainly a comparison to be made between Mr Brian Behan and Salman Rushdie (Limelight, June 20); in fact, a further similarity is that, given the quality of Mr Behan's writing, his life could well be in danger if he did *not* disappear.

As regards the Irish art of cursing, it has fallen on evil days since *The Plough and the Stars* when Uncle Peter told the Young Covey: 'I'll leave you to the day when the all-pitiful, all-merciful, all-lovin' God'll be handin' you to the angels to be rievin' an' roastin' you, tearin' and tormentin' you, burnin' and blastin' you.'

Latterly, a curse is not so much an imprecation as merely strong language—usually our four-letter friend and its variations, or vocal appeals to the best known of the Irish deities, Jayzus.

It is worth making the point that in Ireland the perceived worth of a writer is inexplicably enmeshed with the public and critical assessment of him as a person. Is he, the question is asked, a 'decent skin'? Or could he be—as is more likely, given the Irishman's eagerness to think well of his fellows—'only a bollix'?

Mr Behan's late sibling, Brendan, effed, blinded and bejayzused profusely wherever he went. As a result, it was assumed that he must be—and there is no higher tribute—'one of our own'. And being one of our own, he could not be other than a writer of talent. The logic was and remains unassailable.

It is rare in these unpoetic days that one Irishman will express to another Irishman the pious hope that all of his teeth shall fall out except one, and that the survivor shall be afflicted with an abscess. An aggrieved party is likely to tell you 'May you die roaring for a priest', but that is as far as eloquence is likely to go.

A couple of years ago, after I made a joke about Mr Haughey, the telephone went at two in the morning, and a North of Ireland voice said that I was going to be killed because of it. He did not even bother to accompany the threat with a full-blooded curse, which I thought dull of him.

Brian Behan is to be pitied. Cursing has become a lost art, and it will take a mightier pen than his to revive it. As he will himself know, every Dublin public house has wall-to-wall four-letter words; they hang about at the street corners, on the doorsteps, in the playgrounds and in the very nurseries.

This, alas, is not cursing. It is not even swearing. What it is, is punctuation, and language cannot get much lower than that.

HUGH LEONARD
June 22, 1990   Dalkey, Co. Dublin

It is his friends who begrudge him

SIR—What on earth have I done to offend Hugh Leonard (letter, June 22), the Little Leprechaun Begrudger as he was affectionately known at school?

The last time I saw Hugh he was simpering madly at Terry Wogan, giving a reasonable imitation of a daft Paddy. I must say in Hugh's defence that he hasn't an enemy in Dublin. It is his friends who hate him.

But still your gentle reader will ask why Hugh's outburst against a fellow Dubliner, whose only crime has been to praise Leonard to the skies, while Leonard's condition is known in Dublin as that of the Begrudger. Begrudgers, of whom Leonard appears to be a prime example, are so lacking in self-confidence that they hate everyone in general.

So great is this hatred that it drove James Joyce from Dublin to Paris, vowing never to return. Bernard Shaw as he left described them as narrow-minded bigots who reduce the sublime to the common. In particular your begrudger spares a special hatred for the English Irish—people who have left the Old Sod, survived and even made a success of their lives. Leonard the Begrudger hates above all else the success of my stage play *Boots For The Footless*.

Most English critics, including your own, found the play irresistible and a great night's entertainment. It packed the Tricycle Theatre, taking the most money ever at the box office.

The fact of the play going to the West End is driving the Begrudger mad. He knows that the play tackles issues far beyond his ken. The play pours scorn on the phallic symbolism of the terrorist's gun. It mocks the pseudo-revolutionary and does it with laughter and style. Samuel Beckett lived near Hugh Leonard; racked with sickness he fled from Dalkey to recover his health in London. Was it any wonder he started running faster; he saw Leonard coming.

Last but not least, my heart goes out to Hugh Leonard. He has to pass each and every day under an eight-foot portrait of my brother, Brendan Behan, hanging in the stairway of the Abbey Theatre. It serves every day to remind one of what a real playwright looks like as opposed to a mere television adapter.

BRIAN BEHAN

June 25, 1990   Brighton, W. Sussex

EURO DIRECTION

Sprinkling of nobles among new MEPs

SIR—Two hundred years after the French Revolution it may come as a surprise to realise how many representatives of noble families have been elected members of the new European Parliament. They make only a sprinkling of the 518 MEPs, but the variations from country to country are particularly striking.

Britain and Germany produced the highest totals, but with some significant differences. The 32 Conservative members include three hereditary peers (Lord Bethell, Lord Inglewood and Lord O'Hagan), a life peer (Lord Plumb), three knights and a member of a Scottish gentry family (Edward McMillan-Scott).

The Hon. Sir Peter Vanneck lost his marginal seat of Cleveland and North Yorkshire. But with the exception of Viscount Morpeth, who stood unsuccessfully for the SLD in Northumbria, our political homogeneity makes a striking contrast to the continent.

In Germany, noblemen are spread right across the political spectrum. Bavaria's CSU members include the Archduke Otto, head of the House of Hapsburg, and Franz Ludwig, Count von Stauffenberg, from the same family as the hero of the Hitler bomb plot. Among the Christian Democrats there is Kurt von Wogan, but not Philipp von Bismarck who has retired, and the Free Democrat members include Baron Rudiger von Wechmar and Mechtild von Alemann.

All this might seem predictable enough, but a member of the baronial family of Vittinghoff was elected for the Socialist SPD. Nobles have also been strong supporters of the Greens. Among them is Jakob von Uexkull, a member of another family involved in the Bomb Plot, who failed to retain his seat.

But Italy, despite producing the Marchese Carlo Ripa di Meana as an EC Commissioner with a conspicuously high profile, seems to

have elected no members of its old families. The Christian Democrats there have never really been a gentleman's party; the Contessa
Rangoni Machiavelli even campaigned for David Steel.

In Belgium, François-Xavier de Donnea was elected for the Partie
des Reformes et de la Liberté, and Brigitte Ernst de la Graete for the
Ecologists. Carmen Diez di Rivera y Icaza in Spain and Pedro
Manuel Guedes de Passos Canavarro in Portugal were both elected
for the socialists.

Denmark and The Netherlands both produce a blank, like France,
despite a number of famous names like d'Harcourt and de Rohan still
being active recently in French national politics, along with that of
d'Ornano. (One also notes the success of former President Giscard,
whose family in 1922–23 added the name of D'Estaing in homage to an
ancestor of doubtful nobility.) And, finally, in Ireland, a lone member
of the old Ascendancy, George Salter-Townshend of Castle Town-
shend, stood unsuccessfully as an independent candidate in Munster.

MICHAEL SAYER
July 7, 1989   Sparham, Norfolk

David Steel, the former Liberal leader, came fourth of sixteen candidates in the
Central Italy constituency.

Kant counters 'soulless' federalism

SIR—In his noteworthy article (Feb. 28) George Walden highlighted a 'federation of free states' as Kant's requirement for
peace.

Kant went on to stress that an association or federation of
neighbouring states should retain their independent status as
against a universal ('soulless') conglomeration with the germ of
'despotism' and potential anarchy. Nature, according to Kant,
demands union not by the weakening of competitive forces but
through the equilibrium of these forces in their most active rivalry.

Coming from one of history's most eminent thinkers, is this not a
powerful argument against a potentially domineering 'soulless'
federal state of Europe, a united states of Europe, while favouring
a federation (or commonwealth) of Europe's nationally free states
based on the economic interest of the single market, which latter

would also ensure Germany's co-operation rather than seeking it by
an artificial (and resented) political 'looking in' procedure?

                                    Dr EDMUND GOLDBERGER
March 5, 1990   London W2

Crucial moment in our history

SIR—One does not have to be a member of the Bruges Group, or
even a Government minister concerned about the unity of the
Conservative party, to oppose Jacques Delors's concept of a federal
Europe.

It is extraordinary that when the rest of humanity stresses the
sovereign nature of its different states, the western Europeans
should be willing to abandon theirs for an eventual super state
run by officials in Brussels.

However, it is good that the problem has come into the open and
is associated with negotiations for a single currency. Parliament
came into being to curb the power of the Crown over finance.

If it cedes the symbol of financial sovereignty which is its national
currency it could very soon cease to exist.

As a country, we have to balance our partnership with the
United States, of proven worth in the Gulf crisis, against membership of a federal Europe—demonstrated to be ineffective in every
recent test of defence and foreign policy and, over the years, by no
means favourable to our ideas and interests. Debate over Europe
represents a conflict between the successors of our parliamentary
leaders Pitt and Churchill against the Brussels descendants of the
French royal appointees Colbert and Necker, governing by
decree.

Effective opposition to Delors, however, will not succeed without
considerable changes in national attitudes. The massive balance of
payments deficit which resulted in raising interest rates and the
present recession was largely the fault of the British people.

Until something of the £4.5 billion deficit on food imports has
been reduced and people choose not to borrow ostensibly for home
improvements only to spend a large proportion on short-term
pleasures, our negotiating position will be weak.

We face moral as well as political decisions. It is a pity that the Church as well as the Government is not making its voice heard at this crucial moment in our national history.

Rev Prof WILLIAM FREND

June 19, 1991   Cambridge

'Heart of Europe' is a vain hope

SIR—In the absence of seismic convulsions of a quite unprecedented magnitude, the hope that Britain can be at 'the very heart of Europe' is a vain one. This is not just a matter of semantics.

We are not geographically anywhere near the heart of Europe; and our geography has to a large extent formed our history. Both have played a central part in forming our culture—in the broadest sense—our psychology, loyalties and affections.

Instinctively we look outwards to the oceans, not inwards to the Rhine Valley. Hence the profound mental gulf that so often divides us from our continental neighbours: many of the French, for example, were genuinely affronted that we backed the New Zealanders rather than themselves over the *Rainbow Warrior* affair, taking the view that 'good Europeans' had a duty to stick together.

With a long tradition of parliamentary government and the rule of law, and having escaped occupation by a foreign power, we take a greater pride in our past and in our institutions than do most Continentals, who have a great deal that they would rather forget.

None of this is an argument against aiming for increasing co-operation with our neighbours, but 'at the very heart of Europe' we can never be.

Lord MONSON

July 1, 1991   London SW1

Federal nightmare

SIR—Boris Johnson's report revealing the frantic attempts to draft the dread word 'federal' out of the patently federalist Luxembourg draft treaty (Oct. 4) shows the depth to which some will go. Euro-deception is becoming an art form.

It is not the word 'federal' which matters, but what is being done. The Luxembourg (let alone the Dutch) proposals would involve a massive transfer of power away from the British voter and the British Parliament. They would damage British and European democracy.

The question remains, 'Who governs?' It is a question of power, not semantics. Lewis Carroll summed it up in *Through The Looking Glass*.

'When I use a word,' Humpty Dumpty said in a rather scornful voice, 'it means just what I choose it to mean—neither more nor less.'

'The question is,' said Alice, 'whether you can make words mean so many different things.'

'The question is,' said Humpty Dumpty, 'which is to be master—that's all.'

Will we, too, wake up in time?

BILL CASH, MP (Con)
October 7, 1991   London SW1

~

Too much fuss about 'F' word

SIR—It is hard to understand why Mr Major and Mr Hurd are making such difficulties over the use of the word 'federal' in the Maastricht negotiations.

Apart from anything else, the word is vague. For some people it triggers fears of a centralised system of government—a European state ruled from Brussels. But, for most, federalism means the exact opposite, with as many decisions as possible being taken locally.

For every other member country 'federalism' evokes the idea of a Community which is alive and kicking. They regard Britain's reluctance to accept the word as further evidence that our hearts are not in the business of building Europe.

The result will be that Britain's refusal to make concessions to the other 11 countries over the use of this word will mean that we shall have to give way on matters of much greater practical importance to us, such as the Common Agricultural Policy and the timetable for a single currency.

As the European Community becomes larger, something will have to be done to ensure decisions are taken if we are to avoid interminable deadlocks of the kind that has persisted for years over reform of the CAP. The crude way of arriving at such a consensus is by weighted majority voting—the direction in which member governments, including, albeit reluctantly, the British Government, seem to be moving.

It would be far better to entrust the European Commission with the task of trying to evolve a consensus. They would be more fruitfully employed doing this than busying themselves with annoying details which interfere with our day-to-day lives.

We may not achieve this in my lifetime, but politics is the art of the possible, and I have confidence in the ability of Mr Major and Mr Hurd to achieve as much as possible for this country and for Europe. Still, it is a pity that they have made their task that much more difficult by refusing to swallow the 'F' word.

Sir ANTHONY MEYER, Bt, MP (Con)

November 19, 1991 London SW1

All smiles on the German front

SIR—I am a self-employed publican in Heidelberg employing 10 people, and I often mix with other self-employed people. I was interested in Robin Gedye's report on small traders in Meckenheim, comparing them to their struggling English counterparts in Reigate (July 20).

The traders could be doing as well as they claim, but I found myself smiling broadly. Their talk could have come from any 'fly-on-the-wall' recording of conversation at a barbecue among the German self-employed: all confidence, broad smiles and Porsches; each trying desperately to outdo the others with 'I'm doing very well, thank you'.

I know from experience that these comments bear little relation to the truth. Woe to the man in Germany who says: 'Well, I can still pay the rent, but we aren't saving much.' You just don't say that sort of thing. In a bankruptcy case in Germany, the last two things to go are the confident 'I'm raking it in' smile and the black Porsche—in that order. I am noticing the recession, and I am not alone. With our present interest rates I thank God every day that I haven't any debts, but many small traders have.

Three years ago we were coining it, but times have changed. My rent has risen by 12 per cent in six months, beer by up to 15 per cent, and council charges by up to 20 per cent—and all this with stagnant takings.

While I can admit this in an English newspaper, you will find me smiling and talking rubbish with the rest of them at the Sunday afternoon *grillfeste*—and I still drive my ridiculously expensive BMW. If you do not exude this slight air of Teutonic arrogant confidence your customers might feel they are dealing with a loser, and you don't deal with a loser.

SIMON WAKELING
July 29, 1992   Heidelberg, Germany

~

Don't marginalise us again

SIR—As a historian I view with the deepest dismay the growing crisis in the European Community, with the apparent possibility that the original signatories to the Treaty of Rome (less Italy) may form an inner economic and monetary union.

As it happens, I have recently been reading for a new book the Cabinet papers which document the Labour Government's reluctance in the late 1940s to join in the creation of the Coal and Steel Community (the precursor of the Common Market) and the Conservative Government's equal reluctance in the 1950s to join in the creation of the Common Market itself.

Today's Euro-sceptics—like Tebbit, Ridley, Gould, Budgen and Shore (to say nothing of Lady Thatcher)—depressingly trot out the same arguments, such as all that chuntering about 'sovereignty', used in the 1940s and 1950s in favour of keeping clear and leaving the Europeans to get on with it.

But at least it is understandable that, back in 1945–57, the politicians could believe that Britain (thanks to the existence of the British Commonwealth, the sterling area and the Anglo-American 'special relationship') was still a great power, indeed a world power, and thus able to go it alone. No such excuse can justify the quite amazingly inflated view of Britain's international importance and capacity to exercise 'sovereignty' cherished by today's Euro-sceptics.

Have they not noticed that since the 1940s Great Britain has almost uninterruptedly lost world-market share as an industrial country, persistently sunk down the league table of GNP per head, and seen her currency depreciate from 11–12 Swiss francs to the pound to just over two?

To me, therefore, it is utter folly, and potentially dangerous folly, for the Euro-sceptics to urge us to repeat the mistakes of the 1940s and 1950s in the fallen British circumstances of the 1990s, and once again relegate ourselves to the touchline while the original Common Market countries get on with the game.

CORRELLI BARNETT

September 29, 1992 Churchill College, Cambridge

Ignore these edicts, mes amis Anglais

SIR—As a long-time Anglophile, I am increasingly saddened when I visit your beautiful land to behold the small-time regulations and restrictions imposed upon you both by your Government and the EC administration in Brussels.

I am equally saddened that you alone of the members of the EC abide by these ridiculous edicts. In France we have always ignored those directives of which we have disapproved and implemented only those we have considered to our advantage. It is the French way.

But now our own *belle France* has succumbed. We have banned smoking in public places and, even more terrible, have no-smoking areas in our cafés.

I am desolated beyond belief, and I write this as a committed non-smoking Frenchman, for a basic French freedom is at stake here.

Through the abundant courtesies of your column I would urge your readers to remember that we French have always been a difficult people to govern, and we value our independence of action. The EC and our own incompetent government will long ago have gone up in smoke before the smell of Gauloise ceases to pervade the platforms of the Gard du Nord.

HENRI DUVAL
November 3, 1992   Cheriton, Hants

Quite right, Capt Upham!

SIR—I was particularly interested in the remarks made in 1962 by Capt Charles Upham, VC and Bar, about British entry into the Common Market (obituary, Nov. 23).

Nobody, surely, would deny that Britain has been 'gradually pulled down and down', or that 'the whole English way of life' is in danger. Yet consecutive administrations, mainly Conservative, have taken the country deeper and deeper into Europe, with ever spiralling cost.

Capt Upham's view that 'your politicians have made money their God but what they are buying is disaster' holds true today. One has only to look at what has happened in the privatised utilities to see what he meant, the current British Gas furore over executive salaries being just one example of how a private monopoly runs itself.

I have voted Conservative all my adult life but, along with many friends, have no intention of doing so at the next General Election.

A. C. AYRES
Enton Green, Surrey

SIR—Capt Upham's deeds make this old soldier feel very humble indeed. It should be made compulsory reading to those men who are now complaining of stress, etc, brought on through service in the Gulf war.

What a pity more of us did not fight against entry into the Common Market which resulted in us turning our backs on him and his fellow countrymen.

JOHN EASTBURY
November 26, 1994   Cromer, Norfolk

The New Zealander Captain Charles Upham won the VC on Crete in 1941 and a Bar at El Alamein in 1942.

An 'unnatural' anniversary

SIR—I applaud the sentiments of your leader on the exploitation of one of the world's most momentous battles (June 16). The truth is that Waterloo has been hijacked by commercial interests and by European politicians.

Why is this 'unnatural' 180th anniversary being celebrated unless it is to promote *son et lumière* and battle re-enactments for commercial gain? What possible justification can there be for hoisting the 'inglorious flag' of the European Union over the battlefield unless, of course, you wish to promote that 'Union'?

We are currently assured that Napoleon Bonaparte was the architect of modern Europe. How can the man who enslaved most of the Continent, who caused the deaths of two million Europeans, and who appointed a general to oversee the systematic looting of the treasuries of other countries, be described as such? Napoleon proved himself a military genius, except at Waterloo, but as a man he was a tyrannical monster.

I was at Waterloo last weekend to attend the annual general meeting of the Waterloo Committee, which was set up some 20 years ago to safeguard, among other things, the battlefield and its monuments after it was proposed to drive a motorway through the site.

I did not, as a matter of principle, attend the events at the battlefield itself, and I hope we shall, in future, be spared further violation of its historical significance every few years.

We British have a feeling and respect for the past, something that not all nations understand or share. La Belle Alliance, Napoleon's headquarters which once housed a small museum, has recently been turned into a discotheque.

DUKE OF WELLINGTON and PRINCE OF WATERLOO
June 22, 1995   Stratfield Saye, Hants

~

Country betrayed

SIR—Since it is planning to go ahead with its White Paper on Europe (report, Jan. 19), the Government might be interested to know that as a result of the St Tudy petition—which you kindly publicised even as far as Norfolk Island in the Pacific—I am still inundated with letters of support.

I sense several rivers of opinion. Seventy or so Labour MPs (Euro Safeguards Campaign) and an estimated 100 Tory MPs were all regarded by those who wrote to me as patriots. Perhaps just a majority of my correspondents were in favour of the European Union, with the firm stipulation that the Common Agricultural Policy undergo drastic revision and the Common Fisheries Policy be renounced.

But 100 per cent rejected a single currency or the constitutional, legal, economic, defence or foreign policy implications of a creeping federalism. Some thought that the Lib-Dems should in future be known as the European Federal Party, and that others who tended towards a federal policy could be neither true New (or Old) Labour or Conservative.

Four hundred or so letters and uncounted phone calls do not constitute a Mori or Gallup poll. But the question of whether there is to be a federated Europe or a Europe of Sovereign States is all too pertinent. In answering it I, unlike the media, cannot assign the term Left or Right to Messrs Benn, Shore, Austin Mitchell, Cash or Gill.

They seem to share one common belief certainly held by my correspondents. Our country is being (or has been) betrayed. And that betrayal must be reversed, either by this Government or its successor.

Vice-Adml SIR LOUIS LE BAILLY
January 20, 1996   St Tudy, Cornwall

~

A house divided

SIR—My husband and I have just finished our daily debate on Europe. The catalyst for this discussion was Robin Gedye's article (Feb. 7).

My husband—German, pro-Europe and thinking purely in terms of commerce (like most of our politicians)—can see only advantages for all. He just can't understand how so many people, myself included, can feel such anger over 'trivialities' such as loss of national currency, being dictated to by Brussels on what shape our cucumbers should be, or what produce the WI may or may not sell.

The British, he declares, should just do what Germans would do in the face of such silly rules—ignore them. I try to explain that we, a nation of queuers and keep-off-the-grassers, can't see any point in having rules if you don't intend to obey them.

I, too, can see Helmut Kohl's point of view on monetary union, but that doesn't dispel my doubts about other aspects of the European Community. Having lived on three continents, I have observed how Europeans abroad gravitate naturally to their 'own sort'. I have also noticed how, in mixed gatherings, a trivial political discussion can fast degenerate into an acrimonious 'you' and 'we' debate.

It is hard for me to envisage one great big, matey Europe on anything more than a commercial basis.

(Mrs) PENNY BOHRER
February 13, 1996 Chipping Norton, Oxon

～

A fateful crossroads

SIR—Not since 1940 has the United Kingdom's sovereign right to govern its own affairs been in greater peril. The menacing insistence by Chancellor Kohl that his unshakeable goal is the total irreversible integration of the economies of the European Union countries should not be ignored.

We are in serious danger of allowing him to achieve domination over our economy by 'sleight of hand diplomacy', whereas Adolf Hitler failed to do so by military might.

By postponing the decision on a single European currency until after the next election, Europhiles seek to play down the deadly significance of what is at stake. The election will be fought on a broad spectrum of domestic issues rather than on the key issue of whether Britain shall reclaim the controls secretly yielded up to foreign hands by the small print of the Maastricht Treaty.

When the High Court of Parliament at Westminster raged in fierce debate about the proposals of Maastricht, we were never told of the dire denial of our British rights that the treaty involved.

Indeed, overwhelming emphasis was put on the word 'subsidiarity', which was not an expression commonly understood either by Parliamentarians or the public at large. We were given to understand that major issues concerning this country would remain under the complete control of our own government.

Now we have abundant evidence that Maastricht handed over to the European Union massive control over our daily life. We have reached the stage when the United Kingdom must decide either to yield up any claim to control over our own judicial system, and over our economy, or to withdraw completely from membership of the European Union.

No one has yet been able to indicate the economic gain to us because of our membership of the European Union. The Treasury has regularly revealed that our balance of trade with Europe is in the red. It is only because our surplus with the rest of the world has paid for our deficit with Europe, that we have avoided bankruptcy. If we had relied on European trade rather than on global trade, we would have been destroyed.

Parliament must reassert its proud position as the supreme governing authority in this land, and should negotiate our withdrawal from the massive restrictions imposed on us by the Franco-German Alliance in Europe.

With good will on both sides there is no reason why this withdrawal cannot be undertaken in a friendly agreement that the United Kingdom will enjoy the same trading relationship with Europe as that which currently exists for Japan, Norway and Switzerland.

We are at a fateful crossroads in our history. May God help us to liberate this land once again—to restore our faith in Britain's ability to stand on its own two feet!

Viscount TONYPANDY OF RHONDDA

December 12, 1996   London SW1

Viscount Tonypandy (1909–97) was a Labour MP and Secretary of State for Wales before serving as Speaker of the House of Commons from 1976 to 1983.

Say it in English

SIR—If the European single currency is such a good thing—cutting business costs and promoting freer intercourse between member states—why have we heard nothing from the Commission about a European single language?

Think of the benefits and cost savings that would bring. It is absurd to talk about convergence on everything from defence and policing down to weights and measures when the Commissioners can't even speak to each other without an interpreter.

Since English is the most widely spoken language in the world, let us have a treaty and a starting date—Jan. 1, 2010, for instance—for the abolition of all other European languages, with heavy fines for anyone found not using English.

Such whole-hearted integrationists as the French and the Germans could surely have no objection to such harmonisation.

CYNTHIA HARROD-EAGLES
February 26, 1997   Northwood, Middx

Right stripe

SIR—The announcement that Euro MPs are about to learn that heated underpants may help children to get better exam results (report, Feb. 26) may not be as technologically revolutionary as is claimed.

I recall former schoolmasters applying local heating with an appropriate instrument to inattentive boys who were making inadequate progress in mathematics or Latin; science masters would sometimes use a piece of rubber tubing from Bunsen burners that had been misused to make fireworks.

Good marks were achieved, though perhaps not of the type envisaged by the bosses of Brussels, and would be proudly displayed to one's contemporaries. No doubt it was ruinous psychologically.

BRIAN HUNTER
March 3, 1997   Camberley, Surrey

LIVING LEGACIES

Remaining colonies

SIR—Your front-page headline 'Britain's farewell to empire' (July 1) is, of course, an exaggeration. We may have given up our last major foreign possession—Hong Kong—but there are still colonies—Bermuda, Ascension Island, the Falklands, Gibraltar, the Turks and Caicos, Tristan da Cunha and St Helena.

They are sufficiently far flung for the old boast that the sun never sets on the Empire to be still true. The way that the Falklands became important with the discovery of oil should make us wary of dismissing any of them as worthless.

But while we still have specific responsibilities for the people of these territories (which we are sometimes tardy in fulfilling, as in St Helena), we also have a moral duty to provide leadership in multifarious forms for all who share our English-speaking British culture around the world.

The Government could begin by showing a little more enthusiasm for the Commonwealth, which two countries, Pakistan and South Africa, have rejoined; another, Fiji, hopes to reapply for membership. But the rest of us could perform a valuable service by refusing to be bamboozled into believing that any institution, such as the law or our parliamentary system, must be changed to conform with other models. If we do not, we shall discover that we have slipped irretrievably into the empire of Europe.

EDWARD BURKE
Bath

SIR—It is indeed a surprise to see how little the Queen's visit to Canada has been reported in Britain (letter, July 1). The Queen has been received rapturously wherever she has gone, and a visit by

Prince Philip to flood victims in Manitoba has been especially appreciated.

The whole tour has been an upbeat occasion, such as has not been seen here in recent times. It has served to underline that the link between our two countries remains strong and important.

PETER NEARY
London, Ontario

SIR—Now that Britain has handed Hong Kong back to China, is it not time for China to hand back Tibet to the people of Tibet? The United Nations should commence negotiations on behalf of the people of Tibet for withdrawal of the invading forces.

ANDREW JONES
July 2, 1997 Didcot, Oxon

Make the Rock a dominion

SIR—There is a relatively simple way of answering the call for a new power-sharing agreement between Britain and Gibraltar made by Mr Joe Bossano, the colony's chief minister (report, Nov. 25). The Gibraltarians should be permitted to tread the same path as the Canadians, Australians and New Zealanders towards dominion status.

As a self-governing dominion, the Rock would not only have the chance of enjoying full internal self-government; it would be internationally recognised as fully independent while retaining British institutions under the Crown.

This would give Gibraltarians much needed reassurance that they are members of the British family of nations, who are not about to be cast off but rather made welcome as mature members of the Commonwealth.

Most important, it would be a way of enabling Gibraltar to become independent without Spain having the opportunity to exercise its right to reclaim the peninsula under Article 10 of the Treaty of Utrecht, 1713. It was this factor which prevented Gibraltar from seeking independence along with other colonies in the Sixties.

As a former Governor of Gibraltar, I can confirm that the Gibraltarians have no wish to become Spanish, particularly since they were cut off from Spain by the 15th siege, from 1969 to 1985. Britain has pledged in the preamble to Gibraltar's 1969 constitution that there will be no change of sovereignty against the Gibraltarians' 'freely and democratically expressed wishes'. There has been a steady process of constitutional evolution ever since 1945, under which the local government has achieved more and more responsibility for Gibraltarian affairs as long as there was no conflict with the military needs of the Fortress.

Now that the Rock's strategic importance is diminishing it is surely time to call a new constitutional conference which gives some effect to Mr Bossano's belief that Gibraltarians are more than ready to handle their own affairs.

Gen. Sir WILLIAM JACKSON

November 26, 1993   Gibraltar

General Sir William Jackson was Governor of Gibraltar, 1978–82.

Pensioner's lament at frozen justice

SIR—We congratulate and envy our compatriot old-age pensioners in Britain and 28 other countries where, next month, their British pensions will rise by 10.9 per cent.

The 28 countries are where 40 per cent of British expatriate pensioners are domiciled and where their pensions are index-linked to Britain's cost of living. We in Canada are 95,000 of the remaining 60 per cent of expatriate pensioners whose pensions remain frozen by the ice-wand of Britain's prestidigitator-government.

When I peered through the periscope of my tank on Normandy beach in June 1944 I did not know that my counterparts in the tanks to the left and right of me were smarter because, one day in the future, they were going to work and/or retire in Germany, the United States, Sweden and the Philippines, rather than Canada.

I failed to realise that my contributions to the National Insurance fund during war service or working life in Britain would be regarded by the Government as possessing less cachet (less cash, eh?) than theirs in some future computation which rendered, year by year, my pension as progressively dwindling to a fraction of theirs. Some of our frozen pensioners receive £2.50 a week from Britain.

Depreciation, renunciation, humiliation, deprivation—they have a remarkably similar taste on our palates.

The Government says it would cost an unaffordable £87 million to index fully our pensions; so we ask our fortunate fellow-country-men to raise their voices in righteous indignation at our plight and help us to end this un-British irrationality in the matter of our frozen pensions . . . quickly, before the Government hurls another few billion pounds at some other conflict around the globe in defence of principle, honour and justice.

BENSON ZONENA
March 21, 1991   Toronto

~

Racial surrealism

SIR—Why is it that South Africa always provides this curious mixture of grief and hilarity? I ask the question after reading your correspondent's report (Feb. 4) from Mossel Bay on the South African celebrations to mark the first rounding of the Cape by Bartholomew Diaz 500 years ago.

Because Coloureds and Blacks boycotted the festivities, White volunteers with suitably blackened skins and wearing fuzzy wigs played the parts of the welcoming Hottentots. This is really most appropriate and deeply revealing. At least it might seem so at first glance. It is all part of the tragic pantomime of South African life—Whites playing Blacks on a Whites-only beach (as your correspon-dent notes, the warning signs were still in place).

If this were all, it would be strange enough—but there is no end to strangeness in South Africa. Consider the following: when Diaz first set foot on South African soil in 1488 he was indeed met by a party of the indigenous inhabitants of the Cape, known as Hottentots, or Khoikhoi. But the natives were far from friendly: a stone was thrown, and Diaz replied with a crossbow, killing the stone-thrower. The first riot had been contained and the tone set for future relations between the races.

The anger of the Hottentots was long-lasting. When Diaz's compatriot Vasco Da Gama made landfall north of the Cape nine years later, the Hottentots attacked him violently. At the festivities in Mossel Bay, according to your correspondent, it seems that the latterday Portuguese who waded ashore on the Whites-only beach did not have to face the wrath of the Hottentots. They were met instead by President Botha, who spoke darkly of international boycotts and brightly of the spice trade with India. The surreal quality of South African life is once more laid before us.

Because the fact of the matter is that neither the bewigged Whites nor the boycotting Blacks were equipped to play the roles of the Hottentots, because it was the Hottentots after all who were the original possessors of South Africa—they were the most populous and widely dispersed of the original South African people. And it is they who were the real losers: they had the double misfortune to find themselves caught between invading White settlers and encroaching Black tribes. Today, at least in the Cape, they are extinct.

CHRISTOPHER HOPE
February 6, 1988 London WC1

Old and bold

SIR—President Mandela's new South Africa sets a fine example of ignoring the modern curses of ageism and background.

My father, Robert Snowden, has just been elected to the Western Council of Kwa-Zulu Natal as a member representing the Inkatha Freedom Party. This is despite the fact that he is a former member of the British Colonial Service, and has just celebrated his 81st birthday.

He served in the Second World War as a cavalry officer, worked for the World Bank in West Africa and was private secretary to the first governor-general of the Solomon Islands. Would he have had a similar chance to use his experience if he had opted to retire here?

NEIL SNOWDEN
July 10, 1996 Chislehurst, Kent

Politicians ruining Zimbabwe

SIR—There is no controversy in Zimbabwe about whether land should be made available for resettlement (report, March 20). Ample land is already available. The problem is that President Mugabe's government is using that precious commodity as a vote-catching gimmick to win short-term popularity.

When the white man first arrived in this country 100 years ago, every black was a subsistence peasant farmer. The population was about 300,000. Today it is almost 12 million. We have the largest rate of population increase in the world—more than four per cent—and our numbers double approximately every 16 years.

While large numbers of blacks have become urbanised, it would be difficult to find one who, deep down, does not retain an urge to return to the land. Clearly, redistributing land is not going to resolve the situation.

The humiliating truth is that, for the first time, we have run out of food, and this is months before the impact of the current serious drought will be felt. What was once the bread-basket of Central Africa has now been forced to join the queue of Third World countries begging for food and financial aid.

This is the result of incompetence, corruption and other evils associated with a one-party dictatorship. Over the past decade the acreage planted to maize, the staple food, has been reduced by approximately two thirds, because maize production has become a sure road to bankruptcy for the farmers concerned.

One would have thought that a government claiming to represent the people would have learned from experience. But where the opposition is denied access to the media, where Parliament votes millions of dollars of taxpayers' money as a direct subsidy to the governing party funds, where civil servants are compelled to become members of the governing party in order to safeguard their positions, this has the effect of promoting complacent arrogance in dictators.

Zimbabwe is a classic illustration of Lord Acton's dictum: Power tends to corrupt, and absolute power corrupts absolutely.

Responsible opinion from every sector of our community is strongly opposed to the Land Acquisition Act, which can only hinder the government's efforts to implement its economic structural adjustment programme. Agriculturalists and conservationists are deeply concerned at the devastation that will ensue from the process of transferring land from experienced and efficient farmers to incompetent squatters.

Even before this obnoxious legislation was introduced, the government had secured four million hectares for distribution. Three million hectares have been allocated and ruined, due to inadequate government back-up and incompetent farmers. As a consequence, the government has been floundering, undecided over what to do with the remaining one million hectares.

The only winners at this game will be the party politicians who, to date, have succeeded in brainwashing the poor unsuspecting voters. Nevertheless, people are openly saying that the time has come for Zimbabwe to repeat what happened in Zambia last year—turn out the government via the ballot box.

IAN SMITH

March 25, 1992   Harare

Ian Smith was Prime Minister of Rhodesia, 1964–79.

SENIOR DOMINION

Web of deceit

SIR—When the Prime Minister returned triumphant from Maastricht, one of the victories he claimed to have achieved was that foreign policy and defence would not be subject to the provisions and mechanisms of the treaty, but would be dealt with under the vaunted 'Three Pillars' agreement on a purely inter-governmental basis.

We now learn that the European Union has broken off relations with Canada, and is contemplating imposing sanctions. Are these decisions being taken with the agreement of the British Government, after government-to-government discussions, or are they being orchestrated by the European Commission? Will the web of deceit with which our rulers have bound us to Brussels prove stronger than the ties of blood and kinship?

J. H. GIRLING
Crewkerne, Som

Sir—Like Leo Weston (letter, March 11), I wholeheartedly applaud Canada's defence of its fishermen's right to earn a living.

It is indeed sad that in this country we are saddled with a government whose twin preoccupying and overriding obsessions—grovelling to the rest of the world and enriching a handful of people in the financial sector—are matched in magnitude only by their complete and utter contempt for the people whom they are supposed to represent.

RICHARD CLARKE
Croydon, Surrey

SIR—As the grandson of the First World War prime minister of Newfoundland, the 1st Lord Morris, I must express 100 per cent support for Canada.

My grandfather dispatched the cream of the island's youth to fight alongside Britain under the imperial flag; the Royal New-foundland Regiment fought at Gallipoli, then was mown down at the battle of Beaumont Hamel. Britain can never repay the propor-tionate effort and sacrifice made by those Newfoundlanders. But it can do everything to support a Canadian government which has had the courage to attempt to enforce effective fish conservation policies that are badly needed throughout the entire North Atlantic.

Lord MORRIS
London SW1

SIR—Each day when I hear the news I wonder if we have all gone stark staring mad. What is this thing called the EU which is sending ultimatums on our behalf to Her Majesty's subjects in Canada?

Col MAURICE WILLOUGHBY
Storrington, W. Sussex

SIR—If ever an international situation called for the dispatch of a British gunboat it is this—in support of the Canadians.

ALAN McGREGOR
Dundee

SIR—I resigned from the Conservative Party and voted Liberal at the last election. I later rejoined the Tories, not least because I have an excellent backbencher as MP. But if the remarks in the Commons by the Fisheries Minister, Mr Michael Jack (report, March 14), seriously indicate government policy, then I will have no option but to resign again, like Mr Bremer (letter, March 14).

It has been plain for some time that many of the internal problems of this country stem from lack of commitment to the family; how depressing then that the Government now seems bent on demon-strating the same faults in dealings beyond our shores. Canada is part of British family life, culture, history and economic relations in so many ways that people are largely unconscious of them.

I am an example of these connections in that I am a Canadian citizen, born in Norfolk, whose reaction to British entry to the Common Market was to buy a farm in Manitoba which I have run with our farm here in Suffolk for some years.

The later seasons in Canada enabled me to do this reasonably comfortably, but there have been difficulties. In 1979, I delayed my departure for Canada because, as a local Tory chairman, I wanted to make sure my candidate got home in the general election. Once Mrs Thatcher entered Downing Street I set off for Canada where I was in time to vote for the return of Joe Clark's Conservative government.

There can be no division of my loyalties or that of many others in this country, and if Mr Major's government thinks differently it will lose my support permanently. I must stop now. I have to run up our Canadian flag on a castle just down the road.

J. LEADER
March 15, 1995 Syleham, Suffolk

Atlantic trading partners

SIR—A transatlantic free trade area linking the economies of Europe and North America—the idea supported by Malcolm Rifkind (report, Oct. 9)—is an essential step with which to bind our two continents closer now the Cold War is over. The Soviet threat may have disappeared, but trade friction is on the rise.

This search for 'glue' is not motivated by mere nostalgia. Europe and North America have in common a strong interest in re-invigorating the transatlantic economy and maintaining the momentum of global trade liberalisation.

Free trade is the next logical step. Already our two continental economies are highly integrated in investment, services and technology, which are the new arteries of the global economy. For many industries in Europe and North America, existing continental arrangements are no longer broad enough to encompass their interests. Free trade between us is a natural response to pressure for deeper integration.

Europe and North America are logical partners. In the European Union and, to a degree in Nafta (the North American Free Trade Agreement), we have created unique structures for regional economic co-operation and integration. With imagination, these can provide logical building blocks for a yet more ambitious bridge across the Atlantic, one which could be extended more easily than that between any other regions of the world.

If this transatlantic community is to move forward it will need to be driven by a broader vision than either the European Union or Nafta can themselves provide.

It will have to be rooted in a recognition that we are a set of countries that must ultimately stand together, work together and reinforce our shared global interests.

Given the degree to which technological change is altering the foundations of our post-war relationship and creating the potential for friction, we need to rediscover those ties that bind.

However, deeper transatlantic co-operation is not an alternative to broader global co-operation; it is a new, stronger structure which is central to our ability to manage a larger global order.

ROY MacLAREN
October 11, 1995   International Trade Minister, Ottawa

French stamp an insult to Canada

SIR—How dare the French government issue a stamp celebrating General de Gaulle's speech which gave such encouragement to separatists in Quebec 30 years ago (Peterborough, Feb. 20)? De Gaulle never apologised for his affront, but relations slowly improved until we believed that France was a friend to Canada again.

If the Quai d'Orsay permits the issue of the three-franc stamp, which the French press expects to show the general standing in front of a banner proclaiming *Au Québec tout en Français*, it will be effectively endorsing a programme of 'linguistic cleansing' that was condemned by the United Nations Human Rights Committee in 1993.

What makes this proposal all the more distressing for English Quebeckers is that it comes at a time when their federal government has been ignoring provincial transgressions against the Canadian constitution, and even taking Quebec's side in cases that have been brought before the UN committee.

Only last week a federal minister urged Anglo Quebec to ignore the continuing oppression which has reduced its numbers by hundreds of thousands over the years.

Yet the victims are the 800,000 non-Francophones who have done more to keep Canada together than any other group in the country. As a minority amid six million French speakers, they are concentrated along the Ontario border and in the western region of Montreal.

It is hardly surprising, therefore, that the present persecution is leading to increasing demands from them that, if Quebec separates from Canada, the present province should be further divided. They want it to be split into a separate eastern francophone zone and a western free zone, which desires to remain in Canada where freedom of choice in language matters prevails.

If your readers have any doubts about the significance of the French affront, they should consider what would be the reaction in France if Britain issued a stamp that encouraged the 'heroic efforts' of the Basques to be free of French rule.

CHRISTY McCORMICK
February 22, 1997   Montreal

~

Why knights of road now an extinct species

SIR—As a former 'knight of the road' who has lived in North America for almost 40 years I must agree with John Hiscock (article, Aug. 16) that the hobo is now an extinct species.

The last hobo in the area of Canada where I now live was a character who rejoiced in the name Barbwire Bill. He died, ironically, when hit by a car some 10 years ago.

Today's so-called hoboes are merely the hitch-hiking poor, people on the run and drug addicts, as well as a few wealthy businessmen travelling incognito for kicks.

Although I had moved up in society when I arrived in Canada in 1952, I became an Australian bagman—or amateur swagman as we were known—when I lost my job on a farm and went 'on the track' in northern New South Wales from the autumn of 1929 to the spring of 1932.

The life of a 'baggie' was much the same as that of a hobo, involving jumping on to trains, riding in cattle trucks, and being hustled on by police at every stop, made to search for a spot of work and a bite of something to eat.

But a key reason why there are no true hoboes today is that they are able to draw the old age pension, and it is easier to do that if they stay in one place.

The hobo was a unique breed who vanished, along with so much else, in the mist of change that followed the 1939–45 War.

DUDLEY ST JOHN MAGNUS
August 19, 1989   Kilworthy, Ontario, Canada

Dudley Magnus (1911–97) was a journalist in England, India and Canada, and wrote a novel about the Depression in Australia, *Hanabeke*.

LOYALTY DOWN UNDER

Aboriginal forgiveness

SIR—Following your recent reports about the treatment of Aborigines in Australia today, I am writing to tell you my family's story.

In Western Australia during the 1930s my grandmother—a full-blood Aborigine but married to a white man—was separated, rounded up by police on horseback at Landsdowne Station and made to walk for about three days to Fitzroy Crossing in chains with her sister. The police in those days were only obeying orders. Gran and my great-aunt had chains around their wrists and necks. They were linked to each other by a chain from neck to neck. At nightfall when the police set up camp, Gran and my aunt had chains tied around their ankles to prevent them from escaping. My mother, then a child, followed them to Fitzroy.

A few years later at Fitzroy Crossing, my mother—then seven years old—was separated from Gran and taken away to a government settlement about 100 miles east of Fitzroy. Mum grew up there, married and raised a family. In 1955, the settlement closed down and I was sent away as a boy on the back of an old Blitz truck to a mission station near Fitzroy Crossing. I remained there for five years. During that time I was reunited with my mother, and Gran, who died in 1957.

We do not harbour grudges or ill feelings towards those who treated us unkindly in the past. They are forgiven. We cannot condone what happened—but neither can we condemn the innocent white race of today and try to force them to pay restitution for events they played no part in. We, of today, are responsible for the present and for the future, not for the past.

My story is only one of hundreds of Aborigines who have suffered similar circumstances in the past, but who have also forgiven.

October 5, 1989

RODNEY RIVERS
Toowoomba, Queensland

Abolishing honours in a tantrum

SIR—I may no longer be Premier of Queensland, but that does not mean that I cannot recognise the foolishness of the State's new Labour administration in announcing that it will no longer make recommendations for the Imperial honours list (Peterborough, Dec. 5).

A combination of Labour supporters and the Left-wing media, which has driven Imperial honours out of every other Australian state, is now doing all it can to ensure that no subsequent generations of Queenslanders will be tainted by the honour of being a Knight Commander of the Order of St Michael and St George like myself, a KBE, CBE or OBE.

No doubt they will not be satisfied until they have turned our country into a republic. But they will not make Australia a better place for abolishing these harmless distinctions. No country anywhere has ever found a more satisfactory way of recognising a person's genuine worth and service without placing a financial cost on the community.

This great distinction, unique to the British nations of the world, is being wantonly thrown away in a tantrum. It is a sign of a small-minded nationalism that was never more inappropriate than today, when we Australians are struggling for economic survival in Pacific markets and need our cultural links with the Mother Country as much as ever.

December 11, 1989

Sir JOH BJELKE-PETERSEN
Kingaroy, Queensland

Sir Joh Bjelke-Petersen was Premier of Queensland, 1968–87.

An Aussie with one in the eye

Sir—Jeremy Leasor's story about the Australian soldiers who placed pennies in their eyes (letter, Feb. 3) should not give the idea that there has been a blanket abhorrence Down Under to that dignified appendage, the eyeglass.

Sir George Reid was a genial premier of New South Wales, but an indifferent Prime Minister, known as 'Yes-no' Reid because of his ambivalent attitude to the federation of the Australian colonies.

Whereas his brief prime ministership was hardly a success—he was accused of residing on 'a necklace of negatives' during his few months in office in 1905—he became a successful first Australian High Commissioner in Britain and died a Labour MP at Westminster in 1918. He would be horrified by some of the antics of his successor Paul Keating.

EDWARD BURKE
February 12, 1993   Bristol

Still loyal

SIR—As a former Lieutenant-Governor of South Australia and a fourth-generation Australian of British descent, I would like to point out that the republican issue has been raised abruptly to satisfy minority political concerns and apparently to distract the country from its abysmal economic state.

Some Liberal parties in the states have been so badly shaken by the failure of the federal party in the recent national election that their leaders have made injudicious statements. But the vast majority of those Liberals (and, indeed, others) will get over this, not least because their Country Party cousins will have nothing to to do with it.

Suggestions that Australia might become a republic by 2001 are fanciful. We have been independent of Britain in all essential things for a century. No pro-republican has been able to give me any authentic case of Britain interfering in Australian decisions, certainly since the 1926 Balfour Definition of inter-imperial relations. And none has been able to explain clearly what Australia would gain by becoming a republic.

Soft headed, so-called intellectuals point out that our national identity has changed recently with substantial immigration from continental Europe and, more recently, from Asian countries.

But while it is true that these immigrants show some degree of indifference to the monarchy and the British connection, they recognise them as the basis of our stable system of government. The great majority of Australians, even those of non-conservative political persuasions, are deeply appreciative of the Queen's role in the past four difficult decades.

They realise that Australia owes to the British connection our legal system, political traditions and administrative techniques: all are directly derived from those in Britain.

Now that the question of a republic has been raised, it is right that there should be public discussion leading to a referendum; decisions should not be limited to the political party in power. But the situation calls for a civilised debate, not for the passionate rhetoric of second-grade politicians.

Sir WALTER CROCKER
April 8, 1993   Adelaide, South Australia

Sir Walter Crocker joined the Nigerian Administrative Service in 1930 and was Australian ambassador in Italy, 1967–70.

~

Keating's Asian quest doomed

SIR—Robert Chesshyre's uncritical enthusiasm for the Keating campaign to replace the Queen as Australian head of state with some elected or appointed politician (Magazine, Aug. 28) at least reveals some 'hidden subtext', as the 'politically correct' supporters of this far from 'inevitable' development say.

This campaign is not fuelled by the simple desire of a modern, fully independent nation to have its own native-born state-president rather than a locally resident and constitutionally impartial governor-general.

In fact, it owes its origin to the 'multi-cultural cringe', which not only hates the Poms in England, but also the British heritage shared by New Zealanders and many Canadians. There is the usual university-inculcated and media-reinforced element of guilty Anglo-Saxon ethnic self-hatred in it, with the Queen as an unfortunate scapegoat at an equally unfortunate moment in our own royal history.

The replacement of the EC (including Britain) by the Pacific Rim (including the Japanese commercial empire) as the future focus of trade and strategic 'partnership' is, of course, another suicidal illusion. It is aggravated by the demographic projections since the White Australia policy was abandoned, with New South Wales slowly turning into a new South China.

As Professor Paul Kennedy tartly observes in *Preparing for the Twenty-First Century*, there will be great waves of migration: 'Australia, whose population is expected to rise gently to 22.7 million by 2025, lies next to Indonesia whose population is forecast to grow . . . to 263 million in the same period'.

Australian republicanism could do more than dig a grave for the monarchist Diggers. The Aborigines may be fighting for their land rights with Hindus, Javanese, Chinese and Japanese. The present Fenian bandwagon may prove to be another Western hearse.

TITANIA MASON

Thuringer Wald, Germany

September 1, 1993

No shame about British origins

SIR—Peter Cochrane, a historian at Sydney University, claims that being Anglo-Saxon is 'out of vogue' in Australia and that most Australians of British background prefer to call themselves 'Anglo-Celt' (report, Dec. 5).

Just how many Australians of British descent Dr Cochrane interviewed was unstated. One cannot help suspecting that they were all cronies of a similar persuasion.

It is true that the expression 'Anglo-Saxon' is out of vogue in Australia, as it is in Britain as a self-description, but 'Anglo-Celt' is at least as obsolete, as I confirmed by questioning a few neighbours and friends of British origin in Cheltenham, Winchester, Marlborough and Rugby streets here in the Malvern suburb of Adelaide.

Almost all of them describe themselves simply as unhyphenated Australians. None used either Anglo-Saxon or Anglo-Celt. None repudiated or felt shame in Australia's British origins.

Australian higher education and media have largely been captured by the politically correct who, like Dr Cochrane, routinely represent 'Anglo' as implying 'oppressor'. Not many subjected to such misrepresentations are fooled, however, including members of ethnic minorities. The large majority of non-British immigrants came here because Australia has free political institutions and economic opportunity. It is mainly countries that derive their way of life from Britain which offer those advantages.

I have just carried out a little research with students and colleagues from Asian countries. When asked whether they would prefer to live in an Asian country, other than their land of birth, or Britain nearly all chose Britain. Most even placed Britain before their land of birth.

It is a pity that Dr Cochrane cannot argue the republican case, which has some merit, without denigrating the political traditions to which he owes freedom of debate. Fortunately, other republicans, such as Dr John Hirst, a historian of outstanding calibre and a member of the national committee of the Australian republican movement, are fair in argument and a credit to the political traditions Australia inherited from Britain.

GEOFFREY PARTINGTON
December 10, 1994   Bedford Park, South Australia

A hat with winning ways

SIR—I am sure that all Australians will join me in praising the decision to allow Australia's soldiers to wear our traditional slouch hat on United Nations service in Rwanda (Peterborough, Oct. 13).

The hat has been used by Diggers in campaigns from as far back as the Boer War. Distinctive, highly protective in rain and sun, we proudly use it as a work hat, as well as on ceremonial parades, and even as an object of barter or gift. Well established in Australian literature, song, poem and myth, the slouch hat is simply 'Australian'.

The 'turned up' side needed for certain rifle drill movements has furnished many stories about the recruits' 'sunburnt left ear' and 'two-tone sunburnt face', the latter stemming from the fact that the quarter-inch chinstrap leaves a white mark down the exposed left side of the face. The hat's 'turned up' side also provides an ideal place for embellishment—our light horsemen wore emu plumes to present a dashing figure on horseback.

Our Diggers proudly wore the slouch hat in the many Pacific Island campaigns of the Second World War, though the soft shapeless bush hat has proved easier to manage in more recent close jungle actions.

Made from the fur of rabbits, which are not native animals, the hat is a by-product of British settlement in Australia. Since there is a plague of rabbits today, it seems clear that the raw material for our beloved 'slouch hat' is inexhaustible—and that's just *beaut*.

Maj-Gen W. B. (DIGGER) JAMES
National President, Returned and Services
League, Brisbane, Queensland

October 14, 1994

Thank you, Chirac, mate

SIR—Suzanne Lowry (Paris Life, Aug. 10) clearly does not appreciate that President Chirac's proposal to hold nuclear tests in Mururoa has had some very useful fallout. The tests have united Australia and Australians in a way that, frankly, we have not seen since the Queen's first Royal tour.

All of a sudden traditional enemies have kissed (though not on both cheeks) and made up: they are talking to each other. The great debates that divide our society—Australian Rules versus rugby; Melbourne versus Sydney; Packer versus Murdoch; feminist versus feminist—are suddenly forgotten as we rally to confront the French.

Australians are even getting on with New Zealanders who, traditionally, view us as arrogant bastards insufficiently separated by a stretch water—in much the same way as you British view the French.

It has also given us the chance to let off steam. Australia is a country where 180 nationalities, and every known religion, live in comparative harmony, where the forces of a Racial Vilification Act and political correctness combine with our notorious tolerance to produce stifling politeness. No one tells uncouth jokes about other people any more, not even about the Poms.

So you can imagine how happy we are to have, albeit briefly, an opportunity to be racists again. Now we can all jump on the French, and even call them Frogs. Vast amounts of pent-up bigotry can now be freely, joyously expressed without risk of being charged under the new act or tut-tutted at by the forces of political correctness. For the first time since we dumped the White Australia policy in the 1970s bigotry is officially sanctioned.

While we are abusing the French we cannot, of course, talk to them. So perhaps you might pass on the thanks of a grateful nation to any Frog emerging from the Chunnel.

PHILLIP ADAMS

August 17, 1995   Sydney

PLAIN TALES

African cream

SIR—Thane Prince's inclusion of *crème brulée* in the Glyndebourne hamper (Weekend, July 16) is an excellent choice. But I am concerned lest picnickers share the embarrassment of the Governor of the Gold Coast who was served this *pièce de résistance* (sic) when, on travelling up country, he was the guest of a District Commissioner who fancied himself as a *bon vivant*.

The DC had gone to great pains to ensure that the chafing-dish, to be handed first to His Excellency as protocol demanded, was prepared to the accepted Cambridge standards and had even borrowed the required salamander (not a 'very hot grill') to melt the wafer thin caramel crust.

In spite of all rehearsals the DC's chef—like Thane Prince—found it 'much easier to melt . . . (the) sugar . . . in a saucepan' and, pouring it over the creamy delight, sent it to the table.

When His Excellency had failed utterly to make any impression on the caramel carapace, and his host too had buckled the last of the silver plate, the chef was summoned with the wood axe to uncover the golden harvest beneath. But where in all conscience does one find a wood axe at Glyndebourne?

JAMES MOXON
July 22, 1988   Ludlow, Shropshire

~

Moustache to beat all Handel's bars

SIR—Your agency report '7ft moustache man beheaded' (Jan. 4) prompts me to recall the deceased, whose correct name was Karna Ram Bhil. He was allowed to keep his 7ft 10in moustache whilst serving a prison sentence in 1979.

A colourful character of imposing stature and possessed of a fiery temper, Karna Ram Bhil was famous throughout the Thar desert of Rajasthan in northwest India as a professional flute player, specialising in the playing of ethnic flutes for film and TV scores. I never knew him but became acquainted with his exceptional playing of the peasant flute *narh*—an end blown flute similar to the Arabic *nay*. He had perfected a phenomenal technique whilst serving custodial sentences for his exploits as a professional *dacoit*, or highwayman.

This technique consisted of circular breathing, producing a constant line of complex flute playing, accompanied by a vocal drone bass—interspersed by him telling a story in a vocal monotone. His recordings, made in the prison at Jodphur, earned the Grand Prix Internationale du Disque. They can be heard, and the moustache seen, on Flutes du Rajasthan, Le Chant du Monde (LDX 74645).

ADRIAN BRETT
January 8, 1988   London W1

~

Unwashed extra

SIR—The letters about the late John Fothergill (Sept. 14, 18) bring to mind the Tororo Hotel on the border between Kenya and Uganda before the 1939–1945 War.

Over the entrance to this one-storey building, the notice 'Henry Herbert Aitken licensed to sell Beer, Wines, Spirits and Tobacco to whom, at what time and at what price, he pleases' usually stopped the customer in his tracks.

Above the reception desk was inscribed the following tariff:
Bed, Bath and Breakfast—12.50 shillings
Bed and Breakfast—15 shillings (East African)
The explanation for this difference was that dusty travellers who did not bathe must pay extra for laundry.

JOHN BONHAM
September 9, 1989   Thurlstone, Yorks

~

Benefit of a peg after work

SIR—Your article on alcohol and heart disease (July 26) reminds me of when I was a civil servant in Pakistan in the early days after independence in 1947. Our work in the Pakistan secretariat involved long and arduous hours in the humid climate of Karachi, with the result that quite a number of senior officials were struck down in their offices by coronary attacks. All of them were Pakistanis.

When we were talking about this one night after dinner in my home, a Begum Sahib, the wife of a very senior official whose intelligence matched her beauty, said: 'Our British officers work just as hard as our own men, if not harder, yet not one of them has had a heart attack.

'I put it down to this: at the end of the day, the British officers relax with a couple of pegs of whisky and soda in the Sind Club or at home, whereas our men just come home, sit down and go on worrying about their office problems. If only they would relax with one or two pegs of Scotch like the British.'

Sir ERIC FRANKLIN
Cambridge

August 1, 1991

The croc that ate my watch

SIR—I was much interested by the account of Eric Newby's Rolex watch, which was rescued from an Afghan mutton stew (Weekend, Jan. 2). My own watch had an even more remarkable experience.

It was similar to Newby's Explorer, but had a revolving bezel which could be used while diving in the Red Sea. Called a Turn O'graph, it cost the princely sum of £65 in London in the mid-Fifties.

At the time I was military attaché at our embassy in Khartoum, and the first task the watch had to perform was to time the arrival of Group Captain 'Cat's Eyes' Cunningham's record-breaking, non-stop flight in a Comet from London.

Shortly afterwards, when I was sleeping on a flat roof, a thief crawled up the drainpipe—a not infrequent occurrence—and stole it from beside my bed. I duly reported the theft to a member of the local police who took down the details while remarking, with flashing teeth, that nobody who had the black skin of the ordinary Sudanese would want to buy a watch with a black dial. Nevertheless, some months later the watch was returned to me by the police with an amazing tale. The thief, or possibly the person to whom he was lucky enough to sell the watch, had been eaten by a Nile crocodile, which was subsequently shot by the Deputy Commissioner.

Inside the beast's belly was found my watch, still going merrily and keeping perfect time. The movements and digestive juices of the crocodile had been sufficient to maintain the automatic mechanism in action, and the piece also had the advantage of being waterproof.

I put the watch back on my wrist, where it has been working perfectly ever since; from force of habit, I no longer take it off at night.

Unfortunately some fungus in the crocodile's stomach affected the black dial. This was gradually eaten away and has had to be replaced, though sadly without its wonderfully luminous dots for the numerals.

It is ticking away on my wrist as I write.

Col MAURICE WILLOUGHBY

January 14, 1993   Storrington, W. Sussex

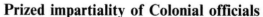

Prized impartiality of Colonial officials

SIR—I confirm Derek Davies's statement (letter, April 6) that Colonial Office rules only very rarely allowed civil servants to retire to live in territories in which they had served. The main reason for this was to ensure that officials retained a reputation for impartiality and fair dealing with no personal axe to grind.

I encountered this when serving in Baluchistan in 1944. I was in charge of Nasirabad district but lived in Jacobabad, some five miles across the border in Sind. When the only Europeans in Jacobabad, the District Commissioner and the Chief of Police, were replaced by Indians, I remained the sole European in the area, 200 miles from my headquarters in Quetta.

After some 18 months I suggested to the Agent to the Governor-General that I, too, should be replaced by one of our Indian officers to 'Indianise' the whole area. This was agreed but when my successor was announced the local landowners besieged my bungalow and demanded that I stay. Asked why, they said it was because I came from England and would retire to England. Furthermore, I had no local connections.

Although they might not have agreed with all my decisions they knew that I was impartial and unbiased. They felt that my successor, however, could well be influenced on religious or tribal grounds. The change went ahead but three months later my successor had a mental breakdown and had to be removed immediately. I returned to hold the fort until another European officer could take over.

The strength of administrators in the British Empire was that they came from overseas, retired overseas and had no physical interest in the territory they administrated. It is mutual distrust, especially among those from different tribes, that has contributed to the general breakdown of law and order in most ex-colonial territories when left to govern themselves.

H. P. HALL
April 13, 1993   Ringwood, Hants

An earlier walker through Africa

SIR—Your report on Ffyona Campbell walking across Africa (Aug. 28) reminded me of Diana Carlisle, a young Australian who arrived in the small township of Mandera on her walk from Cairo to the Cape back in 1953.

I was District Commissioner of Mandera, a sparsely populated district in the north-east corner of Kenya bordering Ethiopia and Somalia. Diana Carlisle had already completed a third of her journey in a few months, on foot, alone, with just a light pack on her back, relying on the hospitality of the mainly tribal people she met along the way.

The three British bachelor police officers and myself, a 'husband-in-exile', entertained her briefly until urgent radio messages were received from headquarters, 500 miles away, instructing us to send her on her way (safer among the nomads).

I remember there was no fuss, no cameras—just the challenge.

THEON WILKINSON
September 2, 1993   London SW15

Before Ffyona

SIR—Theon Wilkinson is right (letter, Sept. 2). I traversed the length of Africa, largely on foot, 40 years ago.

I was a doctor's daughter from Australia who had worked as a nurse in England before taking a job in northern Ethiopia. On deciding after a few months to walk south, I went through Addis Ababa, Nairobi and then into South Africa.

Unlike Ffyona Campbell's highly packaged effort I had no back-up organisation, publicity machine or sponsorship; no companions were following nearby. The world was a different place then. I carried a bag containing little more than a spare pair of jeans. Often I slept in the open and was supplied with food in villages.

Back in those pre-independence days the people, who had never even seen money, treated me like a white goddess, and often conducted me on to the next village. I was never attacked by animals and never had a day's illness, though I drank some foul water and had no purifier.

The only time I had any trouble was when I treated myself to a hotel room in Nairobi and had my money stolen, though a policeman later recovered it. This, however, was also the occasion when I had the fortune to meet Col Ewart Grogan, who had walked from Cairo to Cape Town between 1899 and 1901.

Later I took trains, hitch-hiked, rode a mule but largely walked into South Africa. When I reached the Cape I never contemplated walking into the sea. I finally took ship from Durban to India where I travelled around for several years and worked in Calcutta with Mother Teresa before returning home to Australia.

Why did I do this? I was young, poor and liked travelling.

(Mrs) DIANA CRAUFORD
October 2, 1993   South Caulfield, Victoria, Australia

Beware of the cats

SIR—One cannot help feeling very sorry for John Aspinall that another tragedy has taken place at his zoological gardens (report, Nov. 14). No one knows more about the big cats or is more concerned with their lives or those of their keepers.

Back in 1924, my father J.G. Millais, the author of many books on animal and bird behaviour, took me to stay in Khartoum with Courtenay Brocklehurst, a great friend who was head game warden and keeper of the zoo. Brock took me one morning to see a large and handsome lion called Sayed. He lay on his back while we tickled his tummy. There was an ecstatic expression on his face: his eyes were shut.

But Father was furious when we came back for breakfast. 'Don't you dare do that again,' he told me. I thought Father was exaggerating the dangers involved. But two months later, Sayed's keeper took a rather fat Egyptian friend, who had perhaps heard of the lion's amicable relations with *homo sapiens*.

Unfortunately, this Egyptian made the mistake of opening his umbrella in Sayed's face. They swept up the remains of the Effendi with a dustpan and brush.

RAOUL MILLAIS
November 19, 1994   Chipping Norton, Oxon

Share in wife

SIR—With reference to the African practice of paying *lobola* or bride money (letter, Oct. 14), I recall that some years ago, when on a secondment to the Nyasaland police force, one of my young constables was in difficulties because he was short by £10 of the necessary cash to purchase his intended bride.

I solved the problem by lending him the amount until his next pay day. I then wrote home to my wife in England telling her that she would no doubt be pleased to know that I had become a shareholder in an African wife. As repayment was duly made I did not have to foreclose on the mortgage.

RICHARD FORD
October 17, 1997   Horsell, Surrey

Always caning in Singapore

SIR—Caning on the bare buttocks has always been rife in Singapore (report, April 28). When I was commissioner of prisons and super-intendent of Changi prison, it was frequently used as a punishment for criminal offences and could also be imposed by the prison authorities for acts against prison discipline.

But it appears that, over the past 30 years, the Singapore Government in its wisdom has made a whipping sentence manda-tory for an increased number of crimes. Undeniably, such punish-ment is severe but, in my day, when six or 12 strokes of the rattan cane was the vogue, I never saw any prisoner faint or unable to take the punishment.

Usually, after its infliction, they would take a proffered cigarette and walk away. If any recipient showed undue signs of distress, the Medical Officer would halt the proceedings.

It is true that the rattan cane will break the skin, but in witnessing several score of whippings I never saw profuse bleeding, only severe bruising. I do not doubt that such a sentence is a deterrent and I cannot recollect any offender's returning for a 'second innings'.

PETER JAMES
April 29, 1994   Taverham, Norfolk

~

Looking for just one thing

SIR—Lucretia Stewart's Caribbean travels, *The Weather Prophet*, may be sizzling news in *The Spectator* and seem immensely titillating to British male reviewers (article, Oct. 20). But here she seems only to be reinforcing the legendary Caribbean stereotype: the middle-aged Anglo-Saxon woman who travels alone to the Caribbean for just one thing—a quick black bonk in the bushes.

I am afraid that the sight of fat ladies on the beaches has been a familiar one for the past 30 years. Many of them come from North America, but more recently there have been arrivals from Europe.

Miss Stewart will obviously make a lot of money from all this salacious publicity even if it makes her mother squirm with embar-rassment. But her book has done no good to race relations on this island since it was serialised in three issues of a local tabloid.

These concentrated on her views about black male sexuality and of the white community of some 2,000 people, which feels increasingly vulnerable in a population of around 60,000 whose prejudices were sharpened by the daily broadcasts of the O.J. Simpson trial. This can only harm the respectable tourist trade which I and others have spent 20 years trying to build up. Miss Stewart fails to mention the attendant danger of Aids, although there is considerable wallowing in the other danger—unwanted pregnancy.

I might add that three white ladies on the island—a tourist in her mid-30s, an American resident of 73 and a white Antiguan in her 50s—have been recently raped by unknown black assailants. This is all the more shocking because we were unused to such incidents.

Perhaps we should not blame the rapists; were they only performing a necessary service?

ANITA ELPHINSTONE
October 31, 1995   Antigua, West Indies

Taking a visitor to the cleaners

SIR—Your report on Nigerian scams (Aug. 29) reminds me of one called 'wash wash'. A typical scenario involves a foreign businessman in Lagos chatting in the hotel bar when a Nigerian offers him a 'business opportunity'. The Nigerian brings to his room a briefcase full of what are said to be $100 bills covered in a black gunge.

The story is that the bills have been coated in this way so that they can be smuggled in from a neighbouring country, and the gunge can be removed with a 'special' fluid. A small bottle of the fluid is produced which does indeed remove the gunge to reveal a $100 bill.

The problem is that the fluid is 'difficult to obtain', but the Nigerian knows where to get it, if the businessman will put up £1,000 cash: they can then wash all the notes and share the proceeds. If greed takes over, and the businessman does not think of a host of commonsense alternatives, the instant the £1,000 is handed over several policemen burst in.

It is explained what a heinous crime he has been involved in and that 15 years in a Nigerian prison is the least he can expect. However, for a 'small consideration', say £500, they will leave the back door open if he wants to make good his escape. This is invariably gratefully accepted and the businessman is soon on a plane, glad to be out of the place and without a fuss, £1,500 poorer, but wiser.

JAMES HARDWICK
London WC2

September 4, 1995

IN THE FACE OF DANGER

Verdict hangs over battlefields

SIR—If a coroner's court is empowered to conduct inquests into deaths from friendly fire (report, May 19), may they also investigate those which result from other errors in battle?

John Keegan (article, May 20) estimates that 10 per cent of our casualties in past wars were caused by our own troops. Many more have resulted from 'commander's error'—the disastrous attack, the flawed defensive plan, the useless operation. On a macro scale, Gallipoli, the Somme and the Dieppe raid are subjects of continuing public debate. Less known are actions when junior commanders have misjudged situations and sent men to their deaths.

If parents learn that a son has died through a tactical blunder, their grief and anguish may well be exacerbated. If not satisfied by official explanations, can they bring their case before a coroner's court? Have they the right to question the responsible officer?

When making decisions in battle, leaders never have enough information, and much of what they do is inaccurate. Speed is often vital. Whatever they do, casualties result. If they make a mistake, they and their men may end up dead. In future, if they survive such an error, will they have to face a coroner's inquest? Such a threat would add intolerable stress to battlefield leaders and may well result in over-cautious, hence bad, decisions.

As an infantry company commander, my orders resulted in casualties to my men. About each I thought deeply to discover whether I could have prevented his death or injury. To this day I am not sure whether or not I made a preventable mistake; but if I did, it was certainly not with malice toward my men.

I know of many small scale disasters in battle but never of an officer or NCO responsible who was not deeply affected by it. When being shelled by New Zealand artillery in Korea or bombed by the RAF or the Americans in Normandy, I may have cursed but I will never believe that they were trying to kill an ally.

There are many implications of the Oxford inquest, but it would be a sad day for military morale and effectiveness if it became a precedent for coroners' courts to investigate every death on the battlefield. If it did, and if casualties were heavier than in the Gulf, how many special courts would be needed, how many coroners, how many lawyers?

JEFFERY WILLIAMS
May 21, 1992   Ilminster, Som

No therapy at the real thing

SIR—I could not at first believe your story about the BBC calling on the aid of a psychotherapist to help its employees cope with the stress of covering the D-Day anniversary (report, June 7).

I went over to Normandy on D-Day plus one. Mutilated bodies lay all around us on the beach. There was continuous shellfire, and we still feared for the outcome of the battle. It is true that we had been through the blitz in London, so had some experience of danger. But we had a job to do, and we just did it.

If it had been suggested that we broadcasters needed counselling, our first thought would have been that it was a joke, or perhaps some fiendish ploy of William Joyce, Lord Haw-Haw, to upset the Home Front. If we had then discovered that the suggestion was genuine, we would surely have considered it an insult to all those servicemen who were doing the fighting.

I can see that television today, unlike the relatively simple medium of wartime radio, can induce stress, as when the satellite transmission of Dame Vera Lynn's concert failed. But when I left the BBC's employ 45 years ago. I never considered stress anything to speak about in public. We had fatigue periods of about four or five days to get over any strain, but no psychotherapists. I see no reason why it should be any different today.

STEWART MacPHERSON
Winnipeg, Manitoba

Stewart Macpherson (1908–95) was a mainstay of the radio programme *War Report*.

SIR—Post-traumatic stress syndrome was not unknown, though rare, during the war years. Then it was known as LMF, lack of moral fibre, and treated as such.

Perhaps the old remedy of gritting their teeth would work wonders for today's generation.

MAURICE SHEPLEY
June 9, 1994   Hull

MULES AND MYTHS

Using mules against the Mau Mau

SIR—I have followed with interest your learned correspondence about Hannibal, elephants and the Alps (April 12, 14, 15, 16). It calls vividly to mind a more modern (1955) epic involving mules in Kenya. As a National Service second lieutenant in the King's African Rifles it is true I was not yet the equivalent of GOC, Carthaginian Forces. However, being younger than Hannibal, I felt time was on my side.

We were ordered to cross the Aberdare Mountains (height 9,000ft) in one night and take the Mau Mau silently in the rear. Mules were to carry our supplies.

We were almost shot by, I think, the Glosters because nobody had told them we were coming. The mules were frightened of the dark and bolted. The mountains were so steep the loads fell off and the mules had to be both pulled and shoved.

They were too fat to squeeze between the bamboo which had to be cut down. Eventually on to the plateau, their hooves sank into the peat. We had to dig them out, without spades and carry them. Then we had to go back and carry the loads.

What was meant to take one night took five days. We went so slowly that, between mule carrying, I read two paperbacks on the march. What was meant to take place silently took place amid a cacophony of noise, oaths in Swahili, the sound of falling trees and noises off from elephant, rhino and buffalo as they crashed in fright through the forest ahead of us. Only MacNamara's band could have added to the pandemonium. A Mau Mau informer told me later he had heard us two days before we arrived.

If this was the best army in the world, what, we reflected, could the worst be like? Hannibal probably felt the same, only more so. Carrying those elephants must have been no joke.

JOHN WARD
April 22, 1988   Newcastle upon Tyne

Stalwart Cypriot breed

SIR—In sharp contrast to Mr Ward's experience of the inefficacy of mule transport in Africa (letter, April 22) was the splendid service of my 12 Cypriot mules, and their muleteers, at the Battle of Keren in Eritrea.

The track up Mt Dologorodoc to my medical post just below the fort was a fearsome place where many men were killed, mostly by mortar fire. The mules never seemed to flinch. They stepped over the dead bodies of their comrades and plodded uphill, later to carry wounded men down.

We were very short of water and, having washed oneself from a mug of water, one would offer it to a mule—which drank it!

Robert Flemyng, the well-known actor, served with the mule transport company and later visited my unit in Nazareth.

Maj-Gen F. M. RICHARDSON
April 27, 1988   Edinburgh

Maj-Gen Frank Richardson (1904–96) won a DSO while commanding a field ambulance during the Eritrea campaign in 1941.

A soldier's love

SIR—Legend has it that the mule is a stubborn, difficult and ill-tempered animal. So am I, if I am maltreated. Like Maj-Gen Richardson (letter, April 27), I have the greatest admiration for these splendid animals, which I first encountered when serving with Wingate's Long Range Penetration Groups in late 1942.

The mule, if treated with consideration and respect, was 'man's best friend' in the scenario of the war in Burma. Ask any British soldier who was a mule leader—and I have seen some fine, tough men in tears when their mule had been wounded 'beyond repair' and had to be put down.

The mule is immensely strong, phlegmatic in temperament, highly intelligent and loyal to his handler if treated correctly. Most of us owed our survival to our mules, who carried our heavy weapons, ammunition, wireless equipment, charging engines and a host of other items vital to our ability to function as a fighting unit.

We had heavy-duty 'Artillery' mules, bred in the Argentine, to carry our heavy wireless equipment. Most had put up with an operation on their larynx to prevent their braying disclosing our positions in the jungle. These large animals took a maximum load of 200lb, carefully balanced at 100lb each side of the saddle. If the total load exceeded 200lb, or if the load was unbalanced, the mule would not budge —and rightly so, as a gall would result and the animal could not be worked. Readjust the balance, or reduce the load to the correct maximum, and the mule would respond by marching on and on over near impossible country, while his human masters were dropping with fatigue.

I know I would not be here today had it not been for the mules which carried the radios which called for the air supply drops which kept us alive and fighting during the Burma Campaign.

Lt-Col ROBIN PAINTER
April 29, 1988   Poole, Dorset

Good parachutists

SIR—Col Painter, in his most interesting letter (April 29) mentions artillery mules used in Burma and states that they were bred in the Argentine. Some at least of them came from the United States; and a friend of mine, a lieutenant-colonel in the Royal Army Veterinary Corps, went from India to America to buy them, armed with a lease-lend cheque for $1 million.

Wingate's idea of a long range group supplied entirely from the air included mules delivered by parachute. The mules were tranquillised and tied down on pallets. When they landed they were cut loose and got up, unconcerned by the experience.

R. BORWICK
May 12, 1988 President, British Mule Society, Ashbourne, Derbys

Bear who went to war

SIR—Your caption (Weekend, Nov. 12) implied that Voytek the brown bear 'served' in the British Army; in fact he was part of the Polish forces, albeit under overall British command, and even had a Polish army number.

Some Polish soldiers, who had been released from a Soviet labour camp, bought him at the age of three months in Persia. At first they had some difficulty as he did not eat meat or bread, and had to be given condensed milk and warm water. Nevertheless, Voytek accompanied them through Palestine, Egypt and Italy.

Always an early riser, he loved to bathe in showers with the soldiers, and on one occasion entered a bath-house at dawn to evoke a loud scream. The guards rushed in to discover an Arab, part of a band of munitions thieves, on his knees begging to be spared. Voytek's reward was a bottle of beer.

On another occasion he raided a Polish women's signals company and proceeded to purloin all their precious non-army issue underwear.

As a member of 22nd Transport Company of the Polish 2nd Corps, he was frequently in the front line at the battle of Monte Cassino in 1944. At first Voytek was afraid of the noise of the bursting shells but he was soon happy to work for long periods unloading heavy artillery shells and boxes of ammunition.

At the end of the Second World War the veterans of the Polish army felt unable to return to a Soviet-occupied Poland. Voytek joined them in exile and died, aged 22, in Edinburgh Zoo. He left his bones, like many other Polish veterans, on British soil.

MICHAEL GEORGE OLIZAR
November 22, 1994 London SW15

Why a set of wings produces the girls

SIR—With reference to your report 'G-force effect on sex selection' (Feb. 20): the reason why fighter pilots tend to father girls rather than boys is that they usually have a dominant personality.

After the 1914–1918 War, I remarked that none of my fighter pilot friends had male children. Any exception would be if, at the time of conception, the dominant parent sank his dominant personality, his wife thus becoming dominant, and a male child resulting.

If any of your readers wish to check my claim, I suggest they look discreetly among their friends, or, having themselves only female children, allow the little wife to become the dominant personality.

After all they can always take over command again after the resultant male child has been born.

T. G. M. MAPPLEBECK

February 24, 1988   London SW7

Tom Mapplebeck (1894–1990) served in the Royal Flying Corps in the First World War and was in charge of RAF welfare for the Middle East in the Second.

It isn't G-force

SIR—It is not only astronauts and fighter pilots who tend to father daughters, but helicopter pilots and divers, so the G-force theory of the Texas University researcher (report, Feb. 20) goes through the floor.

In the 1950s a Lieut. White, in charge of the naval diving team in Malta, who had two daughters himself, made a study of the subject when nine out of the 10 babies born to his 10 divers' wives were girls. It transpired that the tenth baby had been conceived when the father was unable to dive because of an ear infection.

Some years later, in discussing the phenomenon with the nursing sister girlfriend of one of my officers in a ship based at Portland, she reported that most of the babies born in the local hospital to the wives of aircrew from the helicopter station were girls (so I predict a daughter for the Duchess of York).

The G-force certainly isn't the deciding factor; stress may be, but I think there is more to it than that. In very general terms, the more extrovert a man is the more likely he is to have daughters. One of the most extrovert men I know has four, and the theory works for most of my friends. My wife and I have one of each.

Cdr BRUCE NICOLLS

February 29, 1988   Portsmouth, Hants

Submariners' lore came unstuck

SIR—I read with interest Cdr Bruce Nicolls's letter (Feb. 29) about the fathering of daughters. I agree that it isn't 'G-force' but I question whether stress or whether one is an extrovert are relevant either.

I entered submarines at the close of the 1939–45 War, and was seriously advised that 'submariners have daughters'. Looking around the squadron and tallying up the 'boy–girl score' it did indeed appear that there were about two daughters for every son. So I braced myself for a few giggling young ladies.

I served a full career 'in the boats' and was commander of three of them. A quarter century later I surfaced for the last time and to my amazement I found that I now had nine sons and two daughters. I was of course flabbergasted. Where was all this submarine tradition?

The last three children appeared after I had gone into nuclear boats—but this didn't seem to have much effect either. The score was still 2:1.

Cdr Nicolls suggests that stress may be a factor in favouring daughters. Submarine operations have been known to be stressful on occasion but this didn't do anything for me. I also question whether 'extroverts have daughters' since this suggests that introverts have sons. I've never seen an introvert behind a periscope nor have I seen an introverted submarine commander in *any* navy.

The job doesn't attract the contemplative type. If extroverts have daughters then introverts have sons—ergo, I am the only introverted submarine commander in naval history. My father was the seventh son of nine children. I suspect this fact has more to do with my own family than either my occupation or my personality.

I regret I can only offer such a limited data base. I did my best!

Cdr H. BOTHWELL, US Navy (Retd)

March 2, 1988   Bath

~

Rescuing of damsels leads to daughters

SIR—On sounding opinions in this military area over the delicate question of whether fathers holding stressful jobs tend to have daughters rather than sons, I find that in the Army this often occurs because there is a tradition of rescuing forlorn damsels who are threatened by predators but have no sturdy brothers to defend them.

As often as not the knightly rescuer falls in love with the hapless girl and marries her. When they subsequently have daughters rather than sons it is wrongly assumed that this is because he is in a stressful occupation, but it is in fact because male births have declined in the girl's family owing to some factor of heredity and that she was vulnerable because she was an heiress and thus surrounded by predators rather than protectors.

In medieval times powerful families died out in the male line because the sons frequently married forlorn heiresses, apparently unaware that the reason why they were heiresses was because there were no male heirs.

Until Henry VIII established a precedent families would die out, in the legitimate line at least, while amateur genealogists would desperately try to establish a claim to the title and estates which would otherwise fall into abeyance and be absorbed by the Crown.

BRIAN HUNTER
March 8, 1988   Camberley, Surrey

Welsh hospitality to U-Boats

SIR—Submariners, it would seem, suffer from an insatiable thirst. Your report (Jan. 18) on the U-boat milk raid on a New Zealand farm has a parallel in the folklore of Wales.

During the First World War, not a single soul in the south Cardiganshire coastal village of Cwmtudu could distinguish the difference in language between one Saxon (English) and another (German). To them both languages were merely foreign gibberish.

Consequently, when the crew of a U-boat put ashore in search of fresh water, the local people not only supplied the supposed Englishmen with fresh water, but also invited them to the local pub, where a rousing time was had by all, the language barrier being demolished by a potent mixture of song, goodwill and strong ale.

I am informed that in recent years the area was visited by a German lady who was curious to see the place where her grandfather had snatched a few happy hours enveloped in a Celtic mist.

BERNARD KELLY
Wolverhampton, West Midlands

SIR—On holiday in Majorca in 1970 we met a German couple who had never visited Britain. Yet the husband described, in detail, a cove in Cardigan Bay near a handful of houses, a pub and a standpipe.

He told me his name was Werner Bergmann and that he had served in a German U-boat during the Second World War. He said U-boats on the Liverpool run regularly called at Cwmtudu to take on water, sometimes fresh vegetables, and often a crate of beer from the back of the pub.

It's difficult to believe they weren't noticed, but if the beer was paid for, no self-respecting Cardi was likely to tell.

ALAN BATEMAN
Haverfordwest, Dyfed

January 22, 1994

Legends flourishing

SIR—The exploits of German submarines have captured the popular imagination since Sir Arthur Conan Doyle first published *Danger! A Story of England's Peril* in the *Strand Magazine* in 1912.

Your report about the German U-boat that sent sailors ashore to pinch milk and do some flirting in New Zealand in 1945 (Jan. 18), together with two letters recounting German submariners' visits to Wales in the First and Second World Wars (Jan. 21), provide further evidence of this growing folklore. Similar stories haunt the coasts of both North and South America, as do tales of phantom U-boats with 'Nazi' gold and treasure.

Whatever the locals and whichever the war, the scenarios are fairly consistent: dances and theatre ashore, scrounging in the fields, chit-chat with the locals in pubs and bars and, in some cases, capture on the high seas with the damning evidence of ticket stubs and newspaper clippings in their pockets. Only the Newfoundlanders have an added twist: Germans marched down the main highway outside St John's 16 abreast, while a cod-fisherman on the Grand Banks saw a U-boat flying through the air.

Corroboration is possible only by examining deployment records and log books. None of us researching German submarines has yet found the tales to have any substance, except of course for covert operations in which spies were landed (never taken off), where automatic weather stations were built in arctic barrens, or incidents in which U-boats operated close inshore to pick up escaped prisoners of war.

That stories of brazen landings in populated centres exist at all bears eloquent testimony to the psychological impact of submarine warfare. Sorry for the cold water; I'm a sceptic by trade.

Prof MICHAEL HADLEY

January 26, 1994   Victoria, British Columbia

WAR IN THE GULF

Sad standards set by CNN's success

SIR—As an old news agency hand, I welcome the irony with which Noel Malcolm portrayed television coverage of the Gulf war (article, Jan. 24). It rightly balanced the way the exploits of the American Cable News Network have been hailed as justifying those pretensions which Malcolm rightly lampoons—'a new level of media coverage . . . worldwide and instantaneous'.

The other night—giving way to media narcissism and turning the cameras on its own kind on the assumption of huge public interest in the antics of the electronic hacks—BBC2 presented a close-up of CNN. During this exercise, a CNN functionary boasted that, no matter how loudly television traditionalists demurred, the network's spectacular doings ensured that television news methods would never be the same again.

Doubtless this is true—and it may not be a wholly bad thing, given the contrived quality of some orthodox television coverage of the Gulf. The sight of a helmeted, battledressed Martin Bell, for example, riding atop a desert tank, flinty eyed and jut-jawed in the best Rommel manner, was fatuous in the extreme and a mockery of a deadly serious situation.

But the new 'immediacy' merchants apparently pride themselves not only on instantly reporting the news but in helping to make it. Moreover, journalistic confusions have actually become a virtue, part of the show. So we have CNN's valiant Peter Arnett in Baghdad reporting from what he calls a war-damaged powder-milk factory; and moments later the US military insisting, on air, that he should have called it a heavily defended chemical weapons factory.

Enthusiasts of such television novelties might take note of the less sensational practices of those self-effacing workhorses of world journalism, the news agencies. I have worked for both Reuters and America's Associated Press.

At both, before a story goes out, its solidity in terms of sources and accuracy must be validated. Both manage to square this with the exigencies of top speed. Another old agency of mine, the Canadian Press has a rule about dubious material: 'If in doubt, cut it out.'

C. J. FOX
London SE26

SIR—In all the kerfuffle over television coverage in the Gulf, surely the problem is bound up in the two elements—voices and pictures—which make the medium so effective. Whatever editors can do back in a studio, they are severely constricted by the necessity for these.

A print journalist's copy can not only be chopped but also amended to avoid dangerous corners. If you do that to television coverage it could lead to better journalism . . . but never better showbiz.

WILLIAM WILSON
London W5

SIR—If CNN had not been in Baghdad to video-record Iraqi television, we might not now be seeing for ourselves the brutal way in which prisoners of war are being treated.

DAVID SINCLAIR
St Leonards-on-Sea, Sussex

From ashes to ashes

SIR—After hearing that Saddam Hussein is claiming victory, can I suggest that they run up the flag at Lord's and say we won the Ashes.

R. E. S. WYATT

March 2, 1991 Helford, Cornwall

Bob Wyatt (1901–95) captained the England cricket team in 1930 and 1934–5.

Rabbis had dark fears of beauty on parade

SIR—I suspect that the presence of America's female Marines in the front line owes much to those pictures beloved by newspapers of Israeli girls marching with arms. So may I point out that the traditional Jewish attitude to women is that they should be seen but not heard, and preferably not seen either. It is against Jewish law for women to serve in the army or bear arms.

Yet one of the most famous commanders in Jewish history was a woman, the prophetess Deborah, who, in Judges 4, led the Israelites to victory against their Canaanite oppressors some 3,000 years ago. And when Sisera, the Canaanite leader, fled the field he was killed with a tent peg by another woman, Jael.

Deborah and Jael, however, are regarded as exceptions, and when the Israeli government first proposed military service for women the rabbis objected. They were less worried about physical dangers than moral ones, for there is still a fairly ingrained Jewish belief that, for women at least, there is a fate worse than death—and they threatened to tear the country apart on the issue.

Eventually a compromise was reached by which any girl can refuse to join the army on religious grounds, and married women are also not liable to conscription. Others are expected to serve two years in the army or do some other form of national service.

My eldest daughter went to live in Israel when she finished school in London and joined the army on arrival. I attended her battalion's passing-out parade and as Wellington might have put it, I don't know what effect those girls would have had on the enemy, but my God they charmed me. A well-cut uniform does something for a woman and it was more like a beauty parade than a military parade. I should imagine that one reason they continue to conscript women is that it softens the Israeli army's image.

Women are given much the same sort of basic training as men and are taught to use arms, but they are never sent beyond the borders of Israel (unless, that is, they work for the Mossad). They are never involved in active combat and are kept at a safe distance—in so far as the small size of the country allows—from the frontline. Instead, they are generally employed as cooks, clerks, washer-uppers and social workers. My daughter and her friends were exposed to discomfort, but never danger—except for that feared by the rabbis—and, in the main, they were bored out of their wits.

Incidentally, according to Jewish law, a woman taken into captivity cannot marry a descendant of the priesthood, in the not unfounded belief that she might have been ravished.

When conscription for women was first introduced in Israel there was an acute manpower shortage and any help women could offer was badly needed. The manpower shortage is now less acute, especially with the Russian immigrants pouring in by the hundred thousand. But there is a feeling that national burdens should be nationally shared.

There is fairly strong feminist movement in Israel, but it has not yet assumed the bizarre forms common in America, and there is no belief that anything a man can do a woman can do better, or at least as well, and there is no clamour among women for frontline duties.

There is no conscription in America, so that women soldiers are of course volunteers, but the very readiness to send them overseas and into the frontline is taken by Arabs not as a measure of female emancipation, but as a measure of Western callousness and even depravity. This must be one reason why Saddam is confident that he has God on his side.

CHAIM BERMANT

February 2, 1991 London NW11

Chaim Bermant (1929–98) was a journalist and novelist.

REMEMBERING NOW

Changing sides

SIR—I share your horror at the historical ignorance of 16- to 24-year-olds in this country (leading article, Aug. 27) but it is a phenomenon which also exists beyond our borders.

In France, shortly before the 50th anniversary celebrations of D-Day, a prominent visitor to a school near Nancy witnessed a teacher asking her class of 12-year-olds what had happened 50 years before, in June 1944. The reply from one boy, a version supported by his classmates, was that the Germans had landed to rescue them from an American occupation.

The teacher was covered in embarrassment, but this nationalist Freudian slip provides an interesting lesson in how the influence of modern political assumptions can rewrite history so easily, when no basis of knowledge exists.

ANTONY BEEVOR
London SW6

August 31, 1996

Shame at Ypres

SIR—On October 20 we visited the Ypres salient and Somme battlefields. As a party of 15- and 16-year-old GCSE history students we found the experience very emotional, and we were extremely aware of the great sacrifice made by our forefathers in the fight for the freedom we now enjoy.

However, we were disgusted by the lack of respect shown by another English school party at the Menin Gate. We do not know who they were, but they joked and swore during the Last Post, and afterwards complained that there was nothing to see.

We hereby wish to dissociate ourselves publicly from such 'youth of today'. Several of our group held personal links with names honoured on the memorials: we realised that many young men killed were little older than we are now. It could so easily be us. We will not forget.

PETER TOON,
SIMON INGRAM
SARAH COOLING
KATE LANGLEY
Joseph Rowntree School
New Earswick, N. Yorks

November 11, 1996

EAST OF THE RHINE

The fall of communism

SIR—When I look at the television images of jubilant Pragueists, when I see the well-known Alexander Dubcek and next to him Vaclav Havel, on whose face the tribulations of the past 20 years—filled with jail vilification and police harassment—are so clearly imprinted, I don't think about the future of my native country. The future is always unknown. I think about the past 40 years of its history under Communist rule.

Over 100,000 men and women served long terms in concentration camps and after they had been released all they could hope for were menial jobs of the lowest order. They could not return to schools to finish their education or learn a trade. They lost their fiancées who did not wait for them, they never again saw their parents, with whom they could have lived for 10 more years.

First of all, I think of those who lost their lives on the gallows, of Milada Horakova, the Socialist Deputy, the only woman ever hanged by Czechs for so-called political crime. The life of almost everybody was badly marked by the Marxist experiment, lives of innumerable individuals have been radically changed for the worse, lives of several hundreds ended by the hangman's hands.

I also think of the forgotten ones, of the Ruthenians, for instance, whose country, an integral part of pre-war Czechoslovakia, was annexed by Stalin in 1945 without any protests from the West, without any consultation with the country's inhabitants, without permission from the Czechoslovak government of the late President Edvard Benes.

I think of all those things of the past, and then of Milan Kundera's line which he put into the mouth of the central character of his novel *The Joke*: 'There were times when I thought that nothing would be forgotten and everything would be redressed. Now I know that everything will be forgotten and nothing will be redressed.'

Will the recent events in Czechoslovakia prove Kundera wrong? I hope so. I hope so.

JOSEF SKVORECKY

March 27, 1989   Toronto

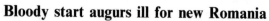

Bloody start augurs ill for new Romania

SIR—The emergence of an opposition party and the promise of free elections in April are good news, but we had better not assume that Romania has changed overnight into a free country.

The Ceausescus' execution (report, Dec. 27) seems as arbitrary and lawless as the assassinations they themselves used to arrange. What authority would a military court have over Elena Ceausescu? Under what law were the couple tried *secretly*? What kind of trial could have been held within hours? In that time, how could the Ceausescus answer the charges, make confessions, name their accomplices?

One answer to such objections is that those who make them do not understand what it is like to be caught up in a revolution. I was in the 1956 Hungarian revolution, and I did not know anyone connected with Imre Nagy's transitional government who approved of summary executions.

My group of students rescued several secret policemen from lynching, and took them to the police station. We wanted to break with the arbitrary violence of tyranny, to establish the rule of law, the principle that everyone has the right to a fair and public trial. Moreover, we wanted those secret policemen's testimonies to be on the record.

Although there were a few lynchings by enraged crowds we tried to stop them, and most people disapproved of them. They understood that a free Hungary could only be built on *due process* and detailed knowledge of who did what during the Stalinist terror.

The summary executions in Romania can only prevent the Ceausescus from implicating the people who terrorised the country on their behalf. The generals who set up the tribunal are the very same officers who less than a week ago were ordering their troops to shoot down unarmed civilians. These men abandoned Ceausescu when the revolt in the conscript army made it obvious that he had no future. Their prompt execution of their masters whom they served so slavishly was nothing but a way of covering their own tracks.

It is also disturbing that the new prime minister, appointed only two days ago, is excusing the generals by making the patently false claim that the summary executions were necessary to persuade the *Securitate* men who were still fighting to give up. But the fighting was nearly over, and showing the Ceausescus in handcuffs on television would have been just as good.

The new provisional government seems to be manned at every level by the same people as the Ceausescu regime. The death of the tyrant is not yet the end of tyranny. Instead, we have the sinister spectacle of his henchmen celebrating his fall.

The Romanian border police, who shot and beat to death more than 200 people last year for trying to cross into Hungary, are telling Western newsmen how happy they are about the dictator's end. Ceausescu's ambassador in London tells us that he is ashamed that he told lies for Ceausescu. But he is not ashamed enough to quit office.

It may not be possible to get rid of all the administrators of the terror any faster without plunging the country into chaos, but just the same this is not a regime that any Western government should be eager to support—or believe.

STEPHEN VIZINCZEY
London SW5

December 28, 1989

Freedom by post

SIR—The Hungarian 5-forint stamp is, I believe, the first to commemorate the recent events in Eastern Europe. In the traditional Hungarian colours of green, white and red, it shows the cut barbed wire with a poppy and cornflower. It recalls the already distant opening of the Hungarian border with Austria to let through East Germans.

STEPHEN SEELY
Sale, Ches

January 15, 1990

A dictatorial taste for Mozart

SIR—Despite reports about the grim situation of Albania, there is one bright spot—for music lovers that is, which all Albanians are. Albania has more resident symphony and opera orchestras than London and New York put together—14 in fact.

A former schoolmaster Hoxha, who had once been a member of the Chinese Marxist group in France headed by Chou En-lai, developed a passion for Mozart and a penchant for opera. On seizing power in the mid-1940s he decreed that the masses should be encouraged to appreciate musical culture.

Thereafter, and to this day, every factory, farming commune and workshop was treated to piped classics performed by any of Tirana's seven orchestras, not to mention the packed concert halls in the capital. The remaining orchestras travel the country giving non-stop performances in towns with a population of more than 4,000.

Albanian conductors never take a bow nor do audiences applaud. Why not? Too bourgeois, I was told.

MICHAEL de HAVILLAND
January 26, 1990   Eastbourne, E. Sussex

~

Polish exiles' Jacobite air

SIR—The prospect of the Polish Government-in-Exile winding up (article, Dec. 4) brings to mind a parallel in our own history: the Stuart government in exile after 1689.

Like the legitimate Free Polish administration which has been based at Eaton Place for the past 45 years, the rightful Stuart sovereigns maintained a government at the chateau of St Germain. This included Secretaries of State, a Lord Chancellor, Black Rod, as well as an elaborate court life.

Until 1697, James II had his own army, composed of troops coming over to France after the Battle of the Boyne and augmented by the Wild Geese from Ireland and English deserters during the Nine Years War.

The first wave of Jacobite immigration was immense—70,000 in France alone. Until the failure of the '15 Rebellion most hoped to go home, but after 1716, when the Stuart Court moved to Avignon and then Rome, they began to integrate in the host countries, becoming merchants, bankers, financiers and innovators in horsebreeding and the textile industry.

Later there was a government-in-exile at Rome, on a smaller scale, with diplomatic envoys at most European courts. Though it was High Treason to correspond with or visit 'James III' or his sons, the Stuart princes were a tourist attraction for British visitors who sought them out in public places.

The difference between the Stuart and Polish exiles, of course, is that the Stuart cause was lost in the end, whereas the London-based President Kaczorowski now has the very real prospect of returning home, provided that Lech Walesa has won the current election.

The turning point for the Jacobites was the '45 Rebellion, when the charismatic Prince Charles Edward landed in Scotland with a handful of retainers, known as the Seven Men of Moidart. It is true, their campaign failed but, Whig mythology notwithstanding, this was by no means inevitable. They swept all before them in Scotland and enjoyed considerable prospects in England which could well have led to success if the Prince had not been forced to turn back at Derby by that bane of all exiled governments, quarrelling and contradictory supporters.

If President Kaczorowski returns to Warsaw to pass on the formal reins of power to the new President Walesa he can be assured that he and the other men of Eaton Place will be remembered as surely as the Men of Moidart, who, incidentally, were almost as old as they are now.

EVELINE CRUICKSHANKS

December 10, 1990 London W1

President Ryszard Kaczorowski of the Polish Government-in-exile returned to Poland on December 22, 1990, the day General Jaruzelski handed over the Presidency in Poland to Lech Walesa.

～

Return of the 'Great Game'?

SIR—Your report (Feb. 4) of the green pennants of Islam flying once more over Kazan, the ancient Tatar capital which for 450 years has been a bastion of Russian Christendom, imparts fresh importance to an earlier history of Central Asia of which the British are joint custodians with the Russians.

Contemporaneously with Britain's final conquest of the Punjab in 1847 the curtain rose on the aggressive Russian drama in Central Asia which is not yet played out.

As late as 1840 there had been no Russian presence south of the Aral Sea but, in the course of the next 60 years, when the 'Great Game' was afoot, Imperial Russia took giant strides, conquering and colonising all the great Khanates including the Little, Middle and Great Hordes of the Mohammedan world, and taking Tashkent, Bokhara and Samarkand, before arriving on the Afghan frontier.

In his memoirs, Field Marshal Lord Roberts of Kandahar said that Britain's Afghan wars were fought essentially 'because of the presence of Russian officers in Kabul'. The time when Russia regarded diplomatic notes with the same apprehension and fear as the approach of cholera passed rapidly. It was demonstrated when Grigoriev, the Russian governor of Western Siberia, voiced concern in 1867 about support from the south 'stirring up a general and combined Mohammedan movement against us . . .' and went on: 'We may remind the English that exciting or fostering revolt is a game that two can play.'

Sir Henry Rawlinson, a member of the India Council, replied, '. . . it must always be remembered that Russia is far more vulnerable than England in this respect and that we could instigate a great anti-Russian Mohammedan movement north of the Oxus with much greater facility than she could stir up the Sikhs and Hindus.'

This, then, is the new, or rather old, drama on which the curtain is going up in Central Asia; but today it requires no stimulus of imperial rivalry. With the Russian withdrawal from Afghanistan has come that disparagement of her power that was also the British experience. Russia's vain visionary ambitions in Central Asia must appear to have come to nothing. In a certain sense she is now the victim of her own victory.

As the periphery is taking its revenge on the former Soviet Union one does not have to be an incurable Cassandra to suggest that events in Kazan illuminate the forecasts of those who consider that the net beneficiary of the collapse of Communism is likely to be Islam.

Islam is an ideology as well as a religion. It must be probable now that the swarming centres of Muslim population will seek there not just a confessional, but a national identity.

MICHAEL CHARLTON
February 6, 1992 Richmond, Surrey

Bachelors under the hammer

SIR—Since arriving in London from Moscow last week, I have been regaled with tales of the injustices suffered by women in the West. In an attempt to cheer up these women, or at least give them food for thought, I have regaled them in return with the news of the bizarre twist in the sex war in Russia—the 'bachelors' auctions' at which women bid for men as sexual commodities.

After 70 years of Communist rule, under which Women's Lib amounted to little more than equal productivity on the factory bench, Russian women have re-emerged forcefully in the battle of the sexes. There may have been no sex in the former Soviet Union (official!); but in Yeltsin's Commonwealth young women of means are prepared to go after what they want.

For years now Russian matriarchs have been disillusioned with their menfolk, who seemed dismayingly content to submit to the system while drawing comfort from a bottle of vodka. It is no coincidence that it is the male of the species that is now under the hammer—nor indeed that the men are making such paltry sums.

At the recent auction held at Tver, in the provinces, the opening bid was but 100 roubles (40p)—less than the cost of a bottle of state-produced vodka. At that same auction the highest price was achieved by a sprightly young journalist, who went for the sum of 10 American dollars.

This low price, I was told, was a reflection of the women's assessment of the poor intellectual calibre of the men on offer. I fear this whole business will turn out badly. Despite the temporary feminine triumph, I am concerned for the women of Russia, rather than for the hapless men. In such difficult times as these, what with food and fuel shortages, we women have more than enough to worry about.

The last thing we need is to know that, at any given moment, our men friends might be lured into putting themselves up for sale. The problem is that many men, already suffering from low self-esteem, are very hard up at the moment. It comes as no surprise, then, that many of them are attracted—not just by the 20 per cent cut of the fee to which they are entitled, but also by the prospect of a free dinner in a hotel restaurant, where they will doubtless only drown their sorrows even more.

VERA SELIVANOVSKAYA

London N7

July 13, 1992

~

Smiling in the face of death

SIR—Sarajevo is about to die. The ammunition is running low, and the besiegers are poised to deliver the *coup de grâce*. On the evidence of Vukovar, Foca, Fisegrad, Rogatica, Zvornik, Vijeljina, and now Gorazde, there seems little reason to suppose it will not be an extremely violent end.

The Yugoslav army's tanks and artillery will pound the undefended city to pieces, this time taking especial care to level every mosque, every memorial to the presence in the Balkans of hated Islam. Then the Chetniks will pour in to exterminate the Muslim vermin, the Croat rubbish, and the 'bad' Serbs. Impatient after their long wait, with their own dead to avenge, they will show no quarter. Three hundred thousand men, women and children will either be killed or, if they are lucky, driven out of the city as part of the ethnic 'cleansing'. Any UN troops or foreign journalists who get in the way will not be spared.

'Good' Serbs who die by mistake will be part of the generation which Dr Radovan Karadzic says he is prepared to sacrifice so that 'future generations of Serbs may live in peace'. Nobody in Sarajevo can believe what is happening. The streets are shattered, with broken shop fronts and gutted buildings. Traffic lights are fallen and vehicles burnt out. The litter of tram and trolleybus cables snakes the roadways, in which a mosaic of broken glass and bits of stone make everything gritty underfoot.

Yet it feels as if this is only a horrible holiday from reality, a nightmare from which the real Sarajevo—the city where I have worked as a translator for 26 years and for which I once produced a guide—will somehow emerge when all this is over.

Life has to go on, even though pedestrians are felled by snipers' bullets, teenagers are taken apart by exploding mortar bombs and a young woman's brains are spilt on the steps of her apartment building while whole families are snuffed out by direct hits on their homes.

We are all unwashed and undernourished, and no longer know what day of the week or what date it is. But women still dress well and keep their poise, and people still smile and enjoy a joke. We all laugh at *'Allo 'Allo* on television—perhaps inordinately so.

I burst into tears yesterday when a UN soldier played me 'Don't cry for me, Argentina'.

WILLIAM TRIBE

July 18, 1992   Sarajevo

MISUNDERSTANDING AMERICA

Root causes of anti-American feelings here

SIR—The American Ambassador to London has commented upon the phenomenon of anti-Americanism. Your columnist (March 14) essays an analysis.

Both men reveal the origin of anti-Americanism to be beyond their grasp. As a result they confuse anti-Americanism with anti-American government and pro-Russian as pro-communist. More profoundly damaging to their case is their insidious insistence on trying to polarise sentiment and compelling choice between two former allies.

The last figures in American politics whom we understood, whatever their faults, were Adlai Stevenson and the Kennedy brothers. After their death power crossed from the New England states to central and southern America and thence to California. The American people resorted to an anti-intellectual, anti-New England, anti-liberal over-simplification which confused rational analysis with sympathy.

The more profound students of world affairs in Europe cannot grasp the yearning for simplicities as articulated by a Johnson, a Reagan, or even a Jimmy Carter, still less the superficiality of response expressed by men elected to government with all the razzmatazz of circus. Furthermore, the cultural manifestations which we receive in Europe are not the highest expressions of American culture but violent homilies full of glamour, visceral sentimentality, and gratuitous violence; that it is cheaper to show *Dallas*, *Dynasty*, etc rather than better acted, better scripted European material is irritating.

Moreover, the ambivalences of America, the subtleties of America, or even the diversities within America are not evident here save to a few. The prism of the media presents an American political establishment which is ignorant of fundamental dimensions of European culture. However repugnant Hitler or Stalin to Europeans or Americans, they are creatures of recognisable European problems and culture which prevail from the Pyrenees to the Urals.

We do not perceive the divisions of Europe as permanent or insoluble. We regret the Berlin Wall, we regret the enmity towards Russia just as we regret the tragic conditions which compromised Socialism in Germany and Russia. But transcending those regrets is a recognition that some of the elements of Russian or German problems are elements of some of our own problems.

In defence of his economic and fiscal policy President Reagan remarked that other economies had to eliminate the rigidities which hampered their progress. Those rigidities are our cultural inheritance; they may not be removed without a deep cultural impoverishment. And for what? *Dallas*, and chewing gum?

ADRIAN H. COWELL

March 20, 1987   Aughton Green, Lancs.

Ambassador Charles Price's remarks on the West's duty to defend common democratic values were discussed in a column by the American playwright and journalist Herb Greer.

Secrets of Thomas Jefferson's family

SIR—I was surprised to read Charles Laurence's report (Nov. 25) on an article in the *Journal of the Early Republic* attributing Thomas Jefferson's alleged relationship with his slave Sally Hemings to wicked British 'disinformation'. It claimed that 'the story was first circulated and influenced by British writers keen to tarnish early American democracy'.

This matter has been exhaustively studied and owes its origin not to Britain, but to the Federalist journalist James Thomson Callender, whom Jefferson had at first befriended but who later served a jail sentence and became embittered. When Jefferson became President in 1801, Callender and his partisan cronies charged him with keeping 'as his concubine one of his own slaves'. What are the facts?

Sally was one of a family of 10 slaves; her mother Betty was the daughter of an English sea-captain and an African negress. Jefferson acquired them in 1774 on the settlement of the estate of his father-in-law John Wayles.

There is every likelihood that Sally, and some of her siblings were the children of John Wayles, and that Sally was thus the half-sister of Jefferson's wife, to whom he was devoted. It was natural that he should ask Sally, then 22, to go with him to France as companion-escort for his two young children, to whom she was thus, probably related.

Jefferson ignored the accusations of Callender who committed suicide a year after publishing his charges, believing that his well-known devotion to his dead wife's memory were enough rebuttal.

If one accepts the slaves' oral traditions, the most likely father of Sally's five children, with their striking physical likeness to the President, was Peter Carr, Jefferson's favourite nephew whom he treated as a son.

Professor ESMOND WRIGHT
December 10, 1987   University College, London WC1

~

Some good advice for Hillary

SIR—Patricia Wilson does not tell us if Hillary Clinton receives any replies in her 'imaginary conversations' with Eleanor Roosevelt (report, Feb. 23). But I have no doubt that, looking down from on high, my grandmother has great sympathy for her.

No one would know better than her that if Mrs Clinton speaks out on public issues—particularly humanitarian ones—in the way my grandmother did in the Thirties and Forties, she can expect to be attacked with a vitriol reserved in Britain for Prime Minister's Question Time. Furthermore, Eleanor Roosevelt always maintained her amateur status (though few doubted her political savvy).

As a practising lawyer, Mrs Clinton will not have that leeway. She will be attacked on a personal level, as the wife of the President, as the First Lady and as a professional who is assigned specific tasks by the President.

In the event that Mrs Clinton has not already heard this, I would call her attention to what Eleanor Roosevelt said in an address about women in politics in 1936: 'You cannot take anything personally. You cannot bear grudges. You must finish the day's work when the day's work is done. You cannot get discouraged too easily. You have to take defeat over and over again and pick up and go on.

'Be sure of your facts. Women who are willing to be leaders must stand up and be shot at. More and more they are going to do it, and more and more they should do it. Above all,' Eleanor said, one 'needs to develop skin as tough as rhinoceros hide'.

My grandmother kept up a brave front, but I know that some of the barbs hurt. And in spite of all the people around the White House, there was no one to really talk to about it. I hope Mrs Clinton can find some comfort, even comic relief, in knowing that it all happened before.

CURTIS ROOSEVELT
February 26, 1993   Deia, Mallorca, Spain

Prejudice on parade

SIR—William Cash speaks truer than he knows when he says Americans tend to see the British as villains (article. May 18).

In Gibraltar on holiday last month, I saw a United States naval commander nearly have a fit when, after accidentally stepping into a restricted area, I declined his shouted order to get out and told him that, as a British subject on Crown territory, I took no orders from US servicemen.

'Don't give me that British shit,' screamed the enraged man. 'We had to come over and fight a war for shit like you.' I was flattered when he added, still at the top of his voice, 'I suppose you are some sort of goddam retired brigadier.'

The excellent Gibraltar Police intervened at this point and the American—whose portly figure and rimless glasses did not suggest he had done much fighting—drove off swearing to have me, and the policeman who declined to arrest me, put on a charge.

To *him,* I was clearly a personal acquaintance of King George III. Readers should remember that the portrayal of Englishmen as film villains springs from a dislike which is deep-laid in some Americans.

CLIFFORD LUTON

May 20, 1995   Poole, Dorset

~

US classlessness a myth

SIR—Robin Lee (Personal View, July 9) is entirely correct in her view that, in many ways, the United States is less of a classless society than Britain is. This country should take justifiable pride in the fact that it has always been a 'classless society' where a butcher's son such as Cardinal Wolsey could, among other activities, aspire to found Christ Church, Oxford.

In so far as America has a meritocracy, we learnt this system from our common ancestors. The key difference, I believe, is that Britain has a public 'aristocracy' or official upper-class listed in such books as Debrett's. Any person of worth and talent can hope to enter their Lordships' house, or at least earn a CBE.

In my country we have no aristocracy recognised by the government. Instead we have a hidden, very private upper-class listed in a book called *The Social Register.*

When working in the Reagan White House's personnel office, I noticed how many appointees were the great-great grandsons or daughters of nineteenth-century presidents, vice-presidents, cabinet officers or senators. Cash-in-hand is really not a big factor in our class system. What matters is how long your family has held on to the loot. A great-great-great-great grandpa in the slave trade trumps a dad in liquor smuggling. How you earn it is a factor: a penurious teacher will outrank a flush junk-dealer. It also counts how you spend it: an authentic country cottage is fine, a mock-Tudor monstrosity will endanger your listing in the right books.

According to sociologist, Digby Baltzell, author of *The Protestant Establishment,* the single most important determinant of class in America is which private school, not university, you attended, such as the elite Groton or St Paul's. As a result, you cannot buy or earn by good works your way into *The Social Register*. If you marry the 'wrong' spouse you can be deleted.

If their Lordships were translated to America, only about half of them would survive the scrutiny of the editors of that demanding listing.

ROBERT SCHUETTINGER
July 11, 1991   Mansfield College, Oxford

~

Trollope right on the US

SIR—Anthony Trollope may have been wrong about the result of the American Civil War (New York Life, May 8) but as both a Trollope biographer and someone born in America I recognise in him a remarkably percipient prophet.

Trollope regarded the United States as those 'wondrous children' of English civilisation; he even once joked that 'nature intended me for an American rather than an Englishman.' But he believed there was an inherent difference between East and West, and predicted that they would separate in his futuristic novel *The Fixed Period*. Recent polls showing the growing discord between Washington and the West may be bearing him out.

Trollope identified the threat to society posed by irresponsible journalists, whom he first attacked in his early novel *The Warden*. He would certainly consider some of the ludicrous babblers on American radio as among the worst examples of what he called 'the tyranny of democracy'.

He also noted another menace. Observing how 'venomous and bloodthirsty philanthropists' had caused the Civil War, he warned that such intellectual fanatics always provoke violent reactions by those whose way of life they undermine.

Trollope once scribbled in his copy of Bacon's *Essays*: 'A country cannot stand high without dignity.' He was mercifully spared the sight of Mr Clinton's jogging: a spectacle which surely destroys any lingering sense of dignity in his office.

Trollope thus foresaw so many of those factors which have set the stage for the tragedy in Oklahoma: the contempt for politicians felt by increasing numbers of people, the tension between the older and the newer parts of America, the unsettling effect of intellectual fanatics and the weakness that springs from a powerful man without any dignity.

Perhaps the recent celebrations of VE Day show how correct Trollope was in another of his views. 'No form of government that ever did exist,' he wrote, 'gives . . . so large a measure of individual freedom . . . as a constitutional monarchy.'

Three of the four wartime allies have presidents who are held in contempt by large segments of their citizens. Only one head of state deserves the love and respect of her people and that was shown triumphantly last weekend. On constitutional monarchy, as on so much else, Trollope was right.

RICHARD MULLEN
May 13, 1995   Oxford

~

Make mine a double first

SIR—You report (Sept. 15) that young Americans are paying $9,000 for pencils with encoded answers to university entrance examinations written on the side. I wonder why they bother.

In the latest madness there, a federal judge has ruled—in a case brought by 10 Boston University 'students'—that university graduation requirements for certain mathematics and language courses place an undue burden on students with learning disabilities. The judge also found that it was unlawful for the university to require students to produce recent diagnosis of learning disability from a physician or a psychologist in order to qualify for special treatment, such as tutoring and extra time to complete tests and assignments. According to the judge's ruling, such requirements were 'high hurdles' that placed emotional and financial burdens on disabled students.

It would appear that three federal laws designed to help those with moderate to severe physical disabilities now cover people who have trouble with reading, trouble with maths, trouble with comprehension, trouble with concentration.

Imagine where this might lead. 'Just because I can't handle maths doesn't mean that I shouldn't be a physicist!' 'Just because I can't spell doesn't mean that I shouldn't teach English.' 'Just because I failed all my tests doesn't mean I shouldn't get a degree.'

Many years ago, when I was teaching in a major American university, I had students in one of my freshman classes who were not required to take (much less pass) any entrance examination. The kindest thing I can say for them was that they didn't snore when they slept through lectures. I was not permitted to fail them even when one of them handed in his test paper completely blank except for his name, not even his student number.

Most things American eventually arrive here. You have been warned.

ANDREW KEVORKIAN
London W1

September 22, 1997

MANNERS

Parisians' polished art of rudeness

SIR—According to Suzanne Lowry (article, June 29), a report by the French Prime Minister M. Rocard has found that foreign businesses seeking European headquarters are put off in France because of Parisians' rudeness.

There are several theories to explain this legendary rudeness (including a general bilious dyspepsia caused by unwise combinations of rich food and drink), but whatever the cause M. Rocard has an uphill struggle if he thinks Parisians can be exhorted to mend their manners. They do not practise rudeness as we know it but as an art form, perfected over centuries. Where else can a mere shrug, a *moue*, a withering upward roll of the eyes contain the information—regardless of words used—that your statement/query/request is clear evidence of the functioning capacity of a brain more appropriate to a unicellular organism. Who else can convey with a simple wagging finger and an '*Ah non, non, non, NON*!' the yawning abyss of one's ignorance and stupidity?

The French are masters of nuance. I suspect that their reaction to being told that people find them rude would be one or more Gallic gestures and a loud '*Nous nous en foutons*'.

FIONA EBERTS
July 3, 1990　　　　　　　　　　　　　　　　London W14

Let this be a lesson on politeness

SIR—The British are noted for their fair play, specially when forming, and waiting in, a queue. Has the following behaviour ever been observed in a British queue?

Scene: San Marino City Post Office entrance, 9.30 am. Robert Cunningham, standing in the sidewalk near the entrance, sees a woman walking up.

He waits for her, and opens the door for her to enter the Post Office ahead of himself. She takes her place in a line of six people just ahead of Cunningham.

He (after waiting several minutes for her to do the right thing): 'Madam, I opened the door for you, but I didn't intend for you to go ahead of me in the queue.'

She: 'But I'm in a very big hurry!'

He: 'So am I.'

She: 'I'll only be a minute.'

He: 'I'll only be a minute.'

She: 'But I'm already late for work.'

He: 'I am too!'

She flounced out of the Post Office in a huff, murdering him with a look.

Moral: Tip your hat, but never open a door for a woman who can walk faster than you!

ROBERT Q. CUNNINGHAM
August 13, 1990   San Marino, California

~

No bar to politeness

SIR—Following your recent correspondence on the disappearance of good manners, I would like to say that I work in a women's prison opening and closing doors for inmates every day, and I am amazed when someone does not smile and say thank you.

Out in the streets and in shops things may well have changed for the worse. But prison inmates are, in my experience, as polite as people generally always used to be.

PAUL DEVLIN
December 16, 1993   Deputy Governor,
New Hall Prison, Wakefield, West Yorks

~

Harding's way

SIR—Hugh Massingberd's experience (article, Dec. 6) of the ill-mannered response of people for whom he held doors open is not a recent phenomenon.

The late Gilbert Harding once held a shop door open for two ladies who passed through without acknowledgment. Seeing that a third was approaching, he said: 'Thank you, madam, for letting me hold the door open for you'. She turned, recognised him, and replied: 'Oh, it's you, you rude man!'

MICHAEL SMITH

December 10, 1993   Presteigne, Powys

Who now will teach us?

SIR—What is so refreshing about Hugh Massingberd's views on good manners is that they are so much at variance with establishment ideas. Dennis Skinner (surely now a part of the Establishment) said recently that good manners were a blind, to be used by the upper classes to put down those lower on the social scale.

We have academics on television and radio prepared to use four-letter words to make their point, without any question of sensitivity entering the equation. Similar objections might be made to our newspapers, especially the quality ones. The cause of courtesy was lost years ago in the tabloids.

We can therefore no longer rely on politicians or the various media forms to back us in the fight to take into account the interests of others before doing or saying anything.

Nor can we rely on technology. After a few years of holding doors open for people to enter the local shopping mall and receiving no acknowledgment, I now find that the doors have been changed to automatic control. There is no longer need for a social transaction of any kind.

Together with Hugh Massingberd, let us start doing something to bring back the good life of decency and consideration.

EDWARD THOMAS

December 11, 1993   Eastbourne, E. Sussex

When the kissing has to start

SIR—Henry Porter (Commentary, July 19) need fear no more. I can give him sound advice on his kissing problem. I too once hated this form of social intercourse, but having converted some years ago now feel about able to call myself a true student of the art. First, it is important to ascertain one's own sincerity in the matter. Aim for the meaningful kisser is no problem since, in order to be effective, one must look fondly at the kissee on approach, thus holding them in position by eye contact. For greater safety and meaningfulness, gently clasp the victim's head; thus ensuring no fast moves.

For the less sincere kiss one needs to employ stealth. The golden rule is to be aware: do not close the eyes even if the kissee is hideous, or if you think you are close enough to relax. Many a disastrous misfiring has occurred at the late stages. It is important to assess the situation correctly.

Be wary of left handers and those who clasp hands with their left instead of the conventional handshake; they are likely to go for your right cheek. Above all, make your own intentions clear; move slowly and deliberately, thus giving an air of authority and giving time for the kissee to position themselves. A slow retreat from one cheek gives time for a swift assessment of whether one kiss is sufficient or not. Never go for the cop out—the lips in mid air facing away from the kissee's eye—as this denotes a slave to convention but a cowardly heart.

I hope this short letter will be of help to Mr Porter. If he requires more information, or practical assistance, I offer my services.

JANE KING
Uley, Glos

July 25, 1991

CLASS

The beer essentials

SIR—I am training butlers this week in Bangkok and, besides this, I have been extremely busy giving my special one-day courses to rich American prospective employers. We call the course 'How to handle your butler' and, apart from the American rich, I have wealthy Australians on the course.

My first butlers will shortly be on their way to Australia. One very wealthy Australian asked me a question: 'If I want a beer does my butler give it to me in a can as I usually have it?' My answer, I feel, surprised him. 'Sir, from now on, your butler will serve you your beer in a cut glass, on a tray.'

IVOR SPENCER
March 27, 1989   Bangkok, Thailand

~

Norway's Mr Men

SIR—Mr Oakley-Hill (letter, May 11) would be happy in Norway. Their only titles (leaving aside those like military ranks) are King and Mr. There is only one King.

MICHAEL ROWLANDSON
May 13, 1989   Salisbury, Wilts

~

Sartorial give-away

SIR—Nowhere is it easier, alas, to detect new money than on the banks of trout and salmon rivers. The vast new bank accounts have led to the purchases of clothes (letter, Aug. 1) that would look bizarre on shooter or shot, let alone on a fisherman.

Breeches are now being worn, coupled to stockings (often highly coloured) and polished brogues. That is the give-away. But they also affect hats that range from the Sherlock Holmes to the Gorblimey (as frequently donned, as a joke no doubt, by the Prince of Wales). They are also inclined, even in the sunshine, to wear new and pristine waxed coats.

Worst of all there can be found in the backs of their cars, often ill-concealed, spinning rods—tools that no gentleman, in any circumstances, would dream of owning, let alone bringing to the river.

Some of these people, I am told, even use plastic bank cards.

DAVID BARR
August 8, 1990   Wisbech, Cambs

Part of nature

SIR—Most people seem to regard class as a bad thing, causing snobbery and injustice. I regard it as a good thing, causing square pegs to be put into square holes and people to diversify without strain.

But whether you consider it a good thing or a bad thing it is an inevitable thing: nearly all animals have a strict class structure. Attempts to alter this fact—as with communism, or money, or political correctness—merely seem to make things worse. Of course you need equality under the law and equality of opportunity but people are generally happier when they know where they are and they are where they belong.

The pilot may seem more glamorous; but you need mechanics and aircraft designers and air hostesses and passengers just as much. Arguments as to who is the grandest are very silly.

(Mrs) GILLIAN BENCE-JONES
July 4, 1992   Nacton, Suffolk

Always to blame

SIR—As a comparatively new member of the middle class (having become a computer analyst programmer) I am peeved.

When I was in the working class (a British Telecom engineer) I got used to being blamed for all the country's economic woes—always being on strike, earning too much, having too long tea breaks and sleeping through night shifts. It was offensive at first, but one got used to it.

Now here I am in the jolly old middle class, and what do I hear? The country's economic woes are still all my fault—this time because I don't spend enough of my money, because I'm still paying for the loans I was encouraged to take out to get us out of the last recession!

No doubt when I eventually become a peer, the aristocracy will find itself blamed for the recession.

August 28, 1992

STEPHEN AXTELL
Newton Longville, Bucks

Inverted snobbery worst

SIR—Max Davidson, in his review of *Scarfe on Class* (Television, July 14), says that anyone asking for the 'lavatory' is a prat with a speech disorder. Well, I am not a prat, nor have I ever suffered from a speech disorder. This also applies to all those of my friends and relatives who speak as I do.

I might also use the words 'loo' or 'WC', but 'toilet' simply does not exist in my vocabulary, as I feel uncomfortable with it. I would never refer to a napkin as a 'serviette', or use the word 'Nan' to describe someone's grandmother: surely a nanny is a person paid to look after one's children?

I say 'How do you do?' and not 'Pleased to meet you', and I never cease to be amazed that children in state schools are taught that their school lunch is a 'school dinner' and that the meal they will have in the evening at home is their 'tea'.

And yes, I do pour my tea in first; I also use a tea strainer, napkin rings, fish knives and forks, and I don't hold my knife 'that way'. I do agree that top people drink coffee—but *not* at 4p.m., Mr Davidson: they usually have tea—Darjeeling, Earl Grey, or Lapsang Souchong.

What is wonderful about this country is that we do all speak and live differently, and we should respect all these differences. Snobbishness may be wrong, but Mr Davidson's inverted snobbery is something those of us who use 'lavatories' are, frankly, tired of.

ANNE GILES
July 17, 1993   South Croydon, Surrey

The inventing of PLU

SIR—We have become aware that the expression People Like Us (PLU) has become common currency, but that it is being wrongly interpreted. May we, therefore, give the original meaning worked out by its inventors, the late Frank Waldron and the undersigned, during the New Year festivities in Montana, Switzerland, in 1946–47.

Montana at that time was a cosmopolitan mix of British, French, Germans and Italians, all more or less based at the Moubra clinic for people with chest problems. Frank was a patient there owing to a war wound.

Surrounded as we were by a *mélange* of all classes and types from *Ancien Regime* to show-biz folk and drunken drop-outs, one formed unexpected and bizarre friendships, and it was in this bohemian night-clubbing atmosphere that the three of us decided that some definition was needed. So we came up with PLU.

It is not a definition of social class. Indeed, we excluded as many people on that count as we included.

We could only give ourselves generalised definitions like 'pleasantly eccentric, civilised, witty, outgoing, broad-minded' but perish the thought of any rigid class divisions.

Marquess of ABERDEEN
JEAN MEADE-FETHERSTONHAUGH
August 10, 1994   Ashampstead, Berks

GENTLEMEN

Cutting remarks

SIR—The pervasive Americanisation of our country manifests itself in so many ways. Apart from the more blatant and obvious influences in advertising and the corruption of language, there is the question of boys' haircuts.

Thirty years ago one could identify an English boy abroad; his hair was groomed, but long from the crown and allowed to follow the natural bone structure of the head. Hence each boy retained a certain individuality.

One very rarely sees the 'English cut' today. Everywhere there is the 'paintbrush' or 'crewcut' which brutalises the individual with its complete lack of sensitivity and subtlety.

Not even our public schools seem capable of resisting this trend, probably because they are so obsessed with academic achievement so that form and style are inclined to go to the wall.

PHILIP FORDER-WHITE
November 11, 1988　　　　　　　　　　Fordingbridge, Hants

Above definition

SIR—May not a gentleman be defined as one who considers it beneath his dignity to attempt to define a gentleman?

RICHARD GAMMAN
January 17, 1990　　　　　　　　　　Hove, East Sussex

Living on

SIR—The attempt by W. F. Deedes to pinpoint the precise moment in history when the English gentleman became dead is premature (article, July 18). His death knell has been sounded many times.

As long ago as the passing of the Reform Bill of 1832, which abolished the rotten boroughs by which all political power was firmly in the hands of gentlemen, the Earl of Bathurst of the day was so distressed that he cut off his pig-tail, one of the caste marks of the superior courtier. 'Ichabod, the glory is departed,' he cried. 'They have let the enemy in upon us.'

The Duke of Wellington agreed with him on the grounds that the government of the people was far too sacred a task to be entrusted to other than gentlemen, just as it was the exclusive right of gentlemen to be officers in the Armed Forces and die leading their men into battle. 'Conduct unbecoming an Officer and a Gentleman' still stands as the most serious offence in the rule book, to be tried by court-martial.

It is true the passing of the Reform Bill marked the beginning of a slow process whereby the power both in politics and the great institutions such as banking, insurance and the law was moving out of the hands of the amateur and into the hands of the professionals—or, as Bill Deedes would have it, from the gentleman to the players.

But this does not mean that the English gentleman, whose word was once taken as his bond, is dead. It is merely that the professionals have sought to disguise themselves as gentlemen and misused his reputation for integrity to their own ends.

A case which perfectly illustrates how the professionals have dropped the baton is that of penniless Czechoslovak refugee, Herr Hoch, who assumed the disguise of an officer and a gentleman as Captain Robert Maxwell, MC. That he was immediately fawned upon by the banks, who opened up their vaults to him, says little for their perspicacity, and even less for the serried ranks of highly paid lawyers who gorged themselves on huge fees to preserve this fiction.

Nevertheless, the English gentleman still lives despite the efforts of those less than honourable men who assume for themselves his reputation for decency and graceful living.

When John Major declared that he would preside over a classless society, it only inflamed the ambition of many to be recognised as being gentlemen as opposed to non-gentlemen.

July 25, 1992

DOUGLAS SUTHERLAND
South Queensferry, Lothian

~

Died in 1971 Act

SIR—So far as the Army Act is concerned, the English gentleman died in 1971. Mr Sutherland (letter, July 25) is quite right to recall that one of the most serious offences known to military law always used to be 'scandalous conduct, unbecoming an officer and a gentleman'.

When the Army Act currently enforced was enacted in 1955, the section dealing with misconduct by officers was still in those traditional words, as was the corresponding provision in the Air Force Act. In accord with the spirit of the times, however, they were amended in 1971 to remove the words 'and a gentleman', which were seen as superfluous, adding nothing to the high standards of behaviour required of anyone having the honour to hold the Queen's Commission. It may also have recognised that a growing proportion of officers plainly were not gentlemen, being ladies!

However, the offence remains, as it always has been, unique in being the only military offence for which only one penalty is provided, namely dismissal, with or without disgrace, in former times cashiering.

It is this which makes it, as Mr Sutherland described it, 'the most serious offence in the rule book' for an officer.

July 28, 1992

JAMES STUART-SMITH, QC
Copthorne, W. Sussex

~

Loosely speaking

SIR—Martin Vander Weyer, referring to 'my word is my bond' in his article 'Sorry, old boy, your word is no longer good enough' (July 21), is apparently unaware that Megarry in his most excellent *A*

Second Miscellany-at-Law states that 'a gentleman's agreement' was reputedly defined by Vaisey J. in 1958 as 'an agreement which is not an agreement, made between two persons, neither of whom is a gentleman, whereby each expects the other to be strictly bound without himself being bound at all'.

ANGUS McLEAN
July 25, 1995   Edinburgh

Macmillan on cads

SIR—I read with interest Nicholas Bagnall's piece about 'cads' (Feb. 21) and the origin of the term 'a bounder'. In his eighties the late Harold Macmillan had a lively definition of 'cads' and 'bounders' which seems hard to beat:

'A bounder is a man who goes to the front and is very brave, and wins every decoration. Then he goes on leave and seduces his colonel's wife. A cad, on the other hand, never goes anywhere near the front, but seduces the colonel's wife anyway.'

In the course of writing the official life of Macmillan, I recall his once musing on whether a woman could properly be designated a bounder or only a cad. He was able to list many of the former, but none of the latter among contemporary women. I wonder if any of your readers could oblige with candidates.

ALISTAIR HORNE
February 24, 1990   London W2

OBLIGATIONS TO SERVANTS

Swinging temerity earns its reward

SIR—Hugh Montgomery-Massingberd's amusing piece on relations between the aristocracy and their servants (March 31) reminded me of the bandleader Tommy Kinsman who specialised in what we in the trade call 'society gigs'. He had astutely gauged the quality's requirements for their coming-out parties, hunt balls and the like and was much in demand throughout the shires.

However, he wasn't above misappropriating bottles of fine wine that happened to be sitting idle (rather like the finding of goods 'wot fell off the back of a lorry'). In the early hours of the morning, at the conclusion of one hunt ball in Wiltshire, her ladyship was graciously thanking Tommy for the excellence of his band's performance as she handed him his cheque when a bottle of champagne slipped from under his coat and smashed on the floor.

Characteristically unperturbed, her ladyship clicked a peremptory finger at a nearby minion and snapped: 'Hoskinson! Fetch Mr Kinsman another bottle of the Bollinger.'

JIM GODBOLT
April 6, 1988   London NW5

~

Footman's skill

SIR—In his article 'Dressed to Kill' (Weekend, Nov. 4), R. W. F. Poole states: 'I am probably the only person left in Britain who knows how to bone boots.' This is not so.

When I was a young house servant in the Thirties with Lord Mildmay of Flete at Flete in South Devon, Berkeley Square and

Shoreham, Kent, I was taught by Mr Fossey, the butler, how to bone riding boots and clean 'pinks and buckskin trousers', ladies' riding habits (assisted by Miss Webb, the ladies' maid).

After learning these duties I was sent to Langham in Rutland for the hunting season to look after the clothes of Mr Anthony and Miss Helen Mildmay. I was proud of the shine on the scratchless boots belonging to Miss Helen and Mr Anthony, later Lord Mildmay. I once spent six hours eliminating a deep scratch.

There must surely be many more ex-butlers, valets, footmen and grooms living who can vouch for the pre-war years of gentlemen's service. I am proud to have served with such a wonderful family.

CHARLES J. COOK

November 11, 1989 Bedford, Notts

Well . . . shot, My Lord

SIR—The footman who rampaged through Lord Derby's household with a sub-machine gun in 1952 (obituary, March 22) attracted so much attention because he reversed the normal order of things. Usually the servants were on the receiving end.

In the 1880s, the Duke of Manchester used to hold lunch parties at which the climax was the driving of every type of game on the estate — deer, rabbits, hare — past the dining room window. The ensuing fusillade often resulted in injury to the long-suffering gamekeepers.

However, the standard rate of a sovereign for every identifiable wound soothed most grumbles plus the proviso that rifles were forbidden.

Perhaps the nearest equivalent to Lord Derby's footman was the member of the Wedgwood family who was shot by his gamekeeper. His tombstone bore the unfortunate legend: 'Well done, thou good and faithful servant'.

Lt-Col N. T. P. MURPHY

March 24, 1990 Gosforth, Cumbria

Duchess's line on breakages

SIR—Of course Godfrey Barker (Sixth Column, May 3) cannot expect his cleaning lady to pay for a breakage however serious or sentimental.

But the Duchess of Windsor's advice to new staff was always that breakages did not happen on purpose and the most important thing was that the domestics should own up at once. (It is a galling experience we have all suffered: to approach a china object, have it fall into six neat little pieces on touch and to realise it has been adroitly placed together in the idiotic hope that we might think we have broken it.)

The guides at Wilton delight in informing tourists that when the Queen dined there and the special china was used, it was agreed that Lady Pembroke should wash it up, and thus any breakages would be her responsibility. If it is the host's duty to provide for the needs of his guest, this must extend to breakages.

Thus I should remain calm if Mr Barker started swaying into my china and wreaking havoc. But I would deny myself the pleasure of inviting him again.

HUGO VICKERS
May 4, 1990   London W8

THE STRONGER SEX

Wrong yardstick

SIR—Minette Marrin has fallen into the common error of confusing equality with identity (article, Sept. 18). She asserts that feminism has failed because comparatively few women hold high-powered jobs, thus suggesting the only criterion of success is that of the male career high-flyer.

But people, male and female, are not born identical in abilities or desires, and equality lies in the freedom of each individual to succeed on his or her own terms. The wife and mother with a part-time job as a check-out assistant is as much a success as the High Court judge, provided each is satisfied with her condition. Using the male career yardstick to measure female achievement is as pointless and misguided as complaining that a Ming vase makes an unsatisfactory petrol can.

CYNTHIA HARROD EAGLES
Northwood, Middx

September 19, 1991

Garrick wife's retreat

SIR—I was interested to read about the proposal to elect women to the Garrick Club (Peterborough, March 3), and much heartened by Lord Cudlipp's response (letter, March 4).

I have been a Garrick wife for 17 years, and an independent career woman for 27 years. I have jostled for my place in a man's world along with the best of them; wined, dined and lunched male guests and clients at a time when it wasn't done all that often, and when I do go to the Garrick I frequently arrive hot and late and with a bulging brief-case.

The soothing balm of having the door opened for you (this after you have just lost the battle for the last Tube seat to a dapper, baby

City tycoon), of retreating to the Ladies Retiring Room which resembles nothing so much as the boudoir of the late Nellie Melba, and then being cosseted into protected indulgence is an oasis in a sweaty old world.

Unlike some of London's other clubs, women are treasured at the Garrick and my only regret is that when they redecorated the Ladies Retiring Room they didn't put the day-bed back in it. I never had occasion to use it, but it was always nice to think that, if the excitement proved too much for me, I could grab a quick 10 minutes' vapours while, at the same time, enjoying the wealth of rare engravings and watercolours on the walls.

I have frequently, while waiting for my husband, been given a glass of champagne by the barman, and have been chatted up in the nicest way by other members who have been concerned that I might be overcome by loneliness or the threat of danger.

I love meeting my fellow female professionals, but I can do that anywhere in London. It is nice, just occasionally, to drop the briefcase and become an adored Edwardian plaything. I'd hate to think of anything changing the style of the place.

DIANE PEARSON
March 5, 1992   London W5

Air of victory on the 7.27

SIR—As a long-suffering British Rail customer, I could only sympathise with an irate lady on the 7.27 stopping service from Brighton to Victoria.

We had ground to a halt at Three Bridges due to 'traction failure', and a muffled voice advised us to cross the platform and join the London Bridge train. One woman passenger thundered up the platform in search of someone appropriate to savage, and caught sight of an unusually smart gentleman in uniform who was casually leaning out of my carriage window.

'Every day of the week you people make my life a misery,' she barked. 'I don't want to change bleeping trains for the umpteenth time—when are you going to get this one moving?'

Unmoved, and with commendable politeness, the gentleman replied: 'I wouldn't know that, madam. I'm an airline pilot.'

MIKE CASEY

June 5, 1992　　　　　　　　　　　　Brighton, E. Sussex

~

Ferocity rating

SIR—My wife was head girl of her school. When questioned by parents as to the suitability of the appointment in view of her diminutive size, the headmistress replied: 'What she lacks in stature, she more than makes up in ferocity.'

The 20 years of our married life have been among my happiest. Discipline is a great virtue.

Sir JAMES WALKER, Bt

September 28, 1992　　　　　　　　Port Soderick, Isle of Man

~

Mild objection to term 'wife'

SIR—Though neither strict adherents to feminism nor uncomfortable in addressing the editor 'Sir', we were surprised to read the headline: '*Wife* finds £15,000 sculpture in the garden' (report, April 29).

As young women aspiring to a generation of indiscriminate recognition we were saddened by the casual (perhaps even patronising) reference to Mrs Paula Godfrey's marital status.

A more thoughtful approach might have been produced in a headline lending rather more emphasis to the unusual occurrence of finding a sculpture in the back garden than to Mr Godfrey's passive achievement.

What would the headline have been if Mr Godfrey's sister's second cousin removed had unearthed the treasure?

JANE HARRIMAN WILKS
KATHERINE AWADALLA

May 4, 1995　　　　　　St Mary's College, University of Durham

~

Decorous term

SIR—The use of the term 'spinster' in your headline (July 29) conveyed quite properly the lady's state, rather than her status. It is a gentle, decorous term, dating from kinder and more rural days, when the Church was less dainty and let its rituals speak.

As a 'spinster of this parish', I married a bachelor, as distinct from a widower, of another parish. I object to the new political prissiness over certain words, which is as censorious as a Victoria matron covering up the legs of her grand piano.

If spinsters go (letter, July 30), so will maiden aunts, who are as invaluable as fairy godmothers.

Are we going to be expected to deny their existence just to please the super-sensitive?

(Mrs) JOSEPHINE PYE
August 4, 1993   West Coker, Som

~

Spare us sex-war skirmishes

SIR—There is only one response to the booklet issued by the Committee of Equal Opportunities at the Central Lancashire University, which cautions married men to not introduce their wives as 'my wife' or their secretaries as 'my secretary' (report, March 16). Hurl it straight into the waste paper bin.

As a former secretary and a current wife, I am not offended to be introduced in either of these ways, and I don't need any legislation to help me to cope with rudeness. The art of putting down rudeness is something every secretary learns quickly.

Certain members of the male sex particularly irritated me by ringing to ask if somebody is there and then saying, when told that the boss was out, 'So nobody's there'. The right reply to that is, 'When he gets back I'll tell him nobody called'.

It is not as if there is anything wrong with titles; they are very useful. When I have to go to see a dentist, I don't want to be introduced to Jane and Mary. I want to know which person is going to take my appointment and which person is going to drill my teeth, so I know who to sue afterwards, if necessary.

While part of the trouble undoubtedly lies in the spreading

tentacles of political correctness, it should be recognised that this flourishes most in committees.

My advice to any committee which finds an attack of PC coming on is to ask the secretary, who is undoubtedly sitting somewhere outside the door, for immediate help. If that does not do the job, then badly stricken male members can ask their wives, who will most likely prescribe a long period of abstinence from all forms of committee work.

Memo to the barmy committee responsible for this booklet: no woman today needs anybody to trump up any little sex-war skirmishes on her behalf.

CAROL SMITH
London, E1

March 19, 1994

Sex war worse in corrected verse

SIR—Stephen Robinson's quotation from e.e. cummings in his article on political correctness (Jan.3) is obviously highly offensive.

To make amends therefore I have written the following, corrected, version of the poem:

> *may i feel said he*
> *i'll appeal said she*
> *may i woo said he*
> *i'll sue said she*
> *shall i go said he*
> *oh no said she*
> *then i'll stay said he*
> *you may said she*
> *let's caress said he*
> *just undress said she*
> *now you're nude said he*
> *don't be rude said she*
> *may i peep said he*
> *go to sleep said she*
> *lovely lass said he*
> *don't harass said she*

> *you sparkle said he*
> *patriarchal said she*
> *you're divine said he*
> *sexist swine said she*
> *you're a tease said he*
> *court fees said she*
> *you're not wearing said he*
> *you'll be hearing said she*
> *any drawers said he*
> *from my lawyers said she*

January 6, 1994

RICHARD DAWKINS
Oxford

Earthy reply

SIR—Just who is this Peterborough? I'll give him 'faintly dowdy earth-mother' (March 27). If I ever had been dowdy, I would have been good and dowdy; nothing faint about me. As it is, what I defiantly lack in conventional chic, of the kind that would commend itself to a Tory newspaper, I invariably make up for with very bright colours, as your wretched little columnist, lurking behind his anonymity, would know if he had ever set eyes on me.

In any case, why should I be subjected to insufferable comments about my appearance just because I'm a woman? Does Peterborough remark on the scruffiness of Anthony Burgess or the sartorial or physical deficiencies of Salman Rushdie? Has he read any of my books? Or is he functionally illiterate as well as rude—and careless?

In addition to getting me wrong, it was 650,000 *dollars*, not pounds, and the British rights will not be 'auctioned'. *The L-Shaped Room* is ancient history, and I wouldn't be in the same bracket, or even the same room, with Jeffrey Archer if you paid me double. Lastly, I plead guilty to being 'sharp-tongued'. A very useful thing to have around some people.

March 31, 1992

LYNNE REID BANKS
Beaminster, Dorset

Some superwoman

SIR—Since the disagreeable Nicola Horlick elected to encourage media participation in her activities (report, Jan. 18), perhaps she might consider expanding this stratagem by allowing television coverage of her exacting daily duties to justify receipt of grossly inflated remuneration and implied superwoman tag.

It could well provide the spring-board for launching a series entitled 'A Week in the Life of . . .', embracing others of her ilk.

The revelations would doubtless afford riveting entertainment for the nation's surgeons, doctors, dentists, teachers, nurses and countless other professionals engaged in equally stressful but financially under-rewarded occupations.

JOHN BLACKBURN
Long Eaton, Derbys

SIR—Anne McElvoy's article (Jan. 20) was spot on, except she called Nicola Horlick 'superwoman'.

In fact, superwoman is the one who stays at home bringing up her own children, or one who works because she has to rather than wants to, as opposed to one who earns a huge salary and employs an army of servants to do it for her.

Mrs CATHERINE BERISFORD
Saffron Walden, Essex

SIR—Surely you must realise that we have had enough of Nicola Horlick? There will be few *Telegraph* readers who do not know a woman whose career, accomplishments and stamina records make Nicola Horlick's life look like Division 4 compared with the Premier League.

DAVID BARR
Wisbech, Cambs

SIR—A working mother, I am horribly reminded of the dreadful Violet Elizabeth of *Just William*'s team, who also threatened to 'theream and theream and theream' until she was 'thick'.

HÉLÈNE DOLDER
Kirkharle, Northumberland

SIR—During the recent, rather unnecessary, debate regarding the problems faced by working mothers, any mention of three notable women has been noticeable only by its absence: the Queen, Lady Thatcher and Cherie Booth.

Perhaps, it is a case of those who can do, and those who can't . . . complain.

HOLLY BELLINGHAM
Wickham Bishops, Essex

SIR—One wonders what is the origin of the phrase so often used to describe failure as 'making a proper horlicks of the job'.

R. BROMLEY GARDNER
January 22, 1997
Malmesbury, Wilts

Mrs Nicola Horlick, a mother of five, was suspended from her post as a high-flying fund manager after it was found that she was negotiating to join a rival firm.

~

Snip, snip, hooray

SIR—Some years ago, travelling in the rush hour by train from London Bridge to East Croydon, a young man sat in the middle of three seats listening to a tape via ear-piece headphones. The noise was deafening.

His neighbours gestured at him to turn down the volume. When he did not do so the woman next to me took a pair of nail scissors from her handbag. She reached across and snipped the wire between the player and the earphones. Silence.

G. M. SMITH
November 6, 1997
Southwater, W. Sussex

~

Dangerous loyalty

SIR—Your article, 'Should men be bullied into the delivery room?' (Oct. 19) reminds me of an experience some years ago when I visited a local maternity ward.

Having talked to each of the mothers. with their newborn babies, whose husbands or partners were with them, I came to the only bed where mother and baby were alone.

Noticing that the mother was wearing a wedding ring, I asked if her husband would be visiting later that day. 'No', she replied, 'I will be visiting him before he visits me.' She explained that he was in the Royal United Hospital, Bath, recovering from a fractured skull and broken arm. He had fainted in the delivery room while she was giving birth.

Rev. BRIAN DONNE
October 22, 1993   Trowbridge, Wilts

A hand for French flirting

SIR—What a gloomy and cynical vision of the relationship between men and women Petronella Wyatt presents if she thinks that Gallic charm comes too easily and that Frenchmen have a hollow gaudiness and do not deliver the goods, namely the financial ones, like diamonds (article, May 15, 1996).

When I first arrived in Britain a few years ago, I suddenly felt like a very old woman. I did not exist for men. No smile, no tender remarks, no rose, no love letters, nothing. At a party, when I complimented a man on his lovely (Italian) tie, he ran away, afraid, thinking that I wanted to seduce him . . .

What a crime! In Britain, everything that is pleasurable is sinful: good food, comfortable and warm rooms, and above all the delight for men and women to get together in an innocent and witty conversation, namely flirting. To flirt came from the French word *fleureter*, which means 'to touch lightly'.

Flirting shows that love is not limited to sex. It is a mischievous, slightly naughty, but not-taking-the-whole-thing-too-seriously game. It enhances life because it keeps the good difference—the sexual polarity between men and women—alive. It is a confidence in mankind as well: very quickly, a flirting young woman will realise that men are not planning to rape, rob, mug or abuse her. For me, flirting is the essence of civilisation.

That is why so many French writers, like Marivaux, or film-makers, like Eric Rohmer, have dedicated their talent to it. 'It is not enough to love, you need to express it with charm and grace,' says a character in *The Triumph of Love*.

I admire President Chirac when he carried his affection to the undemonstrative Brits, by blowing kisses to the London crowd and granting a bemused Betty Boothroyd a *baise-main*. Look at her expression: she loved it!

I suppose that is why so many Englishwomen go, alone, to the Continent: to get their share of Latin romance. In Britain, you need a special day, once a year, for would-be lovers to express anonymously their feelings: St Valentine's Day. What a pity!

If for you, *Miss* Wyatt, men are just providers of diamonds, good for you. May I prefer charm in people and my costume jewellery?

MARIE-FRANÇOISE GOLINSKY

May 18, 1996   London W8

~

Scots showed the way

SIR—It is good to see that English women will now catch up with their Scottish sisters in the equality stakes by being able to enjoy the right to bear arms in their own right (report, May 16).

This means that married women whose husbands are not armigerous will be allowed to use a coat of arms in the way that armigerous unmarried women, widows and those who have been divorced have long been able to do. The reason that married women in England have been barred from displaying their paternal coat under these circumstances seems to arise from the fact that south of the border a married woman had no identity of her own.

In Scotland, where the ladies have ever been of a more independent nature and do not, for legal purposes, abandon their maiden surnames, the heraldic practice is fundamentally different. The former Lord Lyon King of Arms, the late Sir Thomas Innes of Learney, makes clear in his *Scots Heraldry* that from early times they have always been allowed to bear their father's arms, whether married to an armiger or not.

In normal cases, this was based on their derivative right to their father's coat, though it cannot be passed on to their children. However, should they re-matriculate their father's coat (register their arms at the Lyon Court) with any due difference in their own name, then they can transmit it to their progeny with the same relevant surname.

This, of course, makes clear the fallaciousness of the claim that heraldry does not cater for women. What may be more controversial is the question, posed by the more militant among that sex, of why they should bear their arms on a lozenge and not on a shield.

Although in Scotland, heraldic law does not prevent them using a shield, a lozenge (a diamond-shaped figure) is deemed more appropriate to a sex that does not fight.

In my long experience, I have never met any true lady—one of 'ancestry and blood and of coat armour perfect'—who has ever expressed a desire to bear her family arms on a shield, because the lozenge symbolises the head of a distaff which she rightly considers far more appropriate to her.

JOHN GEORGE

May 18, 1995　　　　　　Kintyre Pursuivant of Arms, Edinburgh

My male 'wife'

SIR—Your leader on the use of the word 'partner' (April 19) reminded me of another title which confused. It was used by male undergraduates in residence at Trinity College, Dublin, as recently as the 1960s.

Those who lived in college and who shared rooms with another male student (females were banned from college from midnight) referred to him as 'my wife'. This use was official and was used by the college authorities and the undergraduates alike, without as much as a single blush or snigger.

I am pleased to say that my wife and I both graduated and later married—he in Canada and I in England. The Englishwoman bore me two healthy sons and the Canadian bore my wife two fine daughters.

I. R. SLIM LOWRY

April 25, 1996　　　　　　London, SW3

A SHORTER HUGH

Splitting problem

SIR—I fully understand why Hugh Montgomery-Massingberd has shortened his name to Massingberd (article, Jan. 10).

I, too, have problems with a name of only two syllables. I am frequently addressed, in person and in letters, as Goodolt, Godlio, Goldbolt, Godolt and and Goabit. I am often judaised into Goldblatt and Goldberg.

I am tired of giving my name to receptionists only to be met with 'Sorry, Jim who?', 'Come again' or 'Your name is what?'

So I am seriously considering a change of name to one of the present syllables. I was inclined to the second, but as I might be confused with a certain playwright, I will settle for the first. It will look good on my letter heading.

JIM GODBOLT
January 11, 1992   London NW5

~

Names to roll

SIR—I am sorry that your distinguished correspondent Hugh Montgomery-Massingberd is now to be known as plain Mr Massingberd (article, Jan. 9).

The roll call of double-barrelled surnames in our island's history includes many elegant and distinguished names such as Leveson-Gower, Meade-Featherstonhaugh, Fox-Talbot and Anstruther-Gough-Calthorpe or the quadruple-barrelled Plunkett-Ernle-Erle-Drax.

Classless society my foot; perish the thought!

(Mrs) EGLANTYNE MELBURY-BUBB
January 13, 1992   Cambridge

~

Why don't we all become Smiths?

SIR—The double-barrelled problems of Mr Massingberd (article, Jan. 9) are nothing compared with what we have to face here.

My cousins Carmel and Jerome rejoice, respectively, in the surnames Apap-Bologna-Sceberras-D'Amico-Inguanez, and de Piro-d'Amico-Inguanez. Another distant relative was Count Manduca-Piscopo-Macedonia-Zammit, who on arrival at a hotel in Italy was told there was a reservation for one person only, and that the other three gentlemen could not be accommodated.

One cannot see matters simplifying themselves here in Malta. How would one tell apart the Testaferrata-Bonicis from the Testaferata-Moroni-Vianis or the Testaferrata-Abelas? As for Igino Trapani-Galea-Feriol, it would be unthinkable to see him as plain Gino Galea, or his beautiful baroness as Sylvia Trapani or Feriol.

The Bugeja-Caruanas have, of course, always been known as the 'Caruanellus'; perhaps there lies the solution—nicknames: or we could all change to Smith (with apologies to the Caringtons/Carringtons). One successful abbreviation was Richard England's, who shortened his surname from England-Sant-Fournier, but who would not with a possibility like that?

PETER APAP BOLOGNA

January 16, 1992   Lija, Malta

All barrels

SIR—Hugh Massingberd's abandonment of one of his barrels (article, Jan. 11) reminds me of a story told by a friend of mine who was once an Irish Guards sergeant at Sandhurst.

He swears that on one occasion, a sergeant-major handed him a slip of paper bearing the names Twisleton-Wykeham-Fiennes and Vane-Tempest-Stewart and said, 'I want to see them six officer cadets, now!'

GRAHAM ISON

January 17, 1992   Alton, Hants

One-barrel Smith

SIR—As a Plain-Boring-Ordinary-Smith, I was interested in reading Hugh Massingberd's reasons for dropping a barrel (article, Jan. 11). I agree that one can easily grow into a name, which is why I tried to follow his example.

I wanted to drop the Smith—it's so common—but the Plain-Boring-Ordinary side of the family accused me of being a snob. So I've dropped them instead.

CAROL SMITH
London E1

January 21, 1992

FOUR GREAT CHARACTERS

Uncle Tom maligned in advertisement

SIR—I must protest about the Drambuie advertisement (Magazine, Sept. 16) which suggests that my great-uncle Tom was suspected of stealing his wife's jewels to pay his debts from speculation.

A Sherlock Holmes look-alike is shown holding up the brandy glass from which Tom is supposed to have drunk, declaring, 'As you say, things seem black for Lord Walsingham. His late misfortune on the stock market left him with many debts.'

Tom, the 5th Baron, who lived from 1843 to 1919, had debts because of defaults on the South American railways. He lived apart from his wife latterly, but there is no record in the family of any scandal about jewels.

He went bust in about 1917, largely because of The Ritz (Walsingham House). His manager was a fraudster, and when rumbled shot himself, leaving Tom—a shooting friend of Edward VII, a Fellow of the Royal Society and author of a definitive work on Hawaiian entomology—to pick up the tab.

There is no evidence that he ever touched a drop of Drambuie, which in those days I suspect was regarded as rather vulgar. Tom drank brandy, which perhaps explains why Holmes is holding a brandy glass, not a liqueur glass. There may, in the case of a man already dead, be no case to be argued at law, but surely there is, as Holmes would say, a case of bad manners? Whose? I wonder.

Lord WALSINGHAM
Merton, Norfolk

September 30, 1989

A better example for Mr Waite

SIR—Terry Waite, according to Peterborough (Nov. 22), should take heart from the story of Charles Neufeld, the nineteenth-century German gum-and-gun dealer who spent years as the Khalifa's prisoner in Omdurman and made a tidy sum by selling his memoirs after his rescue by Gen Kitchener and the British Army.

But Neufeld was a pariah because he had helped the Khalifa to build an arms factory. Neufeld's fellow prisoner, Rudolf Slatin Bey, would offer Mr Waite a more inspiring example.

Slatin, an Austrian soldier of fortune enlisted by Gen Gordon as Governor of Darfur, and then captured by the Mahdi, escaped from Omdurman in 1895 with the help of money smuggled in by Major Reginald Wingate, head of British Intelligence in Egypt.

Wingate encouraged Slatin to write his memoirs, *Fire and Sword in the Sudan* (1896), which proved a runaway best-seller in Britain. Slatin's revelations about the Khalifa did much to prepare the public for the British invasion of the Sudan that year.

As the last of Gordon's lieutenants, Slatin was lionised in British society. Queen Victoria entertained him (and his minder, Major Wingate) at Balmoral. She found Slatin a 'charming, modest little man, who no one could think had been through such vicissitudes'. (Wilfred Blunt, on the other hand, wrote sourly: 'He is a mean wretch to have published it, and the Mahdi made a real mistake in not cutting off his head at once when he surrendered.')

Slatin was fêted in Austria and Egypt and ended up Maj-Gen Baron Rudolf von Slatin Pasha KCMG, CB. His chest was so full of medals, according to one story, that King Edward VII told him: 'The next time you come here, Slatin, I shall have to pin the decoration on your backside.'

THOMAS PAKENHAM
November 30, 1991   London W11

～

M. Waddington of France

SIR—Henry Button is right to remind us of William Henry Waddington (letter, Dec. 20). Waddington not only rowed in the victorious Cambridge crew in 1848, he won the Chancellor's medal, was a distinguished classical archaeologist and the second of the seven Protestants who have been Prime Minister of France.

The son of an English manufacturer who had settled in Normandy, he was born in Saint Rémi-sur-Havre, and went to school in Paris before going to Rugby and Trinity College, Cambridge. At Rugby he made the acquaintance of the man who was to be the 15th Earl of Derby, and both became Foreign Minister of their respective countries.

Austen Chamberlain used to recall that at Rugby they used to sing: 'England and France will never be matches/Till Derby and Waddington write the despatches.' At Cambridge he made the acquaintance of the future Marquess of Salisbury, who was to accompany Disraeli to the Congress of Berlin in 1878 where Waddington, as Foreign Minister, represented France.

Waddington's academic and political careers neatly coincided. In 1865 he was elected to the Académie des Inscriptions et Belles Lettres, having acquired a high reputation as a numismatist and epigrapher. In 1871 he was elected deputy for the Aisne, in 1876 exchanging this for Senator. He served in three of the unstable governments of the time as Minister for Public Instruction, became Minister for Foreign Affairs, and was Prime Minister from February to December 1879.

Waddington laid the foundations of the French acquisition of Tunisia in a conversation with Lord Salisbury and, most lasting, created the Ministry of Posts and Telegraphs.

Naturally, he was attacked as being Anglophile. But as Ambassador to London he spent much of his time defending French colonial ventures in Africa and criticised Lugard's activities in Uganda. He was attacked as a Protestant by the Vatican but did much to reduce the effectiveness of the more violent forms of anti-clericalism.

Waddington enjoyed his 10 years as Ambassador in London. But, as a consequence he neglected his electorate in the Aisne *département*. In the senatorial elections of January 1894 he lost his seat. Greatly upset by this defeat he died six days later. He was a Frenchman, after all.

Prof DOUGLAS JOHNSON
London NW3

December 26, 1992

A premier taste in ladies

SIR—Sir Charles Tupper, the Canadian prime minister who was known as 'the Ram of Cumberland County' (Peterborough. Aug. 3), was regarded, with much justification, as a ladies' man.

In the late Victorian era, when women were beginning to make careers for themselves as typists, nurses and doctors, he exploited his opportunities.

Such was his reputation that a railway guard was once posted to his door on a journey to ensure that Sir Charles did not 'get himself or his government into trouble'. On disembarking, Sir Charles thanked the official for his attention, then remarked that the lady's compartment had not been similarly protected.

Such behaviour did not appeal to all his colleagues. Sir John Thompson, another Canadian prime minister, who died over lunch at Windsor Castle in 1894, more than once acted as spoiler for Tupper's attempts to use him as a 'gooseberry'—meaning the cover for an assignation.

Tupper was prime minister for only three months but, as premier of Nova Scotia, he played a key part in creating Canada's confederation and served as Canadian High Commissioner and Nova Scotian Agent General in London.

A lion of a man, with great courage and resourcefulness, Tupper was well capable of making a poor argument seem like a good one by his nearly instinctive use of bluster and brass.

His other principal vice was a lasting preoccupation with the welfare of 'Tupperdom', which included his children and, be it added, his wife.

Professor PETER WAITE
Halifax, Nova Scotia

August 10, 1993

BRITISHNESS

Indians in the face of Tebbit's bowling

SIR—Mr Norman Tebbit has devised a form of *cricket* test (report, April 20) to judge the suitability of Indians to settle in Britain.

If cricket in its general aspect be made a test, nine-tenths of Indians of the westernised upper class would qualify to do so. They are all, without distinction of sex, devotees of the game. My granddaughter, who lives and studies in India, might not be an acceptable immigrant by virtue of her name, which is Papagena, but would qualify for her wholehearted enthusiasm for cricket.

I, on the contrary, in spite of living in England for 20 years and having been abused all my life as a slavish Anglophile by the same class of Indians, have never in my more than 92 years of existence on earth, seen a cricket match. I even switch off the television set when cricket is shown.

But I have other and perhaps surer tests for assessing the ability of fellow Indians to be assimilated into English life. Of these, I shall only mention three: appreciation of *Wind in the Willows*; enjoyment of Stilton cheese in crocks; and going to opera.

By the last test, virtually all Indians would fail. The only occasion on which my wife and I saw fellow Indians at an operatic performance was at Covent Garden for *La Traviata*.

They were a couple in a box, by looks Parsees. Even they left at the end of the second act. To do so after Germont's aria, *Di Provenza il mar, il suol* . . . without staying for the third act (and in a box) was really worse than not going to opera at all.

But the surest test for judging the suitability of Indians as immigrants is to look for the sense of humour in them. It will be a vain search. Mr Tebbit has been threatened with prosecution under the Race Relations Act; an organisation of Indians here threatened to take Chatto & Windus and me to the European

Court of Human Rights for my book on Hinduism. In fact, all Indians in Britain are John Knoxes and their Mary Stuart is Mrs Thatcher. This dour solemnity is, however, perfectly natural, and of this neither Mr Tebbit nor any British politician has any inkling.

All modern Indians have two supreme enjoyments in life, which might be regarded as their *only* ones. These are, first, earning money and, next, nursing endless grievances. They had both during British rule in India. Now that the rule has come to an end, they are trying to recreate the same happy condition of living in Britain. So, they would naturally resent all resistance to their campaign. No one likes to see the props of his life taken away from him.

NIRAD CHAUDHURI

April 27, 1990 Oxford

Pinner Man strikes back . . .

SIR—Jane March, the latest international sex-star, now twinkling in Paris, comes from Pinner in Middlesex, which she has described as 'small and boring', a place from which she was determined at the age of nine to escape (report, Jan. 28).

It is true that the raffish excitements of Essex have never been claimed for Pinner Man or Pinner Girl, but, like so much in England, the leafy lanes of Pinner are not quite as they may appear to a teenage actress with no historical imagination.

What the French media, entranced by Miss March's immature glamour, calls 'a boring suburb of London' is, in fact, a medieval village around which the high tides of London have washed. It still boasts a coaching-inn and half-timbered houses and, once a year, the village streets are blocked by a fair at which the locals disport themselves until midnight.

The daily produce cart for Covent Garden, on which villagers hitched lifts into London, admittedly no longer runs, but the Metropolitan Line aspires to similar standards of regularity and comfort.

If she looked hard, Miss March would find even deeper roots. The mighty River Pinn occasionally overflows, causing blessedly little devastation, as it has since time immemorial. Fringes of trees are part of the ancient Middlesex forest, pierced by bridle paths and footpaths which were old before the Saxons came.

Less than two centuries ago a certain Dr Pell of Pinner Hill wrote: 'We live on the borders of a great wood, with no neighbour within a mile, save of doubtful character. So the family blunderbuss is fired at night about once a fortnight to announce that the household is armed, and a few man traps and spring guns are set in the coverts'.

The population is larger now, but Dr Pell's precautions might still be wise. Pinner has sarsen stones and dew-ponds, hawthorn and honeysuckle and wild roses, robins and finches, owls and foxes.

Concrete lamp standards, shedding their horrible sodium glow, may uglify the main roads at night, but, seen from the hilltop, Middlesex glitters like a huge bowl across which curves the highway to London.

Who—except a teenage sex-star—that could live in Pinner would choose to live in Paris?

ANTHONY LEJEUNE
January 30, 1992   Pinner, Middx

~

Tell it not abroad

SIR—Now that the tourist season is again upon us, doubtless we can expect the usual plethora of unfavourable reports on the conduct of our compatriots from Mediterranean and other resorts.

On this subject, I was intrigued to read the following entry from Kilvert's Diary dated April 5, 1870: 'Of all noxious animals the most noxious is a tourist. And of all tourists the most vulgar, illbred, offensive and loathsome is the British tourist.'

The incident which so exercised the reverend author was not the clink of beer cans being kicked across the piazza nor the clunk of shirtless carcasses falling from bar-stools, but the employment of a walking stick to point out objects of interest.

And the location? Not Benidorm, nor Ostend nor even the departure lounge of Luton, but the ruins of Llanthony Abbey in the Wye Valley.

MICHAEL ALLINSON
July 6, 1992   Lagos, Nigeria

~

COLOUR
CO-ORDINATES

Shady picture practice

SIR—Your front page photograph of the Prime Minister and Mrs Shephard visiting a school where the children are predominantly white (Oct. 31) focused attention, seemingly gratuitously, on two pupils, one black, the other Asian.

I point this out because, increasingly over recent years, whenever reporters from any of the television channels visit a school, university, factory, hospital or superstore the cameramen almost invariably concentrate their opening shots on black or brown faces, even when the person eventually interviewed is white, as is usually the case.

It cannot be in the interest of long-term racial harmony for the numbers of black and brown people to be exaggerated so disproportionately, and so inexorably, in this way. I hope this practice is not now spreading to newspapers.

It is hard to believe that the television cameramen are behaving spontaneously when so many are involved. The only alternative explanation is that they are obeying directives. In either case, what is the purpose of presenting such a false impression?

CHAPMAN PINCHER

November 1, 1996   Kintbury, Berks

~

Negative message

SIR—Peter Herbert claimed that Judge Christopher Hardy's sentencing 'sends an extremely negative message to the black community' (report, April 17).

There is no such thing as the 'black community' which always reacts in a machine-like manner to a given situation. Self-appointed spokesmen like Mr Herbert invariably mean 'black individuals' when they speak of 'the black community'.

These spokesmen seem to approve of almost everything a black person does, whether right or wrong, and are often quick to accuse others of 'playing the race card' yet refuse to admit to doing just that themselves. To claim to speak for all black individuals in this country is to patronise, stereotype and 'play the race card'. What a convenient refuge for the prejudiced 'the black community' has become.

I find nothing 'extremely negative' about the judge's sentencing and remarks. It is one of the most positive messages sent to me by the justice system.

XAVIER PHILIPH ONGOM

London SW17

April 24, 1997

Judges' problem

SIR—The problem with Mr Justice Brooke's assertion that black people face the risk of injustice because judges are ignorant of ethnic minority cultures (editorial, Nov. 20) is that one wonders which aspects of ethnic minority culture should be taken into account.

First, there are at least 200 non-English language groups resident in Britain. Are the judges to be educated in all the cultural variations present in such a conglomeration of values and lifestyles? Second, which aspects of ethnic minority culture are to count as allowable— not dope-taking by Rastafarians or death threats from Islamic fundamentalists, surely—but what else?

Is it really feasible we should be seeking to develop a multi-cultural approach to our courts? Would it not be wiser to encourage immigrant communities to accept that the responsibility for adaptation and change lies with them?

I have known several liberal-minded people who have been subjected to racial awareness proceedings by local education authorities. Without exception they have been left with powerful feelings of resentment, hardly a sound basis for good race relations. In a judicial context, there is a real danger that the whole thing will lead to double standards, that blacks will be dealt with leniently for fear of courts raising cries of 'racism'. Even worse, young blacks may have a quite unnecessary chip placed on their shoulders.

As for Mr Justice Brooke's worry about his black friend being stopped by the police more frequently than he is—is this necessarily to do with racism? Could it not be that different groups have, with regard to crime, produced different public reputations for themselves? Young blacks, according to official figures, are disproportionately involved in crime in inner London.

The price their community pays for this is that the police give it more attention, just as they would if a disproportionate amount of crime were being committed by people with red hair or spectacles. The police have to act on possibilities and probabilities, rarely certainties; this, unfortunately, means that innocent people have to be checked out.

The answer is not to condemn the police, but to urge lower rates of crime on those communities responsible.

RAY HONEYFORD
November 25, 1993   Bury, Lancs

Black truths in the Old West

SIR—How refreshing to see black cowboys getting major parts in westerns (article, Dec. 15). Thousands of blacks—perhaps a quarter of the total—were among the trail riders on the frontier. So fair is fair. However, I hope that the blacks cast as future John Waynes will be spared the manufactured excitement and fictionalised glamour of Hollywood's West.

Whether Anglo, black or hispanic, most cowboys were simply farmhands. Their work was dirty and boring. As a boy herding my father's cattle, I spent many afternoons recasting the drifting clouds into misty versions of Camelot, embattled knights or lofty mountains. If there was glamour, I missed it.

But there still are undeveloped themes for the realists, as I discovered in researching my forthcoming book on remittance men in the West. One is the impact of Britons and their investment, which set the pattern for huge ranches on the western plains. In the absence of British money, the area would have been developed far differently, probably by under-financed farmers on far smaller properties.

Britons also brought their own culture and sense of justice. The chance alliance of stubborn British investor John Tunstall and Billy the Kid led to New Mexico's infamous Lincoln County war.

Although the British gentleman's expectation of finding a servant class ready to do his bidding was material for humorists, there was a counter to this; Britons were less prejudiced than Americans against blacks. Thus, Lord Delaval Beresford, youngest son of the 4th Marquess of Waterford, maintained a common-law relationship with a black woman while ranching in Chihuahua, Mexico.

On trips to El Paso they crossed the Rio Grande River in separate conveyances: racial mixing of the sexes meant jail in Texas. But 'Lady Flo'—Delaval's affectionate name for Florida J. Wolfe—helped him substantially, offsetting his craving for whisky with expertise in ranching.

Between them, they established a satellite ranch in Canada, providing a second haven from Texas's racial laws. When Beresford died in a train collision in 1906, his elder brother, Admiral Lord Charles Beresford, went to El Paso and made a fairly generous settlement on Lady Flo.

This story is real. While it lacks the appeal of a Colt .45 revolver in the hand of a heroic black gunfighter, it says more about the frontier.

LEE OLSON
December 22, 1992   Denver, Colorado

~

Merits of Sambo

SIR—As the only non-white pupil at my Liverpool school in the Fifties I remember finding *Little Black Sambo* very disheartening, to put it mildly. No matter how hard you try, 'Black Sambo' cannot be construed as a polite form of address.

I am aghast to learn that this miserable book may still be in print, not least because the plot makes no sense. Why, to take one example, would the tigers want to steal new clothes? I still feel this allowed the author to portray for no good purpose the abuse and spitefulness endured by black people.

I seriously question how your leader (Sept. 4) could praise as 'charming fantasy' a story involving a lone child left distressed and, in some illustrations, totally naked after being confronted by wild animals. The tale is neither funny nor instructive, and surely the imagery is inappropriate. Despite your assertion to the contrary, I believe that society would also disapprove if the character of a white child was depicted in this way, regardless of the ethnic origins of the author.

To paraphrase your leader, 'Sambo' is of course innocent but very much abused. In my opinion, these demeaning books are fit only for the recycling bin.

PETER BLEVINS
September 11, 1996   London SW17

Golly in Ghana

SIR—I unpacked an old trunk, helped by my neighbour because I am handicapped. She is a black law student from Ghana. On opening it we found three lovely old gollywogs, which once belonged to my three daughters.

They had been banned from the grandchildren—for 'racial discrimination' reasons.

Karen, my black neighbour, howled with excitement. 'I have three gollywogs at home and my sisters, too,' she said.

When I told her about the banishment of gollywogs in Britain and America, Karen shook with laughter, then looked at me and said earnestly: 'Your people must be very, very insecure'.

That is all for 'racism', surely the most stupid brainchild of our civilisation.

(Mrs) ELIZABETH FURSE
October 29, 1996   London SW1

BAR CODES

Botswana's case for tough penalties

SIR—Following the correspondence of Mr Carter-Ruck and Mr Hurd (Feb. 17 and 18), can I support the current proposals going through Parliament to give the Court of Appeal power to increase sentences?

When I arrived in Botswana I was shocked at what then seemed an inordinately high level of sentencing. Three years and 2,500 cases later I have changed my mind. Of course here, as elsewhere, there are many minor cases where imprisonment would be quite unjust. However, I would like to indicate the sort of sentences that frequently are imposed in my court in the type of cases itemised by Mr Carter-Ruck:

The 17-year-old who beat up a bus conductor: two years in the equivalent of what used to be called Borstal in England; if 18, prison for at least that length of time. Corporal punishment would probably be compulsory, depending on the charge. The 46-year-old drugs banker smuggling £500,000 worth of heroin: here the minimum (by law) would be 10 years plus £5,000 in default, three years consecutive plus corporal punishment. Knocking a policeman unconscious: at least three years, plus corporal punishment, depending on injuries.

These examples, which assume that the defendant has pleaded guilty and is a first-time male offender in his twenties or thirties, would not strike a local citizen as particularly heavy.

In Botswana the High Court has power to increase a sentence which is 'disturbingly low'. Experience has shown here that excessive leniency—indeed one might say sentences which are not tough—are quite pointless in most cases. In this respect I cannot believe that the African criminal is so vastly different from his British counterpart.

It is facile for Mr Hurd to say in his reply that 'increasing the maximum penalties . . . sends a clear message to the courts'. For these to have any effect they must be acted upon frequently and result in penalties which are increased in practice on a substantial scale. He says that Mr Carter-Ruck 'spoils his case' by merely using 'a sprinkling of anecdotes'. Not so.

The above examples are typical. Ask any responsible criminal practitioner in England and he will agree that the general sentencing level in a very large number of cases is pitifully inadequate. I am not suggesting that the return of corporal punishment to England should be considered, for that would, almost literally, be flogging a dead horse. But I think, that penologists and sentencers in England could do well to look at the sentencing practice in this so-called Third World country where crime is at a very much lower level than in England.

ANTHONY D. AMSTELL
Chief Magistrate
March 8, 1988   Francistown, Botswana

Trial contrary to international law

SIR—John Demjanjuk has been tried by the judges of Israel and sentenced to death (report, April 25). I would ask these questions.

First, against what law had he offended? Not against the law of Israel. The offences were committed in the years 1942–1943 before the State of Israel existed or had any laws of its own. It was not founded until 1948. Nor were the offences committed against the laws of Germany or Poland. They were committed in the concentration camp at Treblinka and were done by the orders of those in authority in those states.

The only law against which he had offended was the international law in respect of crimes against humanity. It was defined in the Charter of Nürnberg: 'Murder, extermination, and enslavement, deportation and other inhuman acts committed against any civilian population before or during the war.'

Second, what state had jurisdiction to try such crimes against humanity? According to international law a single state after the war might have jurisdiction to set up its special court to try such crimes committed by persons in its custody. The four powers who signed the Charter for Nürnberg acted on this principle by agreeing to set up the Nürnberg Court to try the war criminals then in custody in Germany.

But I know of no principle by which the State of Israel could set up such a court to try crimes said to be committed over 40 years earlier in a far off country by a man not in its custody.

In my opinion it was contrary to international law for the State of Israel to arrange with the United States for the deportation of Demjanjuk to Israel to stand trial there; and for the Court of Israel to try him there for a crime against humanity. If he was to be tried at all it should have been by an international court of justice like the one set up in Nürnberg for he was a war criminal just like Goering and the rest.

I am afraid too that the trial shows signs of racial and political vengeance. Whereas at the trial at Nürnberg the prosecution's case against those convicted was clear on the documents and undisputed, here there was room for doubt. The prosecution's case was rested on identification by witnesses over 40 years later. But we all know how mistakes are made by the witnesses at identification parades here. The accused protested his innocence throughout.

The atmosphere at the trial can be seen by the report that there was 'clapping, cheering and dancing' by the packed 'audience' when he was sentenced to death. When I have sentenced to death there was a hushed calm and solemn silence.

Lord DENNING
April 23, 1988   Whitchurch, Hants

Save us from a Justice Ministry

SIR—When the Law Society concerned itself with regulating the conduct of its own members and disciplining those of them who used the funds of their widow and parson clients as if they were their own, it was a useful body.

Now that its council members—but probably not the majority of its members—think that it should enter the public domain and conduct crusades against legal institutions of which it disapproves, it has become a nuisance. Proposals such as its recent one for the creation of a Ministry of Justice (report, May 22) are dangerous. The less sophisticated politicians might think that the Law Society appreciated what it was doing.

A Ministry of Justice with responsibility for all courts (including, I presume, responsibility for the manorial court of the Manor of Danby in North Yorkshire), the penal system, legal services, law reform and judicial appointments, all under a Cabinet minister answerable to the House of Commons, would be an horrendous bureaucratic monster.

The present carbuncle of a building in Queen Anne's Gate, in which the Home Office is accommodated, would have to be replaced with another one at least three times its size.

Ministers of Justice who changed every time there was a Cabinet reshuffle would never be able to deal with the problems which each of the many departments under their jurisdiction presented.

Pity the Minister of Justice who, in one working week—probably in one working day—had to decide whether money should be spent on plans for new sanitary arrangements in Dartmoor Prison; whether the establishment for police officers in Humberside should be increased by 10; whether the recommendations of the Law Commission for the reform of the law of distress should be implemented; who should be appointed as new magistrates in Cumbria; whether a solicitor who appeared before his local Bench three or four times a year should be given rights of audience in the High Court; and which of the High Court judges (none of whom he had ever met) should be appointed to fill a vacancy in the Court of Appeal.

What in practice would happen is that a civil servant, probably of no higher rank than assistant secretary, would make the decisions for him.

It was easy for the president of the Law Society, Mr Tony Holland, in his recent lecture at Bristol University, to make fun of the Lord Chancellor's division of functions. Lord Mackay of Clashfern performs them admirably. He does so because as a former member of the Scottish Bar he knows how to present a case for the Government.

As one who presides in the appellate committee in the Lords, he can do so in the House itself with dignity and authority. His experience as a Scottish law officer will have prepared him for his administrative functions.

No politician could ever acquire the 'know-how' to perform the functions of a Lord Chancellor, certainly not one who ever since his undergraduate days had lived in or by politics.

May we be delivered from a Ministry of Justice.

Sir FREDERICK LAWTON
May 23, 1991   Skelton, Yorks

~

A Western bourgeois fallacy

SIR—You draw attention to the recent Peking trials of pro-democracy demonstrators (report, Feb. 18), stating that defence lawyers were advised of their clients' guilt before commencement of their trials. This is no surprise to China watchers.

In 1955, when imprisoned in South West Tibet by the Chinese People's Liberation Army, the Butcher of Tibet, General Chiang Kuo Hua, advised me (via an interpreter) that my guilt was established by the fact that the PLA had arrested me in my role as a Western Fascist Lackey Imperialist Running Dog of the CIA.

My protestations of innocence were rebutted with a quotation from the late Soviet State Prosecutor Andrei Vishinsky, 'The concept of innocence before trial is a Western bourgeois fallacy'.

When I asked who would appear for my defence I was told: 'You do not need a defence. Comrade Mao has stated that defence means revolt.'

SYDNEY WIGNALL
February 23, 1991   Old Colwyn, Clwyd

~

Distinguishing head-dress

SIR—Prior to the guidance by the General Council of the Bar in 1974 to lawyers on wearing of wigs, as a new clerk to an elderly solicitor, I inquired—'Why do barristers wear wigs?' His reply was, 'To assist juries in distinguishing them from their clients.'

TOM CHILTON

August 17, 1987   Brighton

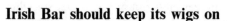

Irish Bar should keep its wigs on

SIR—The Irish controversy about the wearing of wigs in court (report, Oct. 20) is but a preface to a similar movement in England. I hope therefore that the Irish Parliament succeeds in rejecting the proposal to abolish wigs in the Higher Courts—in line with the recent resolution of the Irish Bar Council to retain them.

To the majority of lawyers, litigants and laymen, they are a mark of distinction, dignity and impressiveness. One only has to remember the lack of respect encountered by the English National Industrial Relations Court in the early Seventies when it decided not to use distinctive legal dress under the impression that being 'relevant' was more important than being held in esteem. If wigs are abolished, it should be asked, what about Royal and official robes, clerical wear, graduate degree dress and the distinctive uniform of servicemen, police, nurses, postal workers and others?

After the 1921 Treaty, the old Munster circuit in Ireland unanimously abolished wigs but restored them six months later because everybody concerned with the courts wanted them. The witnesses were obviously far more impressed by the wigs—and therefore more truthful.

Sir JAMES COMYN, QC

October 21, 1994   Tara, Co Meath

Sir James Comyn (1921–97) was a High Court judge and author.

Alien robes

SIR—For most of the time when he is sitting as a judge, the Lord Chancellor (like the other Law Lords sitting in the case) wears clothing which he cannot regard as antiquarian: morning clothes, without gown or bands or wig.

When the arguments in that judicial committee hearing have been heard and judgments are ready, the Lord Chancellor and other Law Lords involved move to the House of Lords Chamber. Traditional robes are put on. The ceremony is brief. It merely puts formally on record the written judgments in the case. If traditional robing for this brief occasion is to be abandoned, the obvious alternative is the simple and very 'modern' attire of the judicial committee.

It would be absurdly antiquarian to adopt instead, as Lord Irvine of Lairg has recently suggested, the much older judicial clothing of an Italian judge—a black robe and bands—a very different legal system unconnected with our common law. It would also be quaintly antiquarian for the Lord Chancellor, when sitting as Speaker of the House of Lords, to adopt that incongruous judicial attire of a legal system unconnected with our common law and which goes back for hundreds of years. If change is thought to be appropriate there too, let the same 'modernisation' be applied.

I add that such changes will not make any difference to the quality of House of Lords judgments (admired and quoted throughout the Common Law world), nor to the quality of public political debate in the Lords.

LEOLIN PRICE, QC
November 25, 1997   London WC2

My lost 'Esq.'

SIR—When I qualified as a lawyer in the 1960s, I was automatically accorded the 'title' of Esq. by the Law Society.

I was very proud of this, and not at all pleased when someone clearly complained several years later, with the result that all women lawyers lost the title, at least so far as the solicitors' body was concerned.

My American clients still write to me in that vein and I much prefer it to Ms (or manuscript, as it is referred to in our household). So does my husband. He in particular objects to those many letters which are written to me as Mrs Erica Stary, because he is not dead and we are not divorced.

The correct terminology, according to Debrett, is thus: if Mrs is to be used, Mrs Michael Stary, as the surname used is that lent by courtesy on marriage. My continental confrères (*consoeurs*) acquire at least the appellation of Mr.

This causes confusion in Britain. One friend had great difficulty cashing a postal order at the Post Office because the payee was (correctly) shown as Mr plus initials, then her surname. It was reasoned that she clearly couldn't be entitled to the cash since she was not male.

Is it not time for the re-introduction of Esq., with a salutation of Mr (for use in letters) for professionally qualified women?

ERICA STARY

April 15, 1997   London N1

ON THE BEAT

University of life best

SIR—Police forces in some other parts of the world live in barracks. It produces the sort of closed-mind isolationism that one writer has described as 'the barracks syndrome'. One of the strengths of the British police service has been that many of its officers live among the community.

They encounter the same problems as other people living in their street; they mix with their neighbours; their children go to the same schools. In short, they are part of the people they police and, as a result, have a greater understanding of their neighbours' problems.

The concept of a police degree (report, Jan. 6) flies in the face of this common touch. Chief Supt Williamson says that much of the course work would centre on ethical aspects of policing and create 'reflective practitioners'. I wonder what that means?

And I wonder, too, what the reaction of police recruiters will be when faced with civilians brandishing this qualification, because students from outside the service will, sooner or later, be allowed to take it, as in the United States. Are these authorities going to have the courage to turn candidates down because they do not possess the many other attributes required of a police officer? Some 20 years ago, entirely as a result of studying in his own time, a young constable under my command secured a place at Oxford University to study philosophy. He asked if he could go off pay so that he could return to his police career on completion of his studies. His application was denied by an assistant commissioner and the service lost a hard-working, intelligent young man who felt disinclined to start all over again after three or four years. I hope that attitudes have changed somewhat since then, but there has always been resistance to in-house training that does not have a direct bearing on police work. That is a mistake.

Surely, a catholic education is likely to be of far greater value than the blinkered and introverted study of police work, no matter what phrases are used to describe it.

It would be better for the police service if young men and women were encouraged to learn more about the world in which they live and which they are helping to police. I just hope we do not finish up with graduates in canteen culture.

GRAHAM ISON

January 8, 1992   Alton, Hants

Softly, softly interviews best

SIR—It is all very well to say that 'police should be trained to be less confrontational and more subtle in their interrogation techniques' (report, April 26).

Some readers will no doubt take this to imply a uniformed bully hovering over some poor waif while intent on an interrogation based on trial by ordeal. But the truth is very different. Villains do not turn up at police station inquiry desks with outstretched hands saying 'Officer, put the cuffs upon these wrists for I have done wrong'. They have to be captured, and that requires information which leads to the hard evidence that puts them in the frame.

The trouble is that the distinction between unsafe and unsatisfactory evidence (and a verdict of not guilty, he didn't do it) seems never to be addressed. If there was less adversarial point-scoring in court and a greater search for the truth, I believe that more trials could come to a rapid conclusion without the guilty having a strong hope that they could get off on a technical point, as happens all too often today.

Avon and Somerset Constabulary runs an interview technique course based on the ethical interview. Its main premise is that when interviewing a suspect, you should take the view that the judge, barristers, jury *et al* are actually present. This shapes your attitude and affects your behaviour.

At the end of the interview will the judge, barristers and jury answer yes to the questions 'Was it just? Was it fair?' If the answers are yes, then it was ethical. Police officers who have tried this out on a week's videotaped course have come out more subtle in their interview techniques and less confrontational.

Inspector **TOM BARRON**

May 8, 1993   Taunton, Som

Leaks are price of a free society

SIR—As a retired inspector and former press officer for North Yorkshire Police, I would point out to those in a lather over the stories about the Princess of Wales (report, Aug. 24) that it is both impossible and, indeed, undesirable to stop all leaks about police inquiries.

The occasional leak is the price we pay for our current freedom and for the police service's modern desire to be seen to be more accountable. In fact most leaks, or tip-offs as journalists prefer to call them, have little or no basis in truth.

They are either rumours, the result of misunderstandings or a misinterpretation of events. But they take up an inordinate amount of time—and money—which those officers involved could be devoting to more important work.

I once spent an entire morning trying to discover which police officer had leaked news of an escape by six prisoners, only to find that the story had been an early-morning joke on local radio. A sleepy journalist had heard it and thought that it was a revelation from an unauthorised police source.

Conscientious police officers and civilian personnel take immense care not to divulge anything which would breach the rules of confidentiality. But no organisation is totally secure. In a police station, where the press mingle with members of the public, a press officer can only do the best he can, sure in the knowledge that this will never do more than stop his superiors grumbling.

I might add that in my new role as an author of crime fiction (*Heartbeat* et al), I have never resorted to the device of employing a police leak in my novels. It would be far too contrived.

Most leaks are little more than unwelcome and annoying drips.

A serious leak is a problem—as John Bunyan said, 'one leak will sink a ship'. But he was writing of *real* leaks consisting of water, not hot air.

PETER WALKER
August 25, 1994   Ampleforth, North Yorks

~

The Aussie way with 'crims'

SIR—I am not sure about the laws in England, but the man who came up before the beak after shooting an intruder (letter, Dec. 6) went about it in the wrong way.

By causing 'severe and lasting injury' to the burglar, he would have left himself open to being sued for damages in Australia. We may not be any worse off here than anywhere else, but we have our share of villains who will do any sort of work, from murder to stealing corn off a blind cocky, for the odd dollar or two.

The New South Wales police instructed me in the proper procedure in a case of break-and-enter when I had a brush with a gang of 'crims' in Lakemba, a suburb of Sydney, a few years back.

I had returned from a night shift just before a car-load of them arrived in my street. My wife went off in our car and, under the impression that the house was empty, two of these creeps, carrying long knives and a 12-inch file, started breaking in.

I encountered them in the side driveway and was aware, as I told them to stop, that I would probably have been carved up if I had not been carrying a loaded rifle. Crying for help, these two ran towards their stolen Ford across the street where four of their mates were sitting.

In Oz, you are not permitted to shoot burglars in the back for some obscure reason. But I proceeded to shoot up the car, much to the horror of the screaming occupants. They were not to know that I had learnt to shoot straight fighting the Japanese during the War, and that the car and its tyres were my targets.

When the car stalled, I had more time to make some alterations to it and the back window took my last slug. Very satisfactory all round. I enjoyed seeing the car wobbling away with three flat tyres.

The detectives who arrived promptly two hours after I had phoned the police informed me of my rights in cases like this. They said care must be taken to shoot miscreants only from the front, after firing a warning shot into a wall.

Then, it is advisable to make sure they are dead, and, if they were not carrying arms, a weapon of some sort should be placed in their hands before calling the police. That, they said, would cover any awkward questions which could be asked later.

There is much talk by do-gooders about individuals' rights but, as far as I am concerned, any stranger who enters my manor uninvited has forsaken any rights he may have had outside.

JOHN GILLARD
January 2, 1995   Cleveland, Queensland

~

Unmanly police?

SIR—I am astounded by the Court of Appeal's ruling that police involved in the Hillsborough disaster have a right to seek compensation (report, Nov. 1). I served as a police officer for 22 years and was pensioned out because I broke my spine, my pelvis, my leg, my ankles and my wrists. I have seen men and women and children and babies in all manner of death. I have seen maggots, brains and skulls blown to hell. I have picked up remains that would keep a grown man awake for the rest of his life. But I chose to do it. There's the rub, isn't it?

Yes, I still dream about it on occasion, and wake up in a cold sweat, and then down a stiff drink. I hang my head in shame at these latest awards given to—what did they call them—policemen?

MICHAEL GREEN
November 2, 1996   Chepstow, Gwent

~

COMMERCIAL FACTORS

Ancients at the top?

SIR—As an avid reader of your business section I have been struck recently by the photographs of senior managers and chief executives.

In almost every case I see gentlemen of mature, if not advanced years, in the driving seats of major organisations. However, as a 51-year-old manager with considerable hard-earned experience I am finding my age a barrier to securing a new top job since redundancy six months ago.

If these same corporations which adopt this policy applied it internally we could expect to see a great exodus of middle to top management forming a line behind me in the dole queue. The same could be said of the Cabinet. Either there is corporate life after 45 or the country is being run by senile, burnt-out incompetents.

PETER TOMPSETT
November 1, 1991   Gresford, Clwyd

~

Downgraded bank managers

SIR—I am writing to express my agreement with Mr David Samuel (letter, June 18) regarding the exploitation of customers by banks. This has only come about because of the change in the organisation of the banks.

Over the past 10 years the status of the branch manager has been eroded. Until comparatively recently he would act on behalf of his customer and argue his case with head office for any loan application he put up.

Most bank managers relished an argument with the regional or head office and were prepared to stake their professional reputations on the applications submitted on behalf of customers.

Because of this, the customer always felt that the branch manager was a friend and ally. Now, with the creation of 'central business centres' (usually away from the high street), a faceless person usually deals with all matters over a comparatively modest sum.

These grey people then issue instructions to the downgraded branch managers as to what they can or cannot lend. There is nobody at branch level who has any authority to argue with the business centres and indeed, because of today's climate, they would not dream of doing so as they are concerned about their own employment and promotion.

The rapport between the customer and the branch manager in most cases has now been completely removed.

Today's problem is that, in the event of an application being rejected, there is very little either the customer or the professional adviser can do. It is difficult to have any close contact with these business centres; nowadays a comparative junior considers an application and passes it on to head office should it rate sufficient points. If it does not fit in with the broad criteria laid down by this central administration you are wasting your time in trying to discuss matters on behalf of any customer.

I am certain that within the next few years the powers within these business centres will need to be handed back to the local branches because of the loss of personal contact between bank and customer. This will result in the immediate strengthening of the rapport between the customer and the branch manager.

J. C. WIDGER
June 25, 1991   Wembley, Middx

Posting parcels in Wonderland

SIR—Now and again, Alice needed to send copies of the same book of fairytales through the post—sometimes singly, sometimes three in the same package. But the postal charges puzzled her greatly. This is what she had to choose from:

- Letter post, three books in separate packages: £1.98;
- Letter post, the same three books in one package: £2.40;
- Parcel post, the same three books in one package: £2.60.

'Why does it cost me more,' asked Alice, 'to send one package than three, when they weigh the same?'

'Because,' said the Post Office, 'your one package weighs 1,000 grams, and must therefore go First Class.'

'But why,' asked Alice, 'must it go First Class when I don't want it to?'

'Because,' said the Post Office, 'all medium-sized packages have to go as fast as possible, whether people want them to or not.'

'But,' said Alice indignantly, 'my three separate packages weigh just as much, and they are allowed to go slowly!'

'If you object to them costing less,' said the Post Office crossly, 'you must send them First Class, then they'll cost you more, and that makes good sense to us.'

Alice seemed to be going round in circles. But then she had an idea.

'Supposing,' she said, 'I send my medium-sized package by parcel post instead of letter post. Will it then be allowed to go slowly?'

'Yes of course,' said the Post Office, 'and it will cost you still more. That will make even more good sense to us.'

Awaking from her dream, Alice was astonished to discover that it was true! So she unpacked the three books from her medium-sized package, and posted them all separately, and all to the same address. It saved her 62p, and the Post Office had to collect, handle, sort and deliver three times instead of once.

MARK JONES

December 12, 1992   York

~

Who is a speculator? You are!

SIR—Why is it that whenever Britain faces a currency crisis some strange group or other, remote from the ken of ordinary people, is blamed for the problem? In the mid-Sixties it was the Gnomes of Zurich.

Now it is the hordes from Essex—the young men such as those shown in your picture (Sept. 17), who are popularly assumed to be in the employ of banks and given to clutching several telephones at once and screaming at the tops of their voices. They are 'the speculators' responsible for the pound's difficulties in the past few weeks, we are assured.

In fact, the foreign exchange dealers so often painted as the villains of the piece are, on the whole, acting merely as conduits for selling pressure which comes from a whole host of sources a good deal closer to the experience of the man in the street.

One of the most powerful pressures has come from the professional managers of savings and pension funds. It is indeed ironic that while many a union leader has complained about Britain being in the grip of 'the speculators', his pension fund has been engaged in the very activity he decries.

Another major source of speculative activity has come from major industrial and commercial companies. Just as many a chairman has bemoaned the activities of the exchange market, so his corporate treasurer has been putting the boot into the pound. Nor is this activity wrong.

All of these people have responsibilities to protect and further the interests of their organisations. And what about the ordinary person going on holiday who wonders whether he should buy his foreign currency now or later? This, too, is speculative.

It is quite misleading for the Government or its supporters to argue that the recent crisis had been drummed up out of nowhere by foreign exchange dealers. The fund managers and corporate treasurers have been able to see as plain as a pikestaff that the DM2.95 exchange rate was untenable and it was only a matter of time before the weight of their money proved them right.

The sterling crisis is an accident that has been waiting to happen for two years.

ROGER BOOTLE
September 18, 1992 Chief Economist,
Midland Montagu, London EC3

Bribery as a way of business

SIR—The four-year sentence meted out to former senior Defence Ministry official Gordon Foxley—for accepting bribes in placing orders with foreign firms (report, May 27)—should make many international business executives uncomfortable.

Bribes paid to public and often private sector officials for illicit favours are against the law, internally, in most nations. However, the bribing of public officials across borders is standard operating procedure for many companies today. So long as company accounting records show the illicit payments across borders as 'business development expenses', or something similar, no company laws are broken domestically. Only in the United States, where the Foreign Corrupt Practices Act specifically bans across-border bribing of public and private decision-makers, are such practices prohibited.

Undoubtedly, through offshore subsidiaries and an excellent network of well placed 'commission agents', US companies' offshore activities have not been visibly affected by this. The accelerating expansion of 'offshore banking centres' has assisted in making such illicit payments anonymous for both bribers and bribed. Tracing the offshore fortunes amassed by corrupt officials of both Eastern European, OECD and developing nations has become virtually impossible, even for nations with an independent judiciary.

Recent Swiss banking co-operation in tracing drug monies has shown the way forward—undoubtedly at the loss of some business to less scrupulous operators elsewhere. The announcement, last month, of a commitment by the OECD to tackle the problem of international bribery is also encouraging. However, statements of intent must be matched by legislative change in the congresses and parliaments of all trading nations and must be coupled with the will and the ability to prosecute offenders—and with isolation for nations not prepared to co-operate.

The proliferation of bribery of decision-makers worldwide encourages wrong, uneconomic decisions to be made and private and public morality to be debased, particularly among the world's poorest nations.

The Foxley case, coupled with the Pergau Dam episode in

Malaysia, should encourage political leaders internationally to reshape the way the world does business.

KARL ZIEGLER
June 3, 1994 Centre for Accountability, London SW1

Excuses, excuses . . .

SIR—As managing director of a large paint company, and having previously held a similar position within a major do-it-yourself business for many years, I am quite accustomed and inured to sales directors' perennial excuses for below-budget results.

As I hear virtually every month, people are using fewer paint and decorating products because the number of house moves is much lower than in 1988. Or, more and more plastic windows, which do not require painting, are replacing the traditional wooden frames. Or even money previously spent on consumer goods, including paint and decorating products, is now going on the National Lottery. And, if all else fails, the weather can be blamed; it is either too hot or too cold.

Until now, all seemed reasonably plausible, if unacceptable, excuses; but at my last board meeting I was completely taken aback to be informed by a sales director, in very serious tones, of the latest reason for a shortfall in sales in Northern Ireland: BSE. Of course, why had this not occurred to me? The rationale was, quite understandably, that agriculture is such a vital component of the province's economy that BSE has consequently had major repercussions on expenditure on non-essential items throughout the whole population. I believed him. For five seconds. Nice try, but no cigar.

I wonder whether any of your readers have encountered similar lateral thoughts from sales staff?

TERRY EDWARDS
May 29, 1996 St Albans, Herts

Flying colours

SIR—Not many years ago BP changed its sign—I am sorry, logo—from the vertical to a very slight angle. I believe the cost of this decision was about £1 million. The BBC has just decided that it should change its initials from a slightly angled to a vertical presentation. The reported cost of this move is £6 million.

British Airways' new decorations, however (report, June 11), reach an entirely new level in being ill-judged, unnecessary and wasteful. Bob Ayling is reported to have said that: 'Some people abroad saw the airline as staid, conservative and a little cold.' Some people also saw British Airways as a prime example of a poorly run organisation being transformed into a world-class carrier.

It is a pity that, apart from the awful daubs on the tail fins, the Union flag, which should be a cause for pride in a British success, has been either removed or reduced to a level rather similar to its present primary role as a decoration on T-shirts and underpants.

GARETH DAVIES
Eastbourne, E. Sussex

SIR—Our national airline since privatisation has become the envy of the world of air transport, and it has done this without the need for the psychedelic offerings which smack of Third World or cut-price bargain flights.

The original paint, I suggest, indicated stability, reliability and, above all, safety. The management of British Airways has only to visit the local stock car race track to see what its new paint job depicts!

Sqn Ldr R. J. RUSSELL
Denver, Norfolk

SIR—The £60 million cost for desecrating the British flag would have been better used in improving facilities for tourist-class passengers.

GUY RAIS
June 12, 1997   London NW9

The flag will fly again

SIR—Lady Thatcher may have been exasperated by the new BA corporate identity (report, Oct. 10), but the logo received acclaim from the design press because it exactly answered the brief from the airline's marketing department, which presumably stated that the airline wanted to be perceived globally and internationally.

It is easy to see where this brief came from and why it was so well received. This is the kind of concept which is easy to sell at board level because most major companies want to be global. However, human nature may throw a spanner in the works.

It is no great secret that, in general, the travelling public want reassurance when they entrust their lives to a carrier company. The 'flag' of a national identity gives this reassurance and, at the same time, lets passengers enjoy a taste of the country of origin. We like to fly Lufthansa because of German reliability and engineering; Swiss Air for punctuality and precision.

History witnessed the creation of the Marina car under a British Leyland with a brief to produce a car for Europe. When the company was true to its British origins it produced Jaguar and Land Rover—internationally acclaimed vehicles exuding the strong British flavour which has been the reason for their success. It is interesting that Rover under German management is now pursuing a policy of Britishness as a selling proposition.

I envisage that, within two years, a new brief will emerge: 'BA wants to be an international *British* company.' The designer will then reinterpret this brief to bring back the Britishness visually.

Let us not forget that the previous BA identity was researched worldwide with a travelling public who expressed a liking for the Britishness of the colours and coat of arms. It is hard to believe that this public has had such a change of heart after four years.

Lady Thatcher's covering of the tail of the BA model painted with a Kalahari tribal pattern went to the heart of the matter.

MARCELLO MINALE
October 16, 1997   Richmond, Surrey

Good 'father' of Yamaichi company

SIR—John Casey offered an interesting insight into the Japanese idea of 'sincerity' and its ritual implications, analysing the president of Yamaichi Securities' public and tearful 'apology' in the face of his company's collapse (article, Nov. 26).

But the president's 'strange' behaviour makes better sense in the light of the sociological character of Japanese organisations and leadership.

Japanese business organisation is fundamentally different from the Western one in that, in the sociologist Max Weber's terms, the former is a 'paternalistic' commune whereas the latter is a 'bureaucratic' association. For example, in the West, to sell a company for the sake of economic interest is considered rational. In Japan, it is somewhat scandalous, perhaps comparable to selling one's family.

Also, there is no such thing as a labour market in Japan. One is not 'employed' by, but rather 'reborn', in a business organisation. Conversely, to be sacked means nothing other than to be excommunicated. Japanese leadership entails a character reminiscent of feudal lordship.

Leaders demand that the ruled should be pious to them, but they have a duty to ensure their well-being. Thus human relationships in Japanese corporations are not purely contractual in the modern sense but also personal. It can be claimed that this traditionalism is disappearing nowadays; however, it remains an undercurrent of Japanese business culture.

Perhaps one should also bear in mind that Mr Nozawa represents the old school of Japanese business. The unfortunate president's feeling towards Yamaichi's employees must have been similar to that of a caring father who has accidentally ruined his family.

Mr Nozawa was, indeed, a good 'father' to his 'family' on the worst and last day in the history of his firm. He said: 'I am bad' or, rather, in Japanese, '*we* are bad', thereby referring to other senior members of his firm who may be responsible for the incident.

Yet he also tried anxiously to protect the majority of employees from any possible allegations of illegal transactions. If there was anything wrong with him, it was simply that he had been the president for three months when his company's fortunes waned dramatically.

TAKASHI SHOGIMEN

November 29, 1997   Clare Hall, Cambridge

Man and overman

SIR—I am sorry to see Boris Johnson use the word 'overmanning' with automatic opprobrium in his article 'Why Labour would imperil the planet's prosperity' (Sept. 4). 'Overmanning' means full employment, high consumption, class and racial harmony, a low welfare bill, a low crime rate, personal choice, contentment and, true, inflation.

'Undermanning' means unemployment, despair, crime, drugs, an alienated youth, overworked officials, a widening gap between rich and poor, a bigger bureaucracy and, yes, low inflation. But nations live well enough with inflation: it can be the lesser of evils.

Overmanning may be bad for an individual business in the short term, but is good for society. What is good for society is, in the long term, good for business. And shouldn't it be 'overpersonning'?

FAY WELDON
September 6, 1996   London NW3

Pay the price

SIR—The rosy Utopian future depicted by Fay Weldon (letter, Sept. 6) with the amazing benefits that would accrue from 'over-manning'—i.e. full employment, class and racial harmony, low crime rates, high consumption and contentment, to name but a few—is deeply flawed.

'Overmanning' immediately renders products dearer. Competition from more economical (and probably foreign) rivals would quickly take its toll, and the firm would lose not only its new workforce, but also its unfortunate original employees. This, extended on a national scale, would certainly not 'be good for society or, in the long term, good for business'.

The employment problem is hugely complex but fairly simple to summarise: namely, too many people chasing too few suitable jobs. This has been accentuated by two important factors:

• Wages form such a high proportion of costs that tremendous efforts have, very successfully, been made to reduce the numbers employed through more efficient technology.

- Women (quite rightly) have vastly increased the numbers of the available workforce.

There are two obvious solutions. One is to create more jobs. This requires expensively developed, new and brilliant ideas, together with the provision of risk capital that would not be attracted unless adequate returns were likely.

The other solution would be to share out the jobs available as fairly and equally as possible among the whole of the workforce. This sounds remarkably like overmanning, but with one important reservation. To remain economically viable, it would be necessary not only to share the work, but also to persuade existing employees to share their working hours and remuneration. This, I think, would be a somewhat difficult and unpopular task.

I can only guess Fay Weldon's political preference, but I wonder which party she would expect to suggest and pursue this particular form of 'overmanning'—and whether she would support it.

EDWARD READING
Wisbech, Cambs

SIR—Surely Fay Weldon's views on overmanning do not conform with true socialist principles.

Karl Marx stated that each worker is entitled to the fruits of his (or her) labour. If the number of workers increases, but the fruit remains the same, then the entitlement of each 'overperson' must be reduced correspondingly.

September 9, 1996

L. C. JACKSON
Uckfield, E. Sussex

~

Korean economics

SIR—I have discovered the reason for the rapid decline of the Far Eastern financial markets (report, Dec. 17) from an example I have been sent of Korean capitalism:

You have *two* cows. You sell *three* of them to your publicly listed company, using letters of credit opened by your brother-in-law at the bank, then execute a debt-equity swap with an associated general offer so that you get all *four* cows back, with a tax deduction for keeping *five* cows.

The milk rights of *six* cows are transferred via a Panamanian intermediary to a Cayman Islands company secretly owned by the majority shareholder, who sells the rights to all *seven* cows' milk back to the listed company.

The annual report says that the company owns *eight* cows with an option on one more.

Meanwhile, you kill the two cows because the *feng shui* is bad.

Dr JOHN GLADSTONE

November 22, 1997   Northwood, Middx

WHEEL WAYS

O my beloved pothole

SIR—Further to Mr Ferdinand Mount's problem over the yellow-lined pothole on the corner near King's Cross (article, July 15), there is a simple Thatcherite solution.

In his book, *A Passion for Excellence*, Tom Peters relates the activities of one Mayor William Donald Schaefer of the City of Baltimore in the United States. It seems that on or before St Valentine's Day citizens of that proud city can buy a pothole for $35 ($5 for senior citizens). The city workers then patch the pothole, paint a valentine on it and send a photograph of the valentine on a 'Pothole Patch Doll' to the loved one of their choice.

The possible marketing opportunities are of course endless. These could include pothole birthdays, pothole anniversaries, even 'get well soon' pothole patches.

COLIN SUTER
July 19, 1988   Northampton

Who's driving . . ?

SIR—I am increasingly puzzled as to why I should be informed by notices in the rear windows of cars I happen to be following that there is a 'Baby on board' or 'Child on board'.

What, I wonder, has this to do with me? Why should they think that any other road user should care about the age groups of the occupants of their car? All I can come up with is perhaps they are asking me not to smash into the back of their car—but I can't think anyone would want to do this anyway, whoever they are following. If this is the case, and I don't want anyone to hit the back of my car, should I get one of those yellow diamonds in the back of my car announcing to the other drivers that 'Middle-aged wife and mother who wishes to remain in one piece on board'?

Looking at the standard of driving of some cars sporting these notices, I sometimes wonder if it's the baby that's doing the driving.

(Mrs) JOAN KNIGHT
January 22, 1990   Tunbridge Wells, Kent

Downhill winners

SIR—An Austin Seven has overtaken a Tiger Moth (letter, March 21), but in 1940 two cyclists overtook two Swordfish aircraft flying into a 30-knot wind on the road west of Crail, Fife. Jock McLellan, a fellow St Andrews student, and I were resting on top of a long brae when the Fleet Air Arm planes came hovering overhead along the line of the road. By pedalling furiously downhill for a quarter of a mile we overtook them. Credit goes to gravity.

G. RANKINE
March 1, 1991   Petersfield, Hants

Driven into the saddle

SIR—I guess it must happen to even the sanest motorist in the end. After years and years of sitting in gridlock trussed up in their cars in some hernia-inducing position with their seatbelts, slowly choking to death on everyone else's exhaust fumes, watching thousands and thousands of pounds seep away on petrol, insurance, parking tickets and tolls they finally, confronted by the sheer improbable madness of it all, completely flip their lids and, like poor, demented Eric Bailey start raving on about the cyclist (article, Sept. 9).

We cyclists have always suspected that motorists are clinically insane, but poor Eric has reached new heights.

It's a shame really because if he knew the serenity of sitting on a saddle listening to the peaceful tick-ticking of ballbearings and the melodic clicks of changing gears on an early morning ride through the city; if he ever knew the keening delight of coasting downhill knowing that you were unlikely to kill or maim someone or poison every tree in sight; if he ever knew the great spasms of oxygenated delight that flood every part of a cyclist's body out in a country lane, then he might have had some sort of chance.

The cyclist has found freedom from traffic jams, stroppy taxi drivers and buses that come six at a time. The cyclist has had his life given back to him and certainly my bike transformed me from a 40-year-old Fleet Street alcoholic into someone who began enjoying life again. Many of my rides have been a lot more fun than sex orgies.

I go weak at the knees when I touch those curves, feel that saddle and crouch down low over the bar. If everyone rode a bike we would immediately begin to understand how heaven could easily arrive on earth.

But Eric and his ilk are destroyers of such visions. They have condemned themselves to an eternal punishment in their horrible motorised steel boxes which will keep them poor and in ill health as they roar around killing everything they come near, including us cyclists.

Can't you transfer Eric to some more appropriate speciality, like the environment?

TOM DAVIES

September 17, 1994   Llandaff, Cardiff

Veering right

SIR—John Parfitt, who has nightmares at the thought of driving on the right in Britain (letter, March 16), is suffering them in vain. Here in the South East, people are already honing and perfecting their Continental driving 'skills' (or, rather, 'skeeoos', as they call them here) by driving only in the right-most lane.

On dual carriageways and motorways here, the nearside lane is frequently empty while everyone crowds into the offside lane. One frequently sees 'Continental-style' overtaking, with cars passing each other on the left rather than on the right.

This is particularly evident on the new four-lane sections of the M25; everyone has shifted one lane to the right, leaving the two left-hand lanes practically empty.

This must be particularly aggravating for the class-conscious owners of certain makes of expensive cars and off-road vehicles who have, until recently, regarded the offside lane as their 'prestige' lane, rather than an overtaking lane.

C. CROFTON-SLEIGH
Rotherfield, E. Sussex

March 25, 1996

Oedipus's road rage

SIR—John O'Sullivan cites Jehu's mad driving (letter, May 31) but the classic example of ancient road rage is surely the disastrous encounter between Oedipus and his father at the crossroads in Phocis.

Sophocles's version, translated by E. F. Watling reads:

'When I came to the place where three roads join, I met a herald followed by a horse-drawn carriage, and a man seated therein . . . The leader roughly ordered me out of the way; and his venerable master joined in with a surly command. It was the driver that thrust me aside, and him I struck, for I was angry.

'The old man saw it, leaning from the carriage, waited until I passed, then, seizing for weapon the driver's two-pronged goad, struck me on the head. He paid with interest for his temerity; quick as lightning, the staff in this right hand did its work; he tumbled headlong out of the carriage, and every man of them there I killed.'

JOHN SPURLING
London N7

June 1, 1996

BETTER HOPES

Seeking eternal sights

SIR—Since the publication (July 18) of the interview Peterborough had with me last week, I have received five or six letters each day urging me to have a cataract removed. My reply to these wellwishers is that, at 85, I have seen enough of Time and the Creatures (Blake) *with* my eye and prefer to see *through* my mind's eye Eternity and God's love.

MALCOLM MUGGERIDGE
July 27, 1988   Robertsbridge, E. Sussex

Malcolm Muggeridge (1903–90) was the greatest journalist of his age.

Biopsy could have prevented my being born

SIR—Prof Robert Winston's argument (article, Feb. 20) in favour of embryo research centres around the question of 'preventing handicap'. As he so rightly says, however, the current thrust of such research is aimed at detecting 'faulty embryos and destroying them, not at either treating existing conditions or preventing them from occurring'.

I have spina bifida, now a detectable, abortable handicap, and thus I have a very personal interest in the whole debate. It is revealing that, had embryo biopsy been available shortly after my conception, it could have resulted in my being tipped down the laboratory sink.

If human rights are to have any meaning, they must be universally applicable to all human beings irrespective of their age, size or location. I thus think all human embryos have the right to protection from harm and to a favourable environment for development. Handicapped people have rights independently of the status other people confer upon them.

In the same way as black people in South Africa are rightly entitled to equal status by virtue simply of their humanity, regardless of what their white oppressors think, so handicapped people are entitled to the most basic human right of all—the right to life. Parents quite naturally want their children to be as healthy as possible, and should take all sensible steps to prevent handicap arising.

However, once it has arisen, be it at three days after conception, three months after conception or three years after birth, the ethical options narrow and consist solely of attempting to alleviate the condition and ensuring that the affected person is treated as their humanity deserves—as a unique, immensely, immeasurably valuable human being for the duration of their lives.

ALISON DAVIS
February 26, 1990 Blandford Forum, Dorset

Oath will prove poor medicine

SIR—A new Hippocratic Oath (report, July 5) is unlikely to be anything other than an oath of convenience and bear no resemblance to the original in the Ancient World.

The Oath has long been better understood by the public than by members of the medical profession who, in this country, have neither studied nor taken it for decades. It specifically and deliberately forbids euthanasia and abortion: 'I will give no deadly drug to any though it be asked of me—and especially I will not aid a woman to procure an abortion.'

Apart from the problems of doctors who take drugs or who feel suicidal themselves, the majority—as adequate members of the profession—still fall grossly short of the intention of the oath. While euthanasia is still generally outlawed, pressure for its acceptance continues to grow.

But it is over abortion that today's doctors fall most short.

Although it is generally gynaecologists who carry out the many thousands of abortions each year, they do so with the signed consent of the majority of general practitioners.

Most GPs conveniently forget that use of the intra-uterine contraceptive device, the loop, is an abortifaceant. They also consider it acceptable to prescribe the 'morning after' pill.

This pill, which is given to thousands of mature women and young teenagers every day, is deliberately prescribed in the knowledge that if a pregnancy exists it will be aborted. No official record is kept of the results, though the Abortion Act requires the signatures of two doctors who have fulfilled specific conditions. Ironically, the ignoring of this embarrassing fact is giving a false impression in the official abortion statistics.

The profession, which started with a strict code, has drifted only in the last two decades into the convenience of situational ethics. It now risks drifting further into an abandonment of ethics altogether.

Hippocrates would not be proud to be the father of medicine in our amoral and secular society some 2,400 years after his time.

In fact, he is probably turning in his grave.

Dr ADRIAN ROGERS
July 6, 1995   Trews Weir Reach, Exeter

Fighting back against polio

SIR—As one who some 45 years ago suddenly collapsed while on patrol in the Malayan jungle, and who a fortnight later was told I had acute poliomyelitis, may I make some comments on the fortitude of Lord Snowdon (article, Oct. 30).

No one who has not experienced it can begin to comprehend what it is like to become instantaneously paralysed—a state of utter powerlessness. But the human being, in both mind and body, is infinitely adaptable. Provided that no irrevocable damage has been caused by the virus, the anterior horns (motor nerves) in the spinal cord will struggle to revive and grow, thus re-establishing the connection between the brain and the muscles, for it is this connection that the polio virus attacks.

However, after 40 years or so of working overtime, the anterior horns are utterly worn out, and they will wither and fade away. It is this that causes what you refer to as the post-polio condition.

Having discussed the problem with leading medical experts in the United States, Canada and here in Britain, I have not the slightest doubt that there is no question of the virus going into remission. Rather, the condition *is* a result of the stresses of long-term disability and the natural degenerative processes of ageing. If it is of any help to fellow sufferers, I pass on the advice given to me some years ago by an eminent neurologist: 'Never stand when you can sit, and never sit when you can lie!'

Lord NAPIER AND ETTRICK

November 6, 1995   London, SW1

Fight drugs the lampoon way

SIR—John Casey is over-optimistic about the benefits of education on drug-taking (article, Jan. 31). Everyone I know was 'educated' about drugs, but that never stopped anyone taking them.

In my experience medical students are no more abstemious than anyone else. Almost everyone my age (26) with whom I am acquainted has tried drugs—I would put the figure at about 98 per cent at least.

No one is going to listen to warnings about drugs being danger-ous. Part of the attraction of drugs, motorbikes, and, for all I know, riding to hounds or being a war correspondent, rests on the same principle.

Death does not cross the mind of most young people, and they are often keen to give the impression that they don't care if they live or die. The challenge is not to convince people that drugs are danger-ous, but that they are uncool, and you can't do that while they are illegal.

If the Government wants to make a serious impact on the esteem in which drugs are held, may I suggest that it puts up posters carrying the picture of East 17's Brian Harvey, replete with his slack jaw, gormless stare, goatee beard and backwards baseball cap, with a slogan along the line of 'Not all the pills on earth could sort out Brian Harvey.'

What teenagers are genuinely scared of is embarrassment. If it was pointed out that ecstasy is extremely unlikely to kill you, but that it is guaranteed to make you grind your teeth together in an unattractive way and to talk gushing, sentimental drivel to people you don't like; if it was pointed out that it would make you a crashing bore, and that in the morning the memory of all this folly, combined with the hangover from hell, would make you wish you had died, then the anti-drugs campaign might strike a chord. As propaganda, it would at least have the benefit of being true.

Noel Gallagher is quite right to slam 'those politicians who simply condemn drug abuse as a criminal activity and think they're doing something positive', and Dr Casey should not apologise for being flippant. If the war on drugs is to make any impact at all it should start to employ the tactics of Dean Swift a little more and those of Judge Jeffreys a little less.

BENEDICT KING

February 4, 1997   Oxford

BOFFINS' CORNER

Science promotes economic growth

SIR—Professor Norman Stone (article, March 26) claims that it doesn't matter that the government is damaging British science because there is not a one-to-one relation between scientific excellence and economic progress and some of the research that is supported is not worth doing. I would like to know what factors he expects to contribute to the future economic growth, if not the educational standards of our people and the quality of our science. Could it be our enormous natural resources, or our love of hard work?

Norman Stone is not a scientist. He says that in the past the Cavendish Lab at Cambridge did fundamental research on a shoestring. That is true, but they are finding it difficult to keep up in modern conditions. How can you compete in laser research if you can not afford the lasers?

It is fashionable to denigrate the university expansion of the 1960s, even though we still have about the lowest proportion of university graduates of any developed country. It is probably true that it led to some second-rate people getting jobs. However, it ill becomes Norman Stone to sneer at it. He, like I, got his first academic position as a result of that expansion.

Professor S. W. HAWKING
April 6, 1987   Cambridge

Anti-scientific rant by writer

SIR—Fay Weldon's incoherent, petulant and nihilistic rant (article, Dec. 2) is the sort of thing I remember scribbling as a disgruntled teenager.

Scientists are not a separate race of aliens, a 'them' to be set against 'us'. We humans, together, have some hard questions to answer about the universe, some nasty diseases to cure, and some formidable environmental problems to overcome. If any discipline ever answers those questions, cures those diseases, solves those problems, that discipline will be, by definition, science.

You cannot eradicate smallpox by injections of literary criticism. The only people who can possibly do a better job than existing scientists are better scientists.

If Fay Weldon thinks existing scientists are doing such a bad job, she should learn some science and equip herself to offer some constructive suggestions for how we can do better. She might make a start by reading the two science books that she derisively mentions as best-sellers. She will find answers to the very questions that she, in the presumptuous name of 'we, the public' (when did we ever nominate Fay Weldon to speak for us?), accuses scientists of evading.

Ironically, these are questions that scientists are widely condemned for not evading. Where did Aunt Maude go when she died? What happened before the Big Bang? What is the ghost in the machine? These questions are often thought, wrongly, to be outside the legitimate territory of all but the most arrogantly grasping scientists. At least it makes a change to be accused of timidity.

What disturbs me more than Fay Weldon's article is that you were prepared to print it—and presumably pay for it. As for the inept Louis MacNeice parody at the end, it made me wonder whether the whole tirade was a joke.

Is Fay Weldon in fact lampooning the anti-intellectual, redneck views she pretends to espouse?

Dr RICHARD DAWKINS
December 5, 1991   Oxford

Greens are 'bad for science'

SIR—Several speakers at the conference of the British Association for the Advancement of Science this week have tried to address the problems of why people—and particularly young people—are developing such negative attitudes towards science, even when their everyday lives are deeply affected by the technological advances of recent years.

But one factor which appears not to have been addressed is the influence on young minds of what goes under the name of 'environmental education' in schools.

The green movement in recent years has grown into something

which is much more than an expression of concern for particular environmental problems: it has become the religion of the secular age. Furthermore, it is not a religion of enlightenment. On the contrary, it is superstitious, irrational and opposed to the expression of human ingenuity through scientific progress.

Green literature is shot through with the most negative images of human beings and their ability to affect the world around them. Humans are described in some widely distributed green textbooks as a form of pollution of the face of the earth ('popullution'). It appears that everything we do is wrong and 'spoils' nature, from the invention of fire onwards.

The consequences of filling young minds with these horrors are only too obvious—as your poll (Aug. 26) confirms. They become revolted by the thought of scientific 'progress'. Small wonder that fewer A-level candidates are taking science subjects.

Poisoning the minds of young people against their own species, and causing them to distrust our ability to shape the environment to fulfil our needs, will affect us all. In a world increasingly dependent on high technology, we will be producing fewer scientists and dropping down the league table of economic growth.

The almost unbelievably rapid changes which technology has wrought in our lives since the last war will become less rapid. Standards of living will rise more slowly; the cures for fatal illnesses will move further into the future.

When I gave a talk last year to a group of students from Sussex University, I tried to counter the gloomy images of environmental decay by explaining that the ingenuity of human beings, coupled with goodwill and properly functioning political and economic structures, could confront all of the problems facing us and continue to make the world a better place to live in.

When I had finished speaking an American student of about 18 said that it was surprising to hear a person of my age feeling so hopeful for the future. I am 39, but this young pessimist made me feel like one of the dinosaurs which the scientists have been discussing at their conference this week.

ROBERT WHELAN

August 30, 1991   Richmond, Surrey

Churchill's icy warning

SIR—May I add to Roger Highfield's excellent report about Mount-batten's iceberg fleet (Sept. 20). Early in the Second World War, aircraft did not have the range to cross the Atlantic. American aircraft therefore had to be shipped across, and many were lost to U-boats.

Geoffrey Pyke proposed to do away with these losses by establishing an airbase made of ice in mid-Atlantic. On being told of this idea by Mountbatten, Churchill declared that he attached great importance to it, but that the scheme would be possible only if 'we let Nature do nearly all the work for us . . . It will be destroyed if it involves the movement of very large numbers of men and a heavy tonnage of steel . . . to the recesses of the Arctic night'.

Pyke enlisted me for the project, because I had learnt a bit about ice during my glacier research before the war, but without telling me what the project was. I should find ways of making ice stronger. When my attempts had failed, I read a report from New York that the brittleness of ice disappears on freezing a mixture of ice and woodpulp, called pykrete by its inventor, the Austrian-born chemist Hermann Mark.

To make pykrete, and to test its properties, Combined Operations installed me with three helpers in a large underground cold store at Smithfield Market in London. We found pykrete to be weight for weight as strong as concrete. Unlike pure ice, it did not shatter on being hit by a projectile, but it sagged slowly under its own weight unless cooled to at least minus 15°C (4°F).

All the same, plans for the bergship went ahead. The Fleet Air Arm demanded a deck 50ft above water, 200ft wide and 2,000ft long. The Admiralty demanded that the ship be self-propelled and that its hull be at least 40 feet thick to withstand torpedoes. The strategists demanded a cruising range of 7,000 miles.

The final design gave the ship a displacement of 2.2 million tons, to be propelled at seven knots by 26 electric motors of over 1200hp each. Its rudder was to have the height of a 15-storey building. Yet it was to be built in Newfoundland in one winter.

When engineers of the US Navy examined the plans, they found that the amount of steel needed to freeze the 2.2 million tons of pykrete in one winter was greater than the amount needed to build the entire ship of steel. It was exactly what Churchill had feared.

Dr MAX PERUTZ
September 21, 1994   Cambridge

RELIGION

Christian socialism

SIR—The debate on the excursions into the realm of morality occasioned by the Prime Minister's [Mrs Thatcher] sermon (report, May 23) centres on two fundamental questions: whether religion or morality is involved in British political action; and how far should it go.

The capitalist system is inherently amoral; that is to say it is based upon self-interest, which can work for either good or evil. But politics are very largely the way things happen; morality must lie at the heart of political action.

If capitalism, as it is, is incompatible with morality in general and Christianity in particular, it is really no good endeavouring to baptise the capitalist system; it should be replaced. Only Christian socialism can constitute a proper replacement.

Lord SOPER
London W1

April 30, 1988

Lord Soper is a Methodist Minister and a former speaker at Hyde Park Corner.

~

Church–State link still justified

SIR—Your leader on the Commons' rejection of the proposal that in some circumstances the Archbishops of Canterbury and York might be permitted to allow the ordination of men and women who have been divorced suggests that the Church of England should, in return for the privileges of its position as the Established Church, be ready to pay the price of parliamentary veto of its own legislative and pastoral proposals.

To those of us who are involved in the Church's day-to-day life it is not altogether clear what these privileges might be. You suggest that the precedence of the Archbishop of Canterbury over all other citizens and the right of some Bishops to sit in the House of Lords, together with a more general prestige, derive from association with the State, and constitute something valuable to the Church.

But whatever value these things may have is slight, and is often offset by the confusion they cause over the Church's real nature and mission. In any case, the rest of the Anglican Communion manages quite well without them, as does the Established Church in Scotland.

It is important, however, that the establishment of the Church should be discussed in other than bargaining terms. The only question worth asking is whether or not in these closing years of the twentieth century the historic partnership between the Church of England and the State can be maintained with integrity and to the advantage of the nation as a whole.

My own view is that the strength of the Church of England, and the level of its involvement with individuals at key moments in their lives and with the general life of the community, is still significant enough to sustain the formal partnership with the State. Moreover, there is a most urgent need for the Christian values, on which the best of our national life is based, to be reaffirmed, and indeed reinforced.

Our political, as well as our religious leaders, have a duty here, and, far from suggesting a separation of Church and State, you, Sir, ought to be advocating a much closer partnership between the two, and the bringing into this partnership of the other Christian churches of these islands. We might then consider together how best this partnership could be formally and symbolically expressed in the twenty-first century.

Very Rev TREVOR BEESON
July 20, 1989   Dean of Winchester

~

Where the old hymns are still welcome

SIR—Following recent letters on the Bishop of Manchester's ban on the singing of 'O Valiant Hearts' at an ecumenical remembrance service next month, can I say that the hymn will be sung at the

Trafalgar and Remembrance Day services in St Peter's Church, Pimperne, Dorset.

The following hymns, all from *Hymns Ancient and Modern Revised*, will also be sung: 351 ('I Heard the Voice of Jesus Say'), 368 ('Praise the Lord, Ye Heavens'), 487 ('Eternal Father, Strong to Save'), 488 ('Holy Father in Thy Mercy'), 629 ('Onward Christian Soldiers'), 579 ('I Vow to Thee, My Country') and the whole of 577 (including the second verse: 'Our Lord, O God, arise,/Scatter our enemies,/ And make them fall;/Confound their politics,/Frustrate their knavish tricks,/On thee our hopes we fix:/God save us all'). The church will be full on both occasions, and the collection at the latter for the Poppy Appeal will be the largest in Dorset.

Sometimes I do just wonder with hindsight if the Corporal, RM, who died in my arms after we had been machine-gunned in the water when HMS *Hermes* was sunk by the Japanese in 1942, really did perish that all might be free.

We, who were at the sharp end of battle, still consider our comrades who died as saints. They gave up all that we might be free to live and worship as we wish. To my simple mind that includes singing hymns that have been hallowed by many years of use.

In the spirit of the immortal memory, I commit myself to Him who made me, and may His Blessing alight on me in my retirement from a Church which no longer seems to serve the just cause which was entrusted to me at my ordination to defend.

Rev. Capt. D. A. FARQUHARSON-ROBERTS

October 17, 1989 Blandford Forum, Dorset

Real heat of hellfire

SIR—The next Archbishop says he believes in Hell (article Feb. 26) and then clarifies it as 'not the burning pit or furnace or anything like that, but a place of separation from God for those who are wilful in their rejection of God'.

The words Christ chose to use were 'everlasting punishment' (Matthew 25 v 46); 'the fire that never shall be quenched' (Mark 9 v 43); and 'a tormenting flame' (Luke 16 v 24); to quote only a few. There are many more.

I expect the modern clergy will answer that Christ spoke in metaphors on these occasions. But even if he did, this metaphor evokes a condition very close to something indescribably painful; the complete opposite of the idea of separation. Christ did not die a cruel and gruelling death to save us from the trials of Robinson Crusoe. One wonders whether *this* equivocation on the substance of the old Gospel betrays a serious heresy.

QUINLAN TERRY

March 12, 1991   Higham, Essex

The architect Quinlan Terry was responding to Dr George Carey's statement that Hell was not a burning pit or furnace but a place of separation from God.

The long road to sainthood

SIR—A dashing bomber pilot, in the person of Lord Cheshire, would certainly be a colourful addition to the calendar of saints (report, Sept. 26).

Cheshire's early life as a roustabout should help: the pattern for the saint as reformed sinner was set by St Augustine in his *Confessions*. Cheshire's early marriage and his military service (including his attitude towards war, killing and, later, the ethics of dropping 'the bomb') would not count for or against him since the Church would look at his life only after he had become a Roman Catholic.

His widow and friends should be warned, though, that all his correspondence will be examined, including his medical and psychiatric records, as will every other aspect of his private and public life. Like politicians, candidates for sainthood must withstand close scrutiny.

Since Christ is the model for all Christian saints, it is well that Cheshire suffered during his life. How he bore his afflictions will be as important as the good works he accomplished. Since a deep prayer life is the common denominator of all non-martyr saints, evidence of this is essential.

As no formal action can be taken on his behalf for at least five years, those who think he is a 'close friend of God' should encourage

prayers to Cheshire asking for 'divine favours' through his inter-
cession, and visits to his grave. These remain time-honoured
measures for establishing that a candidate enjoys the requisite
'reputation for holiness' among the faithful.

In the course of writing my book *Making Saints*, I discovered that
saint-making is the most democratic process in the Roman Church
since—initially at least, it relies on this *vox populi*. Cardinal Hume
would do well to say no more about the cause: his role in such
matters is to observe and judge the parade, not lead it.

The British have a reputation for finding saint-making and saint-
invoking a bit too baroque for their taste, which is one reason why
the cause for Cardinal Newman has taken more than a century. But
if the founder of Opus Dei can be beatified in lightning time—
despite mounting evidence that the process was subverted for his
benefit—surely those Catholics and others who admired Cheshire
owe it to the Church to overcome their reticence.

If you are over 30, however, don't count on seeing Cheshire
canonised in your lifetime. Heaven, and presumably Lord Cheshire,
can wait.

KENNETH WOODWARD
October 3, 1992 New York

~

End of the Oxford Movement

SIR—Two years after Anglicans joined Roman Catholics in mark-
ing the centenary of the death of John Henry Newman, it is not
unfair to ask what the founder of Tractarianism would say about the
recent vote of the General Synod to admit women to the priesthood.

As his biographer I have no doubt that modesty would forbid him
from acknowledging that it is the established Church's greatest crisis
since his own defection in 1845.

Newman saw very clearly that establishment is the glue that keeps
the Church of England together. Such fears as he had as an Anglican
of the problems that might be caused for the Church if Convocation
was recalled have been more than fulfilled by the modern General
Synod, which is increasingly independent of an overwhelmingly
indifferent, secular Parliament.

Without the Establishment to maintain the status quo, the three main parties are left to struggle for control of the Church. For, in spite of the boasted comprehensiveness of Anglicanism, Anglo-Catholics, Evangelicals and liberals hold incompatible views of what Christianity is, and therefore what the Church is.

Of course, there are overlaps, and in this case apparently enough of the more liberal Evangelicals were persuaded so as to secure the required two-thirds majority. The result has been a resounding defeat for the Anglo-Catholic party which, if it even survives, is now completely marginalised. This is surely what Newman would see so clearly: that last week's vote spelt the end of the Oxford Movement.

Like Newman's departure in 1845, the Synod decision is really a triumph for the liberals. Without the Anglo Catholics, will the conservative Evangelicals be able to resist the total liberalisation of the Church of England? More than 100 years ago Newman feared the Church of England would become so 'radically liberalized . . . as to become a simple enemy of the Truth', as it seemed 'only a matter of time, how long the Anglican Church retains any part of the Faith'.

If that 'spell' which Newman thought prevented Anglo-Catholics from recognising the true reality of the Church of England has finally been broken, he would hope that the Roman Catholic authorities will now look as sympathetically as possible at the practicality of establishing, as has been done in the United States, a special rite within the Roman Catholic church for former Anglicans.

When the possibility of an Anglican Uniate church was mooted in 1876, Newman could only welcome any 'means of drawing to us so many good people, who are now shivering at our gates'.

Fr IAN KER
November 18, 1992　　　　　　　　　　　　　　　　Ascot, Berks

〜

Don't defect to Rome

SIR—What saddened me about Fr Ian Ker's letter (Nov. 18) was the assumption that the Anglican Church is a loose connection of divided parties pulling in different directions.

Although I resist the prevalent view of John H. Newman, which is to strain to see the halo on his portrait, I still hold valuable his own vision of the Church as the Via Media between Rome and Dissent. But I cannot make a hero of a man whose idealised view of the Roman Catholic Church caused him to shun loyalty to his own mother church.

In the 1840s it is worth remembering that Newman was the only Tractarian who left to join the Church of Rome. The heroes were the loyal men, John Keble, Edward Pusey and Charles Marriott, who saw that their spiritual life within the Church of England with its simplicity, freedom and honesty, was a strong link.

I hope, as one who voted against the ordination of women to priesthood last year, but who values loyalty and prefers acceptance of a common mind rather than a rigid adherence to Church Order, that Anglo-Catholics (even bishops) will not be tempted to follow Newman to the Church of Rome.

Rev PETER TOWNSEND
November 26, 1992   Oakham, Leics

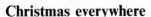

Christmas everywhere

SIR—Many will sympathise with David Barr (letter, Dec. 29). Of 100 of our cards only 15 bore any reference to the Nativity. But *nil desperandum*. A girl selecting cards was overheard to say: 'Lummy, they're even bringing religion into Christmas'.

Dr E. D. Y. GRASBY
January 2, 1993   Hawkhurst, Kent.

The best beauties' books for Lent

SIR—One appreciates the concern of the model agencies for their charges' education (Fashion, March 1), but should not these preceptors seek to diversify the reading in which 'the beautiful eggheads' indulge?

In your photographs three models are holding—in one case perusing—works which indicate an unhealthy concentration on psychology. One is addressing herself to a study of Sigmund Freud: another is clutching *New Pathways in Psychology*; a third has had her attention tiresomely distracted from Foucault's *Madness and Civilisation*. Doubtless these studies are all admirable in their way—but it is a narrow way, without the compensating virtue of straightness.

More profitable Lenten reading suggests itself. *The Cloud of Unknowing* might lift these young girls out of their terrestial slough; the *Confessions* of St Augustine alert them to noxious tendencies of youth; and William Law's *Serious Call to a Devout and Holy Life* help them to avoid the snares which too often lie in wait for those so fatally cursed with beauty.

ROBERT GRAY
March 3, 1993   London W11

Prejudice lives on against papists

SIR—I was surprised at Lord Rawlinson's 'incredulity' at the 'prejudice against Roman Catholics which Peterborough reports' (letter, Dec. 30). My experience has led me to face much bitter and aggressive comment against the Roman Church, although also much support.

At a recent 'distinguished' luncheon party I was informed that my church was 'gloating like the proverbial whore that she is over the decision of the Synod to allow women priests'. At another such luncheon it was suggested that all Romans should take an oath of allegiance to the sovereign.

We Romans are not alone, for the host at that luncheon, a Jew married to a Roman Catholic, consoled me by saying that he too was an outcast from 'the establishment' and considered neither an Englishman nor loyal. Perhaps the saddest occasion was when I preached at a Church of England wedding before a congregation which would certainly be considered 'most distinguished'. As I left the pulpit one member rose and symbolically spat, snarling: 'How dare a Roman Catholic preach in this Church?'

Dom ANTONY SUTCH
January 2, 1993   Downside Abbey, Stratton-on-the-Fosse, Som

Knoxian theology

SIR—Atheistic Anglican priests may be helped liturgically by being alerted to the collect composed by Ronald Knox years ago:

> *Lord, in as much as without Thee*
> *We are not able to doubt Thee,*
> *Give us the grace to tell the whole race*
> *We know nothing whatever about Thee.*

On the other hand, since this refers to an objective reality outside our human aspiration and feeling, perhaps this is for agnostic priests rather than apparent atheists in the ministry.

TIM BRADSHAW
September 10, 1993   Oxford

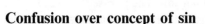

Confusion over concept of sin

SIR—No doubt many people might agree that there are circumstances in which cohabitation without marriage may be relatively innocent (report, June 7). But if the Church accepts it as invariably 'not sinful', regardless of circumstances, what becomes of the Prayer Book doctrinal statement that one of the three important reasons for marriage is 'for a remedy against sin, and to avoid fornication'?

It is significant that anecdotal evidence indicates that many couples coming to be married, if offered a fair choice between the three versions of the marriage service, choose the version in which these words are used—even, in some cases, where they have already been cohabiting.

The Book of Common Prayer is doctrinally normative for the Church. Its implications cannot be lightly set aside.

MARGOT THOMPSON
Prayer Book Society, London EC4

SIR—The Church seems once again to have retreated to its rural roots by contracting a form of foot in mouth disease. When will the bishops and other Church leaders learn not to get swept along by the tide of popular values and secular trends and instead to stand up for traditional and scriptural principles?

Well done Alan Storkey for resigning from the working party and thus distancing himself from this report.

Surely laypeople in the pews deserve better than to be inflicted with reports and statements which seem more interested in being deliberately provocative and controversial than in affirming orthodox Christian beliefs. Or has the Church too become obsessed with the sound-bite alone?

SIMON LEMIEUX
Portsmouth, Hants

SIR—Following its thoughtful report on marriage, there are rumours of a forthcoming Church report on burglary which is said to be circulating.

This comments: 'Some of the reasons for choosing burglary as a way of life were grounded on sober, harsh reality, such as unhappy experiences of working in a regular job. The phrase "criminal" is a most unhelpful way of characterising the lives of burglars. It has the effect of reducing burglary in all its complexity of intentions and forms to a single sensational category.'

Prof STEPHEN BUSH

June 8, 1995   Poynton, Ches

Plug into the Pope

SIR—One wonders what benefits Mgr Gaillot, the former Bishop of Evreux, is expecting to spread in the electronic world with his pastoral letter on the Internet (report, Jan. 17).

Of course, any ecclesiastic with a diocese that is a largely uninhabited dusty area in the Atlas Mountains—canonically described as *in partibus infidelium* (in the territories of the unbelievers)—must have a problem finding an outlet for his energies. In recent months, he has been on a boat near the Mururoa Atoll, presumably hoping to be blown up defying his countrymen's love of nuclear weapons and thereby to earn himself the acclaim of secular martyrdom.

But while one fears that his message on the information super-highway may be no more orthodox than the one he gave to the real world, the good bishop can now do himself a bit of good. He can plug his computer into the bark of Peter, which has also recently joined the Internet to offer papal homilies and discourses. This will enable him to discover what he should have been preaching in the first place.

Mgr BRIAN FERME
January 24, 1996   Rome

TRYING EDUCATION

The importance of learning grammar

SIR—One of Prof. Sir Randolf Quirk's live grouses (Wednesday Matters, May 13) is 'ignorance of sentence construction and paragraphing'; he adds, 'None of these complaints concerns grammar'. This is an astonishing statement: how can one know how to construct a sentence correctly without a basic knowledge of simple grammar?

I with a partner started a new school in 1964. With the aim of establishing the highest possible academic standard we had one period a week devoted to 'Grammar' in order to teach children the correct use of language. We had two outstanding English teachers who concentrated their efforts on creative writing.

Within five years of establishing the school we applied to the DES (or its equivalent at that time) for an inspection with the purpose of obtaining 'recognition as efficient'. H.M. Inspectors were critical of the 'Grammar' period: it was outdated and opposed to the progressive ideas of the late Sixties.

Sadly it was this attitude of the Inspectors and other educationists that has been mainly responsible for the declining standard of literacy. I am in principle in agreement with Dr John Marenbon; and the teaching of grammar need not be dull. Well taught it can be both interesting and fun.

I first taught it shortly after the war when it was required for 'O'-level English Language; I have not changed my views since then of its value both in the learning of other languages and the correct use of our own.

H. E. WATTS
May 18, 1987   Wadebridge, Cornwall

Education aim is a Major decline

SIR—I am surprised to learn that the present Conservative Government is proposing to abolish the distinction between the universities and the polytechnics (report, May 21), but really astonished to read John Major's statement that he wishes 'to break down the artificial barrier which has for too long divided academic education from a vocational one'.

Who told him that the distinction was artificial? Even as a schoolboy in Bengal I wrote 'university *education*' but 'technical *training*'. This was in conformity with the recognised principle that universities existed for two purposes: to foster and extend knowledge and to create a particular human personality, and it was no part of their function to teach the skills needed to earn money. To put the matter in zoological phrasing, universities formed the *homo sapiens* and the technical teaching institutions made the *homo faber*. Both are laudable aims but different.

Even in science the distinction was seen. The two kinds of teaching created or helped two pre-existing aptitudes. To give one pair of illustrations, Faraday was one kind of scientist and Edison another.

Neither had any formal scientific education, but became an equally great and honoured scientist in different ways. The teaching institutions existed to help those whose aptitudes did not rise to the level of genius.

To regard university education in its traditional form as a 'class phenomenon' is silly. If Sir Philip Sidney was at Oxford, so was Wolsey, the son of a grazier. To appeal to statistics, in 1639 some 50 per cent of the entrants to Oxford were sons of the gentry, 41 per cent sons of the 'lower classes', and nine per cent sons of the clergy, a class of mixed social origins.

For a Conservative Prime Minister to make the abolition of the distinction between university education and technical training a part of this programme of creating a 'classless society'—if such a chimera can be conceived of at all, and with the concurrence of the whole party—is of ominous significance for Conservatism. It indicates that Conservative politicians are no longer educated, but just trained like football players.

In contrast, at the beginning of this century, as Lord

Morley wrote, there were five or six MPs in office or in opposition who could earn their livelihood as men of letters. *Mais*—to raise a *lament pour la politique du temps jadis—ou sont les neiges d'antan?*

Second, it also indicates that the Conservative Party by and large has become lower middle-class in its outlook, and is thus possessed by love of money. Actually, the present Conservative party does not want to abolish *all* class distinctions, but only those which are not based on money. There is no denying that the Conservatives of today are as a class the new rich and their opponents the class which wants to filch the upstarts of their wealth.

Politics today has abandoned love of power for love of money as its principal motivation.

NIRAD CHAUDHURI

May 24, 1991   Oxford

Unbeatable aid to education

SIR—Auberon Waugh is mistaken in thinking the beating of schoolboys a peculiarly Anglo-Saxon pastime (Way of the World, July 25).

Suetonius tells us that the Romans went in for it, and Menander, the Greek playwright, said: 'A boy who has not been flogged is not trained.' And a ditty heard in a leading Irish public school—'It can't be helped, it must be done/So down with your breeches and out with your bum'—shows a relish for it among the Celts.

The good and gentle Auberon has good and gentle forebears who differed from him about the beating of schoolboys. Oliver Goldsmith, an Irishman and one of the gentlest men who ever lived, wrote: 'Whatever pains a master may take to make the learning of the languages agreeable to his pupil, he may depend upon it, it will be at first extremely unpleasant . . . Attempting to deceive children into instruction of this kind is deceiving ourselves: and I know no passion capable of conquering a child's natural laziness but fear.'

His friend, the good Samuel Johnson, told Boswell in 1775: 'There is now less flogging in our great schools than formerly, but less is learned there; so that what the boys get at one end they lose at the other.'

George Orwell, who suffered the rigours of Eton in the inter-war years, wrote: 'I doubt whether classical education ever has been or can be successfully carried on without corporal punishment.'

ARTHUR FREWEN

August 3, 1992   London W8

Right creature comforts for the modern Etonian

SIR—Since Eton is already over-subscribed it is unlikely that the *Eton Chronicle*'s suggestion for girl pupils will come about in the next 20 years (report, July 4). As someone who has recently survived the school's Gulag-like rigours beside the Thames, I suggest some soothing remedies.

Etonians are obnoxious only because they are forced to rise too early. So attractive blondes should be employed to awaken boys from their beds with coffee and croissants at a convenient time in the afternoon.

Speakers should be installed in the corridors and soothing music by such artists as Julio Iglesias played while boys slowly enter the washrooms.

The *Chronicle* is concerned at boys on the games field purposely injuring each other and 'swearing and shouting'. This is clearly a result of the pressure endured from strict essay deadlines.

These should therefore be abolished and fax machines installed in the rooms of those Etonians who wish to work. The essays should be vague, poetic, non-political and attractively illustrated with coloured crayons.

Pressures to succeed would be reduced, and boys would be prepared for the real world of the business lunch, Caribbean holidays, the cocktail party and other pressures of high office.

Etonians would become loving, caring, increase their charm and be ready to embrace Europe after 1992.

WILLIAM SITWELL
July 5, 1990   Towcester, Northants

~

Tale of a fair survivor . . .

SIR—As a former pupil of Marlborough College, your article 'Schools where girls are still just sugar and spice' (Jan. 11) reminded me of my own experiences there which were quite different.

Though I had to cope with a ridiculously chauvinistic housemaster—who ultimately expelled me after I had taken my A-levels for staying out after dark (a crime for which a boy would not receive so harsh a punishment)—I was very fond of the place.

I particularly enjoyed getting marked out of 10 on entering the dining hall. This has taught me to take the male sex for what they are: fairly juvenile, quite amusing and, on the whole, easy to cope with.

BELINDA EADE
January 15, 1991   London W12

~

We like boarding

SIR—We, the boys of Eagles dorm at Chelmsford Hall prep school, Eastbourne, read your article on boarding schools (Weekend, Sept. 14) and decided to respond. We held a meeting before lights out and agreed that the article was unjust.

The first thing we decided was that boarding school was not as good as being at home with the family during the holidays. We do miss our parents, but our house staff do their utmost to make our lives as interesting and comfortable as possible.

Tom Stoddart (aged 12), who is boarding for the first time, wanted to do so because he was bored at home and wanted to make more friends and to play more sport at school. Several day boys stay in the evening to join in the activities like push hockey, five-a-side football, tennis and swimming in the school pool, and playing pom-pom for the younger ones. There is also a remote-control car club, indoor games and a train club.

We are all in agreement that our school has a very friendly atmosphere because the house staff and matrons listen to our problems and comfort us when we get upset. They are all very welcoming when we return to school. All the dormitories are colourfully decorated.

We felt your adult readers should have the children's opinion on this subject as our teachers always remind us: 'There are two sides to a story'.

JAL MEHTA, JAMES APPLETON
TIM SUTTON, MATTHEW ILOTT
JAMIE NICHOLLS, TOM FORD
TOM STODDART
BEN VAUGHAN-GAMES
Eastbourne, E. Sussex

September 23, 1991

Two heads not better than one

SIR—You are right to say about the appointment at Rugby School: 'All that matters is that a post should be filled by the most appropriate candidate of either sex, and not promoted to satisfy any politically correct ideal' (editorial, June 15).

The practice of appointing joint heads of school *is* a practice to satisfy a politically correct ideal. I am presently a joint head of school at Framlingham College, Suffolk; there is a head girl, and she and I each has a deputy. We all supported the introduction of this system upon our appointment last year.

However, we have discovered that it is a cumbersome system. One does not have two captains of a sports team—imagine the chaos!

Under the present system, to reflect our status we try to do everything together, even when speaking to the school; our prefects' dinner speech was a *tour de force* of the 'double act'.

In a truly co-educational school, however, there is no need to appoint two heads of school to represent both boys and girls. After all, one doesn't have a headmistress *and* a headmaster. There is no good, for example, appointing a mediocre head boy and an outstanding head girl, passing over a number of other outstanding girls in the process.

No, one needs to appoint the *best* candidate of either sex to the position of head pupil. Next year, on the head girl's and my recommendation, the post of 'joint head of school' is to be abolished—but Framlingham *cannot* be accused of any sexism.

Why? We are a Head Masters' Conference school with a headmistress, Mrs Gwendolen Randall. It is a reflection of true co-education that we do not need to manufacture any positions to be reserved for *either* sex.

MARCUS BOOTH
Woodbridge, Suffolk

SIR—The facts are not in dispute but the problem is summed up in Miss Woolcock's own words: 'I hope my appointment means girls will see themselves as *more* equal'.

B. A. HESKINS
June 17, 1995   Holyhead, Anglesey

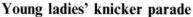

Young ladies' knicker parade

SIR—When I read Allan Massie's story of the knicker inspections at Cheltenham Ladies' College (Commentary, Feb. 2) I thought: 'I don't remember that—but I bet it's true.'

In the Sixties and Seventies the school had a well-deserved reputation for bizarre and restrictive regulations. It also had 12 boarding houses scattered around the town; those in charge of them ran the full gamut of female eccentricity, and they all added their own local flourishes to the school rules.

In this atmosphere of dotty ritual we were inclined to believe every tale we were told of the bees in the various housemistresses' bonnets, and the school was a rumour factory to rival the House of Commons.

As Mr Massie observes, it would be a pity to check such stories and find them to be untrue. However, one of my contemporaries has confirmed that these inspections did take place at Sidney Lodge, where the housemistress was famously prissy, though the details are wrong.

The knickers were bottle-green (not navy), thick brushed cotton (not serge) and the inspections took place indoors (not in the quadrangle). We were supposed to wear these baggy green garments over our regulation plain white pants for gym lessons.

At St Hilda's, my friend remembered, the girls had to descend the stairs to breakfast slowly, in single file, while the housemistress checked that their skirts were long enough (just below the knee) and their hair short enough (clearing the collar).

Perhaps she checked surreptitiously on the knickers at the same time. At St Margaret's, my own house, the housemistress was more interested in seeing that shoes and fingernails were clean, and that we were not smuggling a letter out to the post. She thought our knickers were our own business, but was determined to know who corresponded with whom.

I once saw a senior girl being ordered to kneel in the quadrangle before the formidable Miss Hacking, whose purpose was to see whether the hem of her skirt touched the ground. (It didn't, until she unrolled her waistband three times.)

Any new girls watching would have been told, you may be sure, of the ancient rule about kneeling to Miss Hacking if you passed her in the quad. Untrue? Yes, but no more so than the story of Miss Beale, the founder, tripping over two prostrate drunks in the High Street and decreeing the High Street for ever more out of bounds.

Lady BRIGHT
London W2

February 3, 1993

Jesuits' loss

SIR—I see that unidentified Jesuit with his dictum about the under-sevens is once again being invoked (TV review, May 23).

Jesuits, however, do not, and never did, normally conduct infant or nursery schools. This Jesuit, then, if he ever existed, was surely some cynical old Jesuit engaged in disclaiming all responsibility for Voltaire, James Joyce, or whoever: 'We didn't get him until it was too late to do anything.'

G. K. Chesterton, however, did say that boys are not sent to school until it is too late. He added that the customary bringing up of boys by women in the only years of their lives that matter was a colossal female privilege, against which he declined to rebel.

Feminists, of course, would rather see men bringing up babies and their mothers serving in the Gulf.

(Miss) MURIEL SMITH

May 25, 1991   Holyport, Berks

Bring geography back to earth

SIR—It is not surprising that Claudia FitzHerbert (Commentary, Jan. 16) should be puzzled by the research topics of members of the Institute of British Geographers—among them rural attitudes to female clergy and the views of old people on living 'in the community'.

If you turn to the current *Geographical Journal* you will find the books chosen for the leading review are *Housing and Social Change* and *Landlords and Property*. You will be told that these books deal with such matters as 'the housing policy/housing consumption interface', 'specialised and semi-protected financial circuits for housing', 'the mechanisms or structures which enable landlords to act' and the 'practical ideologies that structure their activities'.

This is the stuff which our leading geographical periodical thinks most deserving of the special attention of its readers—Fellows, for the most part, of the Royal Geographical Society.

Such research has not the remotest connection with geography.

The word means 'earth description', and unless the 'ge' or earth-element is present, it cannot be geography. Surely there is enough to keep geographers busy in the momentous changes being wrought on the rich diversity of the earth's surface by physical forces and human activities intertwined, and in the varied areal patterns and landscapes that result?

Sir Halford Mackinder (1861–1947) succeeded in establishing geography as a university subject in this country, but his success was more apparent than real. As he himself said in 1928, 'the universities established more schools of geography, but at the same time published curricula containing often very little real geography'. Until his death he was constantly trying to call geographers back to their subject—to the earth as the home of man, and how and why it varies from place to place.

How bad the situation is now can be shown from the research interests of members of university and polytechnic geography departments listed in the RGS Guide to postgraduate geography. In most, staff are chiefly concerned with either pure earth science, much of which is more geological than geographical, or techniques such as computer science and remote sensing, sociology and economics.

Among topics professed are 'aerial spraying', 'housing policy', 'urban crime', 'building societies', 'deprivation and advantage', 'modelling and history of planning retailing' and 'feminist geography'. There are some welcome exceptions, notably in Durham, where almost everyone declares a regional interest and they cover, between them, most of the globe.

Does not all this call for an independent inquiry into whether there is not a serious misuse of funds provided by the taxpayer and intended for real geography, and does it not raise doubts as to the intellectual worth of what often now passes for geography in higher education?

Dr W. H. PARKER
January 22, 1992   St Briavels, Glos

Dr Parker (1912–87) was a lecturer at Christ Church, Oxford, and the biographer of Sir Halford Mackinder.

Stoic response from A. J. Wentworth, BA

SIR—I really must ask your contributor Peterborough to be a little more considerate in his choice of items with which to bolster up his daily columns. As recently as March 7 he thought fit to include a reference to a so-called 'history of school uniforms', from which he quoted a number of remarkable excerpts. Of those that most seriously upset my old friend A. J. Wentworth, BA, I will only mention 'rust-coloured breeches' and 'green needle-cord waistcoats with brass buttons'.

And now, a bare nine months later, comes this unfortunate allusion (Dec. 12) to No Smacking Week, which of course caught the eye of Mr Wentworth, naturally a dedicated reader of your paper ever since the *Morning Post* was snatched from his grasp. He is an old man now, rather frail, and shocks of this kind are bad for him, as you would agree if you could see the six pages of foolscap he has written to me on the subject. As it is, I can only give you the gist, if that, of a letter of considerable warmth.

'No such balderdash' he firmly states, 'has come my way since an attempt was made to interest me in a new method of teaching mathematics, which, if I remember rightly seemed to involve measuring the height of a vaulting horse in the gymnasium or some such falderal, though I dare say horses are banned nowadays in case one of the boys splits his rust coloured breeches and begins to cry. Is there to be a No Crying Week, I feel bound to ask? Mind you, we want no Squeers in our schools, at any rate for younger boys. *Suaviter in modo*, eh? Just enough to make them wish they hadn't done whatever it was, was always my guiding principle . . .

'And here's a curious thing. I well remember a lecture I gave to a ladies guild of some kind in America, I think it was, and a more chuckle-headed batch of misconceptions about the teaching of children than they threw up at question time, I never met, not even in my own country. However, that is beside the point. What I meant to say was that right at the end a woman in a purple hat asked whether corporal punishment was still permitted in English schools. I told her that it was very rare, I believed, in state schools, but that of course in private schools, such as Burgrove, where the formation of character . . . "You mean you have to pay to get it done?" put in a lady at the back. I thought her voice had a wistful note.'

Mr Wentworth's letter ends, some pages later, on an equally cheerful note. 'Of course', he writes, 'if this no smacking is only for a week, no very great harm will be done.'

H. F. ELLIS

December 24, 1990   Taunton, Som

INAPPROPRIATE VOICES?

Dialects decision a backward step

SIR—The decision of Sir Ron Dearing, chairman of the School Curriculum and Assessment Authority, to downgrade the importance of teaching standard English in favour of the 'richness of dialects and languages in England and Wales' is a backward step (report, Oct. 22).

The purpose of any language is communication, and that is best achieved when every citizen of a country speaks the same language in the same way. We have not only home-grown dialects, but also those introduced from the Caribbean and the Indian sub-continent. Such diversification of language leads not to richness but to dilution, to misunderstanding and to breakdowns in communication that benefit no one.

Both the School Curriculum and Assessment Authority and the National Association for the Teaching of English should be aware of the results of teachers' failing both to teach and to insist on correct standard English. A 1992 national survey of British undergraduates' standards of English showed that grammar, spelling, punctuation and clarity of expression are all suffering because school pupils are not being taught properly and are not having their mistakes corrected.

There is nothing difficult in a child's speaking both his local dialect and standard English, but the child has to be taught that it is standard English that will enable him to get on in the world. Children need to be taught right from wrong in English just as much as in, say, mathematics.

Without a standard form of English, the next generation of school leavers will find job opportunities more limited, social activities more restricted and life's horizons much lower than they might be had teachers emphasised the benefits of learning a language that can be understood from Cornwall to Co Derry, from Arbroath to Athens.

ERIC HAYMAN

October 27, 1993   London W4

Flow of dialect

SIR—Hugh Massingberd has commented on a new 'classless' dialect known as 'Estuary English' which is sweeping southern Britain (Class Monitor, March 20).

This dialect is probably what my brother, who left these shores some 40 years ago, referred to when he wrote to me recently saying that in all English television news excerpts and current affairs programmes carried by his local network, the participants all seemed to speak Cockney.

I believe that 'Estuary English' is son of 'North Thames twang' which originated in the Rainham–Grays area of Essex—the spiritual home of the glottal stop.

I recall a conversation between two young ladies in my train compartment many years ago, which went something like this:

'Ere, I doan like Pe'er, 'er new 'e torks funny.'

'Worryer mean?'

'Weyull, 'e says all 'is words.'

I have often pondered on that phrase, and hoped that the young man named remained so articulate.

G. CLAYDEN

March 23, 1993   Corringham, Essex

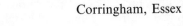

That word again

SIR—One unexpected effect of the end of National Service was that the younger generation suddenly thought it was terribly clever and sophisticated to use the F-word in casual conversation.

Anyone who had been in the Services, during the war or later (and that meant most people), was fed up to the back teeth with the endless, repetitive, pointless F-this, F-you, F-off, even using it in the middle of words: 'Don't you under f-ing stand?'

It was the hallmark of the uncouth and the illiterate; not infrequently it was used by officers who thought (wrongly) that it made them sound on the same wavelength as the troops: how wrong they were.

On demobilisation most people wished never to hear it ever again.

Now it appears 4,000 times in a book about Glasgow, winning what might be rudely, though perhaps not entirely inaccurately, entitled the F-er Prize. Do not our intellectual pundits realise it is the hallmark of the inarticulate?

BRIAN HUNTER
October 22, 1994 Camberley, Surrey

~

Beautifully spoken of old

SIR—The suggestion put forward by the adaptor of the BBC's version of *Pride and Prejudice* and by your correspondent L. E. Snellgrove (letter, Oct. 11) that no one in the modern world can have any idea as to how the upper classes spoke in the time of Jane Austen is quite absurd.

What, for example, about eighteenth-century dictionaries which put the stresses of words such as 'formidable' precisely where the twentieth-century 'U-speaker' would put them?

The popular theory that the English aristocrat used to speak with the accent of his own region is essentially an historical myth. Of course, there are examples of these but they are the exceptions which prove the rule. Thus, in the eighteenth century an aristocrat who spoke with a regional accent like the Devonshire magnate, John Parker, 1st Lord Boringdon, aroused comment.

'I had the pleasure of finding Parker as dirty, as comical and talking as bad English as ever', Georgiana Duchess of Devonshire wrote of him. Parker was known to be very rich and eccentric and so his speech did not matter more than his personal cleanliness; but a gentleman less favoured who had to make his way in the world took more trouble about how he spoke.

Even at the beginning of the seventeenth century the gentleman of fashion spoke with an accent which in its essentials was similar to 'the King's English' or the so-called 'Oxford accent' of later years.

Henry Peacham's classic work *The Compleat Gentleman* (1622) ranks a 'graceful' pronunciation high among a gentleman's attributes, together with 'a plaine and most similar stile', and advises readers to have 'much conference with those who can speak well'.

As for the influence of the wireless, Sir Harold Nicolson looked forward, in 1955, to an age when all classes would 'speak English as beautifully and uniformly as they do upon the BBC'. Forty years on, though, the Corporation has abandoned its old manner of speech in favour of the all-too-aptly named 'classless' accent, which, though certainly uniform, is far from beautiful.

THOMAS BYRNE
October 14, 1995 Dublin

~

Keep word 'gay' in right hands

SIR—Once upon a time, when young girls reached marriageable age, they 'came out' and were carefree and 'gay'.

Nowadays, these previously pleasant and innocuous terms are used to describe the rather less charming activities of ageing clerics, MPs, media celebrities and outrageous people campaigning for homosexual rights—whatever these might be.

Not only do the latter misappropriate the English language—which I should have thought no one has any 'right' to do—they simply will not stop talking about themselves and their sexual proclivities and trying to make others do the same.

Amazingly, they even have 'lovers'. But a lover usually had a lass when I went to school. We sang songs about them, as we did about boys and girls coming out to play.

But, even among heterosexuals, I have never been too happy about this connection between love and sex. Sex may be lovely, but surely it isn't love.

Is it not simply a pleasurable physical exercise indulged in and enjoyed by two people who have discovered they find such acrobatics mutually pleasing? Love must surely be different, something a little more selfless and cerebral.

Could not those who seem so anxious about 'coming out' now go back in—and belt up?

PAMELA STREET
March 20, 1995   London W1

When Hugh Drummond went 'gay'

SIR—Concerning your correspondence about the word 'gay', there is an unusual use of the word in *Bulldog Drummond*, which was published in 1920.

When Captain Drummond and his gang are rescuing Potts, the American multi-millionaire, from Carl Peterson's thumbscrew, Hugh Drummond says: 'Let's get gay with Potts.'

He does not mean light-hearted nor does he mean vicious pleasure. He means 'let's get going'. Gay is used twice like this in Sapper's first Drummond book.

STANLEY REYNOLDS
March 24, 1995   Cheddon Fitzpaine, Som

Tally man

SIR—For those who desire a title for their unmarried co-habitees, what about the derivative from 'living tally' which was common in Bolton, Lancashire, during my childhood there—tallyman or tallywoman?

KATHLEEN ORME
November 26, 1993   Sheffield, S. Yorks

A girl called Lil

SIR—In the West Country the question of a suitable title for 'concubine' has been resolved. Such a lady is introduced as 'Lil' as in 'Meet my Lil'.

It stands, of course, for 'live-in lover'.

AYLETT MOORE
November 30, 1993   Beaulieu, Hants

Seconds out

SIR—Acting on Graham Lord's advice (Notebook, Nov. 19), I introduced my lady friend to a new group of acquaintances as my 'concubine'. Unfortunately, their dictionary, the *Colliers English*, defines this term as 'a secondary wife—usually of lower social rank'.

I now have to buy some expensive perfume and book a table for dinner.

PETER JAKEMAN
November 24, 1995 Mansfield, Notts

~

Layman's guide

SIR—My late father-in-law, a down-to-earth Black Countryman, used to refer to anyone's co-habiting 'partner' as their 'lie-by'.

T. A. UNDERHILL
April 27, 1996 Halesowen, W. Midlands

~

Take your . . . 'er

SIR—May I add to your correspondence on partners by recalling that I was once visiting a woman patient when a gentleman came bounding up the stairs and said 'Good morning, Doctor. I don't think you know me but I am—'er 'im, if you see what I mean.'

I made a mental note that the patient must be " 'is 'er".

Dr A. C. DANIEL
Retford, Notts

SIR—Surely the most common term for a partner is the word 'Ummer', as most people at a loss say: 'I'd like you to meet my, um, er . . .'

STEVE BRENNAN
Milton Keynes, Bucks

SIR—In America, organisers of the 1979 census were said to have used POSSLQ—Person of Opposite Sex Sharing Living Quarters.

HENRY BUTTON
Cambridge

SIR—How about a 'spouse equivalent'?

P. S. JOSSALYN
Ipswich

SIR—While my Canadian cousin and his partner were awaiting divorce he always wrote and spoke of her as his 'playmate'. It conjures up thoughts.

B. C. LEEDEN
April 30, 1996
Broxbourne, Herts

~

In a wife's place . . .

SIR—Anthony Furse refers to his daughter's partner as 'The Outlaw' (letter, April 29). My unmarried daughter and son have provided me with a 'Sin-in-law' and a 'Didn't-ought-a-in-law'!

JUDITH KELFORD
Hinton St George, Som

SIR—My brother referred to his mistress as his 'Overnight bag'.

CHAS BEVERLEY
St Helier, Jersey

SIR—Conventional terms for referring to one's partner have their uses. I recall a married friend who reckoned to keep his spouse on her toes by introducing her with the words: 'I'd like you to meet my first wife.'

TIM GODFREY
May 1, 1996
London SW11

~

Pillow talk

SIR—'Counterpane Chum' is how my grandmother describes the man I live with. Perhaps, in more modern parlance, we could be referred to as a 'Duvet Duo'.

(Miss) DEBORA CASTREE

May 3, 1996 London SW11

~

'Whammy' going down plughole

SIR—H. L. Mencken once wrote a joke piece about how the bathtub was invented. It was taken so seriously that within five years most reference works carried his spoof as solemn fact. Mencken wrote letters of denial, but it did no good.

The same thing is happening to the 'double whammy'. First to misuse it was Chris Patten, with his poster showing two boxing gloves labelled 'Higher Prices' and 'More Taxes'. Patten's clincher was 'Labour's Double Whammy'. A commercial company has copied Patten's poster for its own message, again using the 'double whammy' phrase, and bartenders have been reported as serving 'double whammy' drinks, which one says gives you two kicks in one drink. So now it's not only a punch, it's a kick.

All the above uses of 'double whammy' are wrong. Al Capp is *ye onlie true begetter* of the whammy, single or double. In his cartoon strip, *Li'l Abner*, Capp invented the village of Dogpatch, a hillbilly community, one of whose characters was Evil-Eye Fleagle. (Only someone with the evil eye could shoot you a whammy.)

If Fleagle looked at you with one eye open and pointed a finger, that was the whammy. If he used both eyes and pointed two fingers, that was a double whammy. It was a curse, a jinx, a hex, the Indian Sign, it never involved physical violence, it was just there to bring you bad luck.

If you lived in Dogpatch and feared Evil-Eye Fleagle, the curse worked: it would paralyse you with fear. The moral of all this is, don't trust British politicians to use American slang. They can't. O tempora! O Whammy!

LARRY ADLER

March 19, 1992 London NW1

~

Authentic ring to ducal dam

SIR—The student at Amherst College in Massachusetts should indeed have been awarded full marks since the word 'dam' in this instance was correctly spelt without a terminal 'n' (letter, June 20).

Col Arthur Wellesley (the future Duke of Wellington) first used the phrase 'I don't care a dam' while serving in India. On being informed after a forced march that his field guns would be seriously delayed, Col Wellesley replied: 'I don't care a dam—we will fight without guns.'

The dam (now obsolete) was the chief copper coin current in India; it formed the ready money for the rich and poor alike and was equivalent in value to one halfpenny of this country's coinage of the period. (Two dams were the equivalent of one penny, so that one 'two-a-penny' dam was often mistakenly called a 'two-penny-dam').

The concurrent expression in this country during the 1800s and early 1900s was 'I don't care a brass farthing'. A brass farthing (as opposed to a copper farthing) would have been a forgery and of no value.

KENNETH WARBURTON
June 23, 1992   Bournemouth

Pilger problems

SIR—Auberon Waugh did not invent the verb to *pilger* (report, March 23). He merely gave it a new and rather malicious meaning. It is as surprising that the dictionary accepted this at the time as it is that the entry has now been withdrawn after a complaint by Mr John Pilger, the journalist.

The dictionary had in fact already included an old-established verb, *pilger* and *pilgering*, which has been in use for nearly a century for a certain process in the milling of metal.

Incidentally, the *OED* has also long had a definition of *waugh*: 'An instinctive exclamation indicating . . . indignation and the like.'

This, in the circumstances, seemed extraordinarily apt: and I therefore suggested *waughing*, with the additional definition:

'Indignantly and repetitively banging on against Northerners, anti-smokers, breath-testing and Left-wing journalists.'

So far the *OED* has not taken up my suggestion.

FRITZ SPIEGL
Liverpool

March 24, 1994

~

Good old days, bad old language

SIR—Having watched *The Camomile Lawn*, may I take up the cudgels on behalf of my generation?

In 1939, as Richard Last points out (Review, March 6), no young man would have propositioned a girl so blatantly with an 'F' word as Oliver did within the first five minutes of renewing their acquaintance.

In fact, throughout my career in the WAAF, at Kenley during the Battle of Britain and later London during the Blitz, never once did I hear the word used accidentally or on purpose, by any soldier, sailor or airman during the whole of my four years' service.

At Kenley, the nature of my job enabled me to overhear many heated exchanges in the air, yet even under pressure the enemy was never referred to as anything other than a 'bandit'—not even a bloody one.

My husband tells me that in male company, bad language was minimal compared with the amount in common use today.

Isn't it time we 'thirty-niners' were portrayed as being the exceptionally well mannered, considerate people we were? Or will scriptwriters continue to lull foul-mouthed viewers into thinking that bad language has always been acceptable?

(Mrs) MARIAN MOSELEY
Fowey, Cornwall

March 9, 1992

~

When the air turned blue

SIR—Marian Moseley (letter, March 9) says that she never heard profanity during her four years as a Waaf in the Second World War, and she condemns the dialogue of *The Camomile Lawn* as not being authentic.

Much the same criticism was made when my novel *Piece of Cake* (set in the Battle of Britain) appeared on television; indeed, a senior retired RAF officer reproached me for suggesting that the language and conduct of fighter pilots was not at all times 'exemplary'.

Many Waafs served as plotters in ops rooms. Air Commodore Gerald Gibbs, a senior staff officer in 1940, has recalled:

'In the beginning, we tried to get the girls to leave those rooms in which R/T was broadcast from the aircraft during air fighting—for the language was terrible. But it wasn't idle blasphemy or obscenity. It was the voice of men in the midst of fighting for their lives—and dying.

'The girls refused to leave their jobs and said that they didn't mind the language as much as we thought. They added that it was nice of us to think of their being like that, all the same.'

However, at one point the station commander at RAF Tangmere did disconnect the loudspeaker, believing 'some of the battle comments were too ripe even for the most sophisticated Waafs', as Paul Brickhill recorded in his biography of Douglas Bader.

Bader himself was notoriously profane, both on the ground and in the air. This transcript of part of an actual R/T exchange when Bader's squadron was in combat gives an idea of the sort of language that Waafs heard:

'Get organised.'

'I'm ****** if I can.'

'Four behind and above.'

'OK. I'm looking after you.'

'Look behind.'

'It's only me. Don't get the wind up.'

'Alright, you ****!'

'Don't **** about. We'll have some collisions in a minute.'

No doubt Mrs Moseley's memories reflect her own experiences; but I suggest it is dangerous to argue from the particular to the general. It is possible that men never swore on her station, but they certainly swore elsewhere—well within earshot of Waafs, who were quite untroubled by it.

DEREK ROBINSON

March 10, 1992 Bristol

Genteel prejudices and evasions

SIR—Anne Giles faithfully parades the entrenched verbal usages of the genteel middle or upper-middle class, as famously catalogued in the Fifties by Nancy Mitford (letter, July 17).

A few are based on commonsense, most are pure prejudice, and some strike me as faintly ridiculous. Would Mrs Giles, for instance, apply the ponderous 'napkin' to one of those flimsy bits of paper dispensed in most restaurants?

The French 'serviette' is surely more appropriate. And her restriction of 'Nan' to a person employed to look after one's children reminds me of Evelyn Waugh's advice to an ill-dressed club acquaintance: 'I should change your man.'

The problem with English usages associated with the natural functions is that they are virtually all evasions. 'Lavatory' (literally, a place for washing) is as much a euphemism as the despised 'toilet', the American 'bathroom', and the municipal 'convenience' (not to mention 'comfort station'). 'WC' has a certain honesty, but it is rather clinical for domestic use. 'Loo', a coy contraction of an existing euphemism, seems to me the most ridiculous cop-out of all.

The intractability of this peculiarly English problem is demonstrated by my dictionary (H.C. Wyld, 1936), which defines 'privy' as 'latrine' and 'latrine' as 'privy'.

The best solution—one we adopted many years ago—is to have your own family word. At least, it avoids charges of snobbery, inverted or otherwise.

RICHARD LAST
Woking, Surrey

July 20, 1993

Rallying to the Old Scots cause

SIR—I note with delight your report on the extension of teaching the Scots language at Edinburgh University (Dec. 18). With suppressed nationalities and so-called minority languages reviving all over Europe, the restoration of Scots to the dignity it once held as a national language should be welcomed by all, especially the English.

For in pronunciations like *doon* and *toon*, *nicht* and *richt*, and in vocabulary like *reek* (smoke) and *dicht* (wipe), it is Scots and not standard English which preserves the Old English roots common to both languages. You have much to gain in your ability to express your own culture by tapping this vigour and directness inherent in Scots.

This should have transpired as a matter of course following the Treaty of Union, 1707. But a mixture of English-culture imperialism and the ability of Scots on the make to kiss conscience and culture goodbye for a piece of the action resulted in English, and English only, being valued.

James Boswell was a classic example of the Scottish sook. His father, Lord Auchinleck, was less than impressed when he became Johnson's 'Scotch cur'. He raged: 'Jamie has gaen clean gyte (mad) . . . whae's tail dae ye think he has preened himsel tae noo? . . . an auld Dominie (teacher), wha keepit a schule an' caa'ed it an Acaademy.'

Not all Scots apologised for their language. At a Scots appeal case before the House of Lords, John Clerk of Penicuik naturally pleaded his client's case for the rights to a river in his customary court Scots, referring frequently to 'the watter'. When the Lord Chancellor mocked his speech and condescendingly asked, 'Is watter spelt with two t's in Scotland?' Clerk replied: 'Na, Na, my Lord, we dinna spell watter wi twa t's, but we spell mainners wi twa n's!'

Gradually, the language which had been the medium of arguably the greatest poetry written in Europe from 1450 to the Reformation was reduced to the status of a provincial dialect. It has never disappeared, though. Most folk are, like myself, bilingual in English and Scots. Due to its stigmatisation it is an underground language, spoken by consenting adults in the privacy of their own home. When they do come out and speak it, however, the myth that it is merely a debased proletarian patois is blown away. In a recent series for Radio Scotland, I interviewed, among others, a Unesco prize-winning scientist and a top investment analyst in Scots so rich, it gart yer lugs dirl!

In literature and drama, it is still a tremendously vital language, and some notable publishing successes here lately have been books in or about Scots. In recent decades, Scots' similarity to English means it has been eroded almost without people being aware of the process. Yet this very similarity is what would make its restoration comparatively simple.

Peer Norrie Lamont and wee Robin Cook raxin' oot hauns tae ane anither at the reopening o' the Scots Parliament an' greein' 'East's east, west's west, but hame's best!' Noo, thon is a thocht tae gie us aa a richt herty guid new year, when it comes.

BILLY KAY
December 24, 1991 Newport-on-Tay, Fife

~

M. Toubon's presumption

SIR—M. Jacques Toubon's feelings about the choice of *Le Shuttle* as the name for the Chunnel train (report, Jan. 29) is symptomatic of the greater linguistic xenophobia of the French, characterised in his absurd intention to legislate for the promotion of the French language.

One wonders whether M. Toubon thinks the French language sprang from nothing. Language is an evolving process which will never be restricted by laws. French radio presenters openly mocked the last attempts to force them to wish us a *bonne fin de semaine* instead of the accepted *bon weekend* some years ago.

Even the scantest knowledge of his compatriots, which should be easily supplied by his civil servants in the Ministry of Culture, if he has not already made the discovery for himself, should warn M. Toubon that the French people do not bow willingly to change.

This is particularly true when pressure comes from the government, and even more so when it smacks of interference in their right as private citizens to make their own choices. Needless to say, an attempt to force radio stations to play a certain percentage of indigenous music will immediately be seen as a primitive, barbaric reaction to the evidence—which is that the people who listen to pop music clearly prefer things the way they are.

If the minister really wants to promote the French language, he should get rid of the Academie Française, modernise the spelling of

French, and make learning it more appealing to foreigners. Such a move would immeasurably widen access to the literary heritage of this beautiful and precise language.

I know, as a teacher of French to prep school boys myself, that a mixture of some flexibility with the high standards of, say, Radio 3 announcers, would make many more continue to learn it in adult life.

If instead M. Toubon continues on his present course, he will not only alienate potential students of French still further but, for those who already speak the language, make it even 'cooler' to speak Franglais and listen to anglophone pop music.

NIGEL PEARCE
February 14, 1994   Oxford

'Plain' correction a poor joke

SIR—A reference book that I edited 10 years ago—*The Oxford Companion to the Mind*—has been 'awarded' the Golden Bull by the Plain English Campaign for 'gobbledygook'.

There is a wealth of factual information, and some difficult and unfamiliar ideas, presented with extensive cross-indexing. Technical terms are used—and defined—for their usual convenience and brevity, and for interfacing with the wider literature. It is intended for students and professionals, including medical doctors.

The example cited for criticism is the first sentence of the entry *Neuro-peptides*. 'Analgesia' is given by them as 'apalgesia'—turning a good English sentence into gobbledygook.

The 'award' letter says: 'Although the issue of Plain English is one that we take extremely seriously, the Golden Bulls are issued in a very lighthearted way.' What right has anyone to dispense public criticism lightheartedly? I happen to like jokes, but this is beyond a joke.

As it happens, I have striven to think and write clearly for many years in a dozen books and hundreds of scientific publications. Inevitably, not all are easy reading. Technical writing has to be specialised to present unfamiliar ideas when standard plain English is not adequate—and it can be boring.

New thoughts and information cannot be read without the effort of marshalling one's knowledge, and building cross-connections in the mind—sometimes living with questions burning in the brain for weeks or even years. This is the excitement and challenge of the academic life. It does not suit everyone, but it is too important to be dismissed by criteria of easy but facile understanding from the inadequate vocabulary of 'plain' language.

To apply restrictions of 'plain' for all communication would reduce music to plain-chant, and eliminate Shakespeare and just about everything worth reading except emergency instructions, and perhaps the law, which indeed should be in plain English for all to understand without effort. *The Oxford Companion to the Mind* is a bizarre choice for this 'award' as the full richness of our language is needed to do justice to the human mind.

At first a knitting pattern looks like gobbledygook, but with understanding it offers plain and pearl!

Prof RICHARD GREGORY, FRS

December 17, 1997   Bristol

BETWEEN COVERS

Unsentimental Beatrix Potter

SIR—I disagree profoundly with the spokesperson for Ladybird Books who asserted that my late relative Beatrix Potter would have been more perturbed by current farming practice than by what has happened to her 'Tales' (report, Sept. 15). She was utterly unsentimental about animals.

My father used to recall how, on an occasion when the family had been invited to tea, she cruelly tweaked the neck of a sparrow that was causing some damage in her garden. Generations of children have been chilled by the strongly retributive tone of some of her stories, whilst being charmed by her illustrations and—it is to be hoped—uplifted by the excellence of her English prose style.

It is precisely this blend of fantasy and the hard facts of life, elegantly expressed and beautifully illustrated, which has made the *Tales* such an enduring institution, and which has now been so completely debased by Ladybird.

I cannot imagine parents and grandparents with tears in their eyes presenting to the new baby or toddler copies of books peopled by the vapid cuddly toys shown in your photograph. I doubt whether the new format will succeed—certainly it does not deserve to.

September 19, 1987

MARJORIE HOOLEY (née HEELIS)
Melbourne, Derbys

∼

Earlier protests

SIR—It is not the first time that Frederick Warne & Co. have been perfidious to the memory of Beatrix Potter. In 1956 I had occasion to buy a new copy of *The Tale of Pigling Bland*, the first copy having been lost. My children were indignant when the new copy was read to them, because 'the words are all wrong'. In particular, the 3 ¼-years old was upset because Alexander was no longer 'hopelessly volatile' but had become 'rather excitable'. Another mother wrote to the press about the altered text. Frederick Warne & Co. then confessed that a young editor had considered Miss Potter's text 'unsuitable' and had started to revise the books. The publishers bowed to the protests and reissued *Pigling Bland* in the original text.

Young children love the language of Beatrix Potter, instinctively recognising that her style fits the pictures, and that both are special. There are plenty of supermarket-type books available today, and for Warne's publisher to trot out fashionable clichés, such as it being 'an extremely élitist view' to wish to defend Miss Potter's unique contribution to children's writing, must simply be to conceal the real truth: the firm's present owners wish to make money by such graceless manipulation of her work.

M. JONES
September 21, 1987   Sidmouth, Devon

A resignation matter

SIR—For the past six years I have been the artistic adviser to Frederick Warne for all the Beatrix Potter merchandise, striving during those years to ensure that the reproduction of any Potter image remains as faithful to the original as possible.

Yesterday afternoon I resigned, finding it impossible to reconcile my responsibilities in that field with the Ladybird version of Peter Rabbit and Squirrel Nutkin.

After a lifetime of working in the field of children's books, I cannot be associated with—or indeed understand the necessity for—what I believe to be a debasement of these beloved works of art, a part of our national heritage. I see it as a serious severance of the trust that Beatrix Potter gave to Frederick Warne when she bequeathed them her copyrights, in the reasonable belief that they would be safe in their hands.

For me personally it was ironical that the publication of these bowdlerised versions of two of Beatrix Potter's best loved books occurred while I was in America making known the recently published and exquisite newly originated editions.

Happily, these 'original and authorised' editions are very much available in this country too, and perhaps after the important Beatrix Potter exhibition opening at the Tate Gallery on Nov. 18 our faith in the perpetuation of the true Potter will be regenerated.

JUDY TAYLOR

October 2, 1987 London NW3

Writing into the sunset

SIR—I was amused but far from impressed by David Holloway's article (Weekend, Aug. 4). To my way of thinking it is a re-run of the kind of middle-class, middle-management snobbish thinking which prompted the dedication for my forthcoming, 128th book *JT's Ladies Ride Again*.

The dedication was: 'For all the idiots of the press who have written articles entitled things like The Fastest Pen in Melton Mowbray and filled with the most stupid, snob-orientated pseudo-western jargon *never* to appear on the pages of mine or any other authors' books. May the bluebird of happiness fly over them when it has dysentery, because that is catching.'

I think the basic reason the western has not achieved greater acceptance as high-class literature is because its basic market is working class.

My theory is that people who constantly knock westerns have been lobotomised by parents since childhood into believing that every form of mass entertainment is beneath their lofty intellect, therefore is sub-standard. In the close to 30 years I have been unashamedly writing message-free action-escapism-adventure fiction for the mass market I have managed to sell worldwide around 25 million copies of my books and at least 30 have topped the quarter of a million mark, which to my way of thinking should qualify for me being accepted as a moderately successful author.

Mr Holloway will also find that most people who read westerns have never read *The Virginian* and many I've spoken to said they started it but couldn't finish it.

I feel I should also point out that Zane Grey was supplanted by Louis L'Amour at least 40 years ago and, with all due lack of modesty since his death, I have now taken Louis's place.

The western or the escapist western has never received literary acclaim. Our books just sold and as a professional author that is what counts with me.

J. T. EDSON
August 8, 1990   Columbia River, Oregon

~

London's love of Scots dirt

SIR—In *The Gentleman's Magazine* for 1746 there is a highly aggrieved account of how the Highland Host, otherwise strictly disciplined, had randomly excreted in both home and garden of their seized English billet.

English taste is now more bizarre. While they may not quite have got around to inviting Glaswegian novelists as house guests, from the evidence of James Kelman's Booker Prize (report, Oct. 12) the metropolitan set—for such they are even if two of their number have developed a taste for travelling the road to England—cannot read enough about being dumped on by these gritty Scottish realists.

There was a time when Scots looking in the mirror of English literary culture saw a true image of the stature of their writers. Dr Johnson knew 'Ossian' MacPherson immediately for the phoney he was. Coleridge saw Burns as a great vernacular, democratic poet.

Contemporary English evaluation of Kelman as political radical or creative innovator seems much more suspect. Indeed, if we accept the logic of Kelman's acceptance speech, one could argue that London's endorsement of him as a major writer is symptomatic of the decadence of England's intrusive values.

It is deeply mysterious how the members of Kelman's repetitive line of macho Glaswegians, even in this academic age of self-promotingly paranoid political correctness, have established themselves as icons of suffering humanity. He has nothing of Raymond Carver's pain, tension and vision achieved by a truly pared down style.

Indeed, the real pain of Glasgow is not present in these self-obsessive enclosed works. Much more complex vision is needed to reveal how life is being sucked from men, women, adolescents and children in these drug-dominated vortexes.

At the moment when the Union may be ending, Kelman presents acute symptoms of a deeply disturbing Scottish state of mind. A revisionist history is being fabricated by creative writers and sundry intellectuals which suggests we Scots were not only colonised by the English, but bonded in comparable suffering with the wretched of the earth.

We were indispensable to the British imperial project. The role was not only profitable but to our taste. Heaven forfend an independent Scotland with its intelligentsia in plebeian drag promoting notions of anti-imperial dissent and imperial victimage as our birthright. Heaven help an England so culturally far gone that it endorses such a vision.

ANDREW NOBLE
October 15, 1992   Glasgow

Portrait of a con artist

SIR—Mary Kenny need not agonise over her failure to read *Ulysses* (article, March 19) though it is very brave of her to admit not having done so; it is the Irish equivalent of a Welshman admitting that he is tone-deaf.

Ulysses is in fact quite unreadable for large stretches, and was made deliberately so by its author. 'My wife,' he said, 'has gone to page 27, counting the cover.' The first several chapters of the book are quite enjoyable and written in a perfectly conventional late-nineteenth-century manner.

Many subsequent passages are comic in intent, and some succeed superbly well, but many more are dross. The reason for this is not far to seek: it was normal before the twentieth century got under way for writers to be dependent on the sale of their works to readers, who must necessarily enjoy them, or at least comprehend them, before paying good money for them. A degree of experimentalism (Sterne, Stendhal, Thackeray) was acceptable only insofar as it was successful.

By Joyce's time, however, experimentalism in music and painting had become *de rigueur* for its own sake. If music and painting, then why not literature also, reasoned Eliot and Wyndham Lewis, among others. In order to cash in, it would be necessary only to find patrons (preferably middle-aged ladies with lots of money and no sense) who could be induced to subsidise rubbish that they could not understand for the very reason that there was nothing in it to understand.

In this department, Joyce was the champion scrounger of all time. Textual analysis of *Ulysses* reveals an astonishing correlation between the size of cheques received from these deluded females and consequent obfuscation and self-indulgence (i.e. sloppiness) in the master's work.

No one, therefore, need feel bound to read *Ulysses*, and there are very good reasons why intending writers should not do so. Joyce is not only incomparably the most over-rated writer who has ever lived; he has done more damage to the writing trade than anyone who came before or after him.

We will shortly be celebrating the (bogus) 90th anniversary of Bloomsday, the day on which the action of *Ulysses* is set. It was for some years a mystery why Joyce chose June 16 1904 until solved by myself. This was the day on which he received the first sexual favour he had not paid for, and that from his future wife, Nora.

STAN GEBLER DAVIES

March 28, 1994   Dublin

Stan Gebler Davies (1943–94) was a bohemian Irish journalist.

The Saint's good influence

SIR—The death of Leslie Charteris (obituary, April 17) should remind us of a more general loss. Read the best of his Saint stories, written in the 1930s, and the change becomes immediately clear.

The Saint could be as ruthless as any modern hero ('Damn you, what is your racket?' asked the villain. 'Death', said the Saint in a voice of terrible softness, 'death is my racket'); and his relationship with Patricia Holm would not stand (and did not receive) close examination. But the mood is cheerful, the language—like the

Saint's clothes—immaculate, while the code was chivalrous and the conclusion always triumphant.

Modern thrillers, in contrast, make one feel that there are no good brave causes, that chivalry is a sour joke, that ugly language and brutal behaviour are this world's inescapable norm.

They are, in John le Carré's phrase, 'loser-books' as distinct from 'winner-books', though le Carré's own educated prose and anguished morality saved him from the modern slough. The bleak spirit of modernity and the language accompanying it have spread, more from the highbrow than the lowbrow end of the spectrum—from Graham Greene's 'entertainments' rather than from Mickey Spillane and Hank Jansen.

The literary historian William Vivian Butler once said that anybody who had fallen under the spell of Charteris and his contemporaries, especially in childhood, would be 'forever suspicious of pomposity, subservience and solemnity, and quite powerfully fortified against despair'.

Butler went on: 'Even on his darkest days, he can never entirely silence a mischievous voice drawling that life is a mysterious adventure; that, for all we know, there may be a chuckle instead of a tear at the heart of things; that there's always a way out of the cellar, even if the water's rising past one's neck.'

The truth is that the Saint really was a much better influence than the ungodly who have followed him.

ANTHONY LEJEUNE
April 19, 1993   Pinner, Middx

∼

No wet fish

SIR—Major James Bigglesworth, DSO, MC, DFC, would never recognise himself as the neurotic creature described in your report as rather 'girly' and prone to tears (report, Jan. 28).

True, his creator, Capt W. E. Johns, made him slight, with small, feminine hands, but he was as tough as they came. He might weep over the death of a brother pilot—but then he would fly into battle again.

Biggles was decisive, matter-of-fact and the possessor of a broad grin. In the first story about him, published in 1932, he was a very young RFC officer, feeling the strain of flying in the First World War.

It must be said that he also had an irritating little falsetto laugh, intended to show the tensions of the time. The laugh never recurred in the subsequent 96 books about him.

As Johns is on record as heartily disliking Lawrence of Arabia, whose handshake made him think of wet fish, it seems unlikely he had him in mind as a model for his hero.

However, in *Biggles Flies East* (1935), there is a dashing figure who roams the desert disguised as an Arab—not Biggles, but his arch-enemy, Hauptman Erich von Stalhein.

PIERS WILLIAMS
Bromley, Kent

SIR—Whether or not T. E. Lawrence was W. E. Johns's model for Biggles, Lawrence was certainly the basis of Michael Ransom, in *The Ascent of F6*, by W. H. Auden and Christopher Isherwood (1937), and Private Meek in Bernard Shaw's *Too True To Be Good* (1934).

He was also in part the inspiration of Sandy Arbuthnot in John Buchan's *The Courts of the Morning* (1929). Interestingly, in three earlier Hannay novels the character was based on the MP adventurer Auberon Herbert, who was also the model for the character in the last of the series.

In the course of researching for a new edition of my book, *The Originals*, I have discovered him in D. H. Lawrence's *Lady Chatterley's Lover* (1928), thinly disguised as Colonel C. E. Florence, in whom Lady Chatterley's father 'saw too much advertisement behind all the humility . . . the conceit of self-abasement'.

WILLIAM AMOS
January 30, 1992   Little Langdale, Cumbria

∽

The alternative ending

SIR—The 11 million or so who have been watching *Lady Chatterley* of a Sunday evening should be grateful to Ken Russell for having found a way to end the story at all. Whatever power D. H. Lawrence holds for the reader—and it remains strong, as almost every bookshop contains shelves of even his little-known works—it was not his ability to end a tale.

The three published versions of the story of Lady Chatterley and her gamekeeper all have different, inconclusive endings. In my research for a biography of Lawrence, I have found him to be the bane of current scholars who, with computers, pursue authors in search of the definitive corrected text.

Lawrence himself said, not as a boast, just as a fact, 'I write every book three times'—not copying and revising, 'but literally. After I finish the first draft, I put it aside and write another. Then I put the second aside and write a third.'

This often meant changing characters' names (as indeed the game-keeper is Parkin in the first two versions of *Lady Chatterley*) and certainly altering the fates that overtook them.

What really happened to the fictional Connie and Mellors after Lawrence's final version, which left them parted, but hoping to meet soon, has probably exercised as many minds as what happened to Scarlett and Rhett. Over the years, *The Daily Telegraph's* Peter Simple column, for one, has reported sightings of that odd couple, the Mellorses.

That Russell decided to end his four-part series by packing them off to Canada is not out of keeping with Lawrence's work. Several of his short stories, such as *The Fox* and *Daughters of the Vicar* also end with a passage to Canada.

Emigration is an honourable solution to a socio-sexual impasse in the English novel—as it was, indeed, for Lawrence and the German baroness who, when they fled in 1912, was somebody else's wife.

BRENDA MADDOX
June 28, 1993   London W8

~

Waiting to take the controls

SIR—It is strange that whenever a heroic episode occurs, such as that involving Mr Alan Anderson, the non-pilot who landed an airplane safely after the pilot, his prospective father-in-law, col-lapsed and later died (report, March 31), my phone rings and someone says, 'Hey! What you wrote about in *Flight into Danger* just came true.'

Well, that has happened at least a half dozen times since 1956 when I wrote that story as a television play, later turning it into a novel.

I always congratulate the person concerned for a feat of cool courage and latent skill that only a qualified pilot can truly appreciate and understand.

So here we go again. My phone did ring, and I now snap this ex-RAF pilot's salute to Mr Anderson along with sympathy to the pilot's family.

When I wrote the story of a rusty old ex-fighter pilot—who mentally was me—taking over a big four-engine passenger plane whose pilots had succumbed to food poisoning, then receiving radio instructions from the ground and eventually landing safely, to the best of my knowledge such an incident had not occurred before. It was all my imagination.

As well as those actual incidents, I have had letters from private pilots who have told me that because of my story they had family members learn solely to execute a landing—just in case. And a close friend in California, also ex-air force, for the same reason taught his wife to land their plane. She hated it, still does, but at least knows approximately how.

The trouble is, I've never done it myself outside my imagination.

Occasionally I charter a light plane to go to Florida and relegate my wife to a back seat, seating myself next to the pilot. He's a healthy young fellow, but I wonder: will this time be my turn?

It hasn't happened yet. I'll be 72 next week, and if it's going to, it had better be soon.

April 2, 1992

ARTHUR HAILEY
Nassau, Bahamas

How to study form for the Booker

SIR—Referring to your line-up of the Booker Prize runners (article, Sept. 14), may I offer your readers The Booker Handicap, or How They Brought the Bad News (after Browning):

> *I called in at Ladbroke's, I rang William Hill,*
> *I studied the runners whose chances are nil;*

'Read!' cried the publishers praying for sales.
The bleary-eyed judges sat gravely engrossed,
Deciding which horse would be first past the post.

Oh, will it be Beryl, or will it be John?
Penelope? Brian?—say, who is odds-on?
Will Mordecai lose? Can Antonia win?
The artist thinks rarely of being quids in:
What drives him or her isn't fortune or fame,
But hoping that they will remember your name.

Be kind to the authors, absorbed in their dreams
Of sex, God and Cambridge, and similar themes.
Forget how they bored you, take note of their toil.
Their madness at midnight, their burning of oil.
A tip for the punters: the writer should score
Who goes to the movies and knows less is Moore.

ROGER WODDIS
September 20, 1990   London N13

The satirical poet Roger Woddis (1917–93) was reviewing the finalists for the 1990
Booker Prize for fiction. Beryl Bainbridge, John McGahern, Penelope Fitzgerald,
Mordecai Richler and Brian Moore were defeated by Antonia Byatt with *Possession*.

Don't let James exclude Benson

SIR—In his lively account of the vacant tenancy at Lamb House at
Rye (property page, Oct. 25), Chris Partridge makes no mention of
E. F. Benson's 22 years in the house, from 1918 to 1940.

I suspect this odd omission reflects the selective nature of the
information given to him by the National Trust. Benson was only a
tenant, and because the house was donated by the James family, the
official emphasis remains resolutely on Henry James, with a tendency
to marginalise the Benson connection. This is despite the fact that
James actually lived there for a shorter time (1898 to 1916).

But a potential tenant must be prepared for the fact that
thousands of people visit Lamb House and Rye every year because

Benson lived there and set his much-loved Mapp and Lucia stories in the town: the places are so clearly described that one can easily identify them as one walks about the streets. Nowadays rather fewer people come on account of Henry James—dare I suggest that, however great his work, it just doesn't give as much pleasure to as many people.

Benson's popularity remains undimmed and his six Mapp and Lucia books of the 1920s and 1930s are today as fresh as ever. This is borne out by the fact that a play, *Make Way for Lucia* (starring Angela Thorne, John Wells and Marcia Warren) finished touring Britain only last week, while membership of the Tilling Society hasn't dropped below around 800 for several years.

Benson and James were on amicable terms, and I genuinely dislike finding myself in the position of having to set one against the other in order that Benson be given due recognition. How delightful it would be if the new Lamb House tenant were someone who enjoys *both* authors. Such people do exist.

CYNTHIA REAVELL

November 8, 1995 Rye, East Sussex

Rye story

SIR—While it is true that the National Trust makes little reference to E. F. Benson at Lamb House (letter Nov. 8), the really neglected former resident is his brother, A. C. Benson, who initially held the lease jointly.

Just before the Second World War, when Arthur Mee wrote about Rye in his guide *The King's England*, A. C., novelist and author of the poem *Land of Hope and Glory*, was given a whole paragraph, while E. F. was mentioned only as 'another son of the Archbishop of Canterbury'. Henry James was not mentioned at all.

Viola Bayley, whose home is opposite Lamb, recalls appearing before E. F. in his capacity as magistrate. Then a shy 17-year old, she had been charged with illegal parking.

'It was raining and the gallery was full,' she recalled, 'and he played to it, asking me if I had any previous convictions . . . I felt awful.'

Later that day, Benson came to tea at Ms Bayley's and said to her: 'We had rather a lot of fun this morning, didn't we?' 'I could have killed him,' she observed.

CHRIS PARTRIDGE

November 11, 1995   Petersfield, Hants

Posted from the front

SIR—It does seem sad, and is maybe an indictment of our educational system, that young soldiers in Bosnia and their wives in Germany find it so hard to write letters to each other (report, Dec. 9).

Possibly the Army should introduce into recruit training a basic 'Dear Mum' letter-writing course, on the lines of the obligatory weekly letter home from prep school which, as I recall, was always written on Sunday morning and had to cover more than one side of the paper, after a helpful housemaster had chalked up on the blackboard reminders of the headline events of the week: 'We beat St Cake's 4–0' or 'Matron ran off with the biology master'.

The Navy has always taken writing seriously. Every midshipman had to keep a journal, with sketches, of events on board his ship, which was regularly inspected by his captain. Most mess decks had a resident scribe who, in exchange for 'sippers' or 'gulpers' from the daily tot of rum, would compose suitable letters to send to girl friends.

Letters home are a pleasure to receive, make fascinating family reading in the future, and may be the last remembrance of somebody who did not come home. They may even, like some of the letters from the Great War trenches or Private Wheeler's letters from the Napoleonic wars, prove of lasting historical and literary value.

But in the end, it must surely be militarily essential for serving men and women in the Armed Forces, especially as they become more senior, to be able to express themselves clearly on paper. So why not begin with 'Dear Mum'.

JOHN WINTON

December 10, 1992   Llandyrnog, Denbighs

Dull is the discreet diary

SIR—By bracketing Alan Clark as a diarist with Harold Nicolson and 'Chips' Channon, Julian Critchley confers high praise indeed, and extends the minuscule category of entertaining political diaries (Weekend, June 5).

Politicians make dull diarists as a rule, using the form simply to recast themselves as the unsung tail that wagged the mighty dog of history. Nothing spoils a diary more than an agenda of self-justification.

What distinguishes the few good political ones is—as with all diaries—the character of the writer. This need not be a high character, or even a self-aware one. Reading a great many diaries has brought me to the conclusion that every one, even the most apparently secretive, is written for some kind of conjectural reader, and so presents a slightly heightened image of its writer.

The charm of diary-reading lies not in accepting the version of self which the diarist hopes to present, but reading through that to the real self below. As 'Chips' Channon put it, 'What is more dull than a discreet diary? One might just as well have a discreet soul.' Alan Clark is deliciously indiscreet. The propriety of presenting such indiscretion to the public is a matter of individual conscience, and one can see many reasons why Mr Clark should have decided to do so. Publishers' advances and serial rights may well figure high among them. He has clearly heeded the advice of Mae West: 'Keep a diary and one day it'll keep you.'

Discussing Pepys, Harold Nicolson wrote: 'It is some relief to reflect that to be a good diarist one must have a little snouty, sneeky [*sic*] mind,' but I think he was being unfair to his subject. The quality that Pepys had—and what made him a great diarist—was curiosity. His mind was open to everything, and nothing lay outside the scope of his record.

What makes most politicians' diaries dull is the fact that they are only about politics and restrict other subject matter to details which reflect well on their writers. Refreshingly, Alan Clark has not fallen into this pitfall.

His diaries should, of course, be read with Julian Critchley's recommended accessories: the Fortnum's hamper, the bottle of decent claret and the nubile secretary.

SIMON BRETT
June 8, 1993 Arundel, W. Sussex

Mixing money with poetry

SIR—I write not as a major diplomat but in the much more exalted capacity of a minor poet.

First, I want to thank you for devoting a full leader to poetry and poets (June 21). This was a most generous gesture, especially in these troubled times when most of the space in newspapers is devoted to the latest outrages of the New International Disorder.

Secondly, Al-Mutanabbi, the greatest of Arab poets, declared in a famous line:

> *In this world*
> *There is not glory without money*
> *No money without glory*

I always thought this was a most cynical statement, coming from a poet. Having read your leader on the sad situation of the Poetry Society, I am tempted to think that the old Bard could have been right after all.

GHAZI ALGOSAIBI

June 25, 1993   Ambassador for Saudi Arabia, London W1

LIFE IN PICTURES

British prefer books to art

SIR—Richard Dorment's article (Jan. 1) and David Coke's letter (Jan. 6) on art and its appreciation in Britain make instructive reading.

One may argue with some conviction that some nations outshine others at some form of art—the Italians are manifestly brilliant at composing opera, the Germans showed a genius for writing classical music and the French have maintained a superior record of creativity in the visual arts. Where then does Britain fit in artistic excellence?

The musical and choral traditions of the Welsh and northern Englanders have flourished for centuries and the visual arts have enjoyed sporadic peaks since the mid-18th century.

However, the British achieve their creative apotheosis elsewhere; what must be recognised is that they are essentially a literary people rather than an artistic people. My assertion is supported by elementary market research.

The middle-class homes I have visited often have few pictures—maybe an ancestral portrait or two—and perhaps a watercolour or print or two next to a doggy calendar on the wall; but lo! the bookcases in the room(s) are groaning under the weight of books. This fact reveals the dominant and dynamic element in British culture, which is literature.

The British may be a little different in their art appreciation from the rest of Europe but the respect for artistic creativity is extant. I do not share the belief that we appear to have a disproportionate number of philistines in Britain as compared to the Continent. What we do have is a disproportionately vocal group of philistines whose provocative remarks are sometimes media-worthy.

NICHOLAS STACEY
January 9, 1992   London SW1

Nicholas Stacey (1920–97) was a Hungarian-born businessman specialising in takeovers.

~

The duties of an art critic

SIR—Richard Dorment condemns me for suggesting that those who sponsor the annual re-hanging at the Tate Gallery should put an end to the perpetual confusion there by withdrawing their sponsorship (article, Feb. 26).

The Tate's prime responsibilities are as the national reserves of British art, modern foreign paintings and modern sculpture. In all these fields its displays should offer a measure of permanence that reassures the intending visitor from elsewhere in the kingdom and from abroad.

It is not the business of a national museum to mount a merry-go-round of brief exhibitions and displays that reflect the whimsy and caprice of a director—or to function as his plaything and the instrument of his personal aggrandisement.

Sponsors of the arts, alas largely ignorant of the subject, should not assume that those who are trustees and directors are, by virtue of these positions, creatures of divine wisdom incapable of flawed judgment. They should pay heed to criticism soundly argued, recognising that blind sponsorship is irresponsible.

Without financial support specifically for the exercise, the upheavals at the Tate would cease, and the gallery would be compelled to demonstrate with the permanent display of its finest possessions its claimed 'simple chronological path through the collections'.

This would not in any way prevent it from maintaining a rolling programme of small exhibitions that reveal and review the gallery's extensive holdings of works by less significant artists.

Mr Dorment damns critics weary of contemporary art, and abuses them for discarding the rule of Lawrence Gowing (a wretched painter) that 'the duty of a critic is to lavish unalloyed praise upon the artist'. It is, on the contrary, his duty to use his eye and experience to tell the truth. If he sees nothing of consequence in an artist's work, the critic must betray neither himself nor his readers with timorous pretence. To cry 'rubbish' may indeed be the only honest response.

Mr Dorment, I observe, used the words 'terrible', 'half-baked' and 'blowsy' in one short paragraph on an exhibition that did 'incalculable harm', only last January.

March 2, 1993
BRIAN SEWELL
London W8

Tracing the real Mr Christian

SIR—As a direct descendant and biographer of Fletcher Christian, who led the mutiny on the *Bounty* in 1789, I was intrigued to see his supposed portrait (report, Jan. 12) compiled from drawings of descendants on Pitcairn Island by Merseyside police. Unfortunately, the project seems wildly off the mark.

There is a special case for not using his descendants when looking for the face of Fletcher Christian. Of the three children he fathered by his Tahitian wife, his daughter died a spinster and both his sons married older, full-blooded Tahitian women. Thus Christian's grandchildren were three-quarter Tahitian, and when married to other half-caste Pitcairners, would produce children with more Tahitian than European blood.

Christian was indeed dark-skinned and brown-eyed, possibly an echo of his Celtic background; who is to say that his mother was not the donor of these characteristics? Most Christians on Pitcairn Island have descent from his older son, but there are many more on Norfolk Island, descended from his second son, who might have inherited a stronger dose of Christian genes.

No, the only way to determine what Christian *might* have looked like must be to use images only of his immediate ancestors and relatives. This is precisely what Adrian Teal, a student at Bristol University, is doing. He is reconstructing Fletcher's portrait from those of his first cousins, the Lord Chief Justice Lord Ellenborough and Bishop Law of Bath and Wells, as well as others.

So far, Bligh remains our best guide. He approved the painting by Robert Dodd in which Fletcher Christian stands on *Bounty*'s stern, taunting Bligh in a small boat as breadfruit plants are hurled overboard. Bligh must have advised on Christian's appearance, and must also have agreed to Christian standing precisely where his commander's private latrine should be—a wicked visual pun.

GLYNN CHRISTIAN
London W11

January 20, 1994

Arty fog floating across the Mersey

SIR—As a Liverpool artist who is bewildered by the liturgy of thanksgiving rising incense-like over the Mersey for the new Tate gallery (report, May 24), I would like to add some thoughts in another direction.

The fact that the new gallery is to be a museum of modern art only was not decided by any democratic consultation with the people. It is imposed upon a population of which 99 per cent find most modern art, especially abstract, to be hokum. It has no standards of excellence that can be verified or tested. It simply hands over the keys of power to the art establishment mystagogues whose explanatory texts are as odd and scattered as pelican droppings. Their use of English also has the disadvantage of being about as clear as Sanskrit to most ordinary people.

In the postwar years this particular group has seized control of the inner corridor of artistic power—and this really explains how they control and tease a frustrated and often angry population with exhibits, sculptures, paintings the size of cricket pitches, bricks, old lavatory doors and other such sensitive awarenesses of hidden life on our planet.

The underlying warning is clear as regards the general threat to democratic life in this country by small élites who claim special knowledge and browbeat Government bureaucrats into pliant service. That there is increasingly always some small group who know what is best for us has become such a repeat story that the masses lie trussed up like Gulliver—and in this case forced to pay for an awful lot of ephemeral trash.

The new Tate is an almost weird, indeed kinky, response to a city that only seven years ago could have been burned to the ground because of its grim problems, particularly unemployment. Marie Antoinette could not have bettered this one.

But for many citizens, after several trailers for the opening ceremony with metal scaffold sculpture in the adjacent dock waters—and one cost £15,000—Marie Antoinette's cake begins to look like solid good sense.

In all, it makes one think of another historical precedent—that of Nero fiddling while Rome burned—a classical disjunction of cultural activity with an historic event. The siting of a gallery of modern art on the Mersey has a similar air of misplacement about it.

FRANK HENDRY
May 27, 1988 Liverpool

Timely reminder

SIR—Having attended the opening of the Royal Academy exhibition (review, Sept. 17) I support the inclusion of Marcus Harvey's portrait of Myra Hindley.

Although born after the Moors murders took place, I remember the revulsion it caused my parents when they first explained these heinous crimes to me. My mother felt that Hindley and Brady had introduced a new note of depravity into the British consciousness, and therefore they should never be freed.

Although I wholeheartedly agree with this point of view, I was moved by the portrait. At the height of Hindley's campaign to reinvent and liberate herself, this picture is a timely reminder of the gravity of her offence. The grainy effect, seen from a distance, is her particular fingerprint of evil. The magnificently framed face is a stain of corruption she would somehow wash away. Close to, the tiny handprints are eloquent testimony to the weakness of her small victims.

Lady DALMENY
September 18, 1997 London SW3

Resignation time at the Academy?

SIR—John Ward is a hero. So are the other three Royal Academicians whose resignations you have reported. You can argue about whether or not the stuff in Sensation is art until the cows come home to be dissected by Damien Hirst. This is not the point.

The point is that relatives of children tortured and killed in the most horrifyingly debased way are very much alive and have made it clear that *they* are tortured by the so-called 'portrait' of Hindley (and perhaps its proximity to statues of naked children covered in genitalia). We are human beings first, artists second. Academicians who failed to control the doings of the paid employee should be ashamed of themselves. As individuals they surely would not treat injured people so callously. Why do it collectively in the name of art?

It is surely ironic that this 'portrait', a blow-up of a photograph albeit in hand-shaped 'dots', is defended, while Ward is criticised for painting too many portraits for the good of his oeuvre. Ward's portraits, especially his groups and his girls, are surely among the most distinguished of his generation. Indeed, he was lionised even by the press, for a bevy of them appeared in the RA Summer Exhibition about 10 years ago.

Portraiture is not only one of the most difficult of disciplines, it has also produced some of the world's most universally acknowledged masterpieces: the *Mona Lisa* and the late self-portraits of Rembrandt. The young need encouraging down this difficult path.

Only this year John Ward dominated the distinguished judges on the panel for our Ondaatje Prize for Portraiture, with the result that the youngest and least stuffy finalist was selected.

The RA will be the poorer without John Ward, but he was right to go. If we want the Academy to stand for something decent, the rest of us should terminate our Friends' subscriptions forthwith.

DAPHNE TODD
October 18, 1997   President, Royal Society of Portrait Painters
London SW1

~

My name is . . .

SIR— I find as a past-president of the Royal Institute of Oil Painters— a society always noted by the initials ROI—and as a member of the Royal Society of Portrait Painters (where one's affiliation is marked by the letters RP) that letters can arrive addressed to Mr Pproi or to Mr Rp.

Since painters hope that their names might register with picture buyers, perhaps I would have a chance of that happening if I were to adopt one of these as an alternative to my own less exotic version.

MICHAEL NOAKES
May 23, 1997   London NW8

STRANGE DESIGNS

Power of the architect

SIR—In one sentence, Gavin Stamp (in his critique of the Clore Gallery, April 4) summed up the argument against today's architectural thinking: 'a building ought to be more than an object to be photographed, published and praised'. Today's architects have, for so long, been mounted on pedestals created by constant mutual praise from within their cloistered profession, that they are no longer designing buildings that are practical; they are obsessed by concept.

Architecture is all about organisation of space to fulfill the proposed user's requirements, while ideally at the same time being aesthetically pleasing. Modern architecture has become so involved with intricate concepts that utility and practicality have become totally obscured. Concept has now become an excuse for an architect's inability to transpose a client's requirements into good design. What, for example, does Stirling really mean when he claims that he was 'trying to maintain a conversation between the new building and the old', with reference to the new Gallery? The conceptual rut has now got to such a ridiculous stage that architects can now wax lyrical about their amazing ideas to glassy eyed clients, and actually dictate to those clients how the building should be used. Paradoxically, the clients' requirements should, of course, dictate the design of the building, not the other way round.

It is time for architects to stop covering up gross inadequacies by mutual adoration and the awarding of undeserved Gold Medals, and review their responsibility to society. They are there for their clients' use. At the moment, they have too much power, too much say and the added bonus of having a captive public who are, on the whole, uninformed and easily led by this group of people with massively inflated superiority complexes. It is up to the public to curb this scarring of our urban landscapes with such monstrosities as the Lloyd's building, the Clore Gallery *et al*. Architects must not be allowed to dictate how we live.

IAN RUTTER

April 8, 1987   London SE21

~

Problem of matching facts and legend

SIR—I have read with amusement of events in Rhodes involving the lump of stone supposed to be the hand of the Colossus. A great deal has been written and said about the Colossus in the last few days, but in fact we know very little about it.

The reference book of 1891 (Seyffert) gives its height as 280ft, another of 1938 gives it as 120ft, and 100ft has recently been quoted in the press. In fact, we have no exact data on the height, except that it was the tallest statue of antiquity.

The Colossus did not straddle the harbour, as popularly supposed, but stood to one side. Therefore, when it fell due to earthquake or tidal wave, it had a 50 per cent chance of falling into the sea or onto the land. But we know it fell on the land because the proper casing of the statue was sold off to a scrap merchant. Since the statue was placed in copper, and this was taken away, it follows that all that could have been left were the remains of the armature and the infill material—historically and artistically worthless, and unidentifiable.

The Colossus is listed as one of the Wonders of the Ancient World, along with six others, including the Hanging Gardens of Babylon. However, the excavator of Babylon, Robert Koldway, found that the Hanging Gardens were supported on only two tiers of barrel vaulting, each with a 10ft to 11ft span, the structure overall being about 45ft high.

Perhaps we need to scale down our notions of the Colossus, which are inflated from very sketchy evidence, a form of modern mythology.

If nothing else the recent saga of the Colossus goes to show that the silly season arrives early in Greece. Reputedly, Melina Mercouri asked the chief archaeologist at the Ministry of Culture if the recovered lump of stone was part of the Colossus. He replied: 'Never in a month of Sundays!'

PANOS ARVANITAKIS

July 10, 1987 London SW13

Fantasy foresaw conflagration

SIR—The burning (report, Sept. 1) of Uppark on the Sussex Downs, above the sea, is very tragic. A masterpiece of William and Mary architecture, the house was redolent of historic associations, both upstairs and downstairs.

When first I saw it, Uppark was relatively unknown, untouched, a sleeping beauty, presided over by owners who had inherited in a most romantic manner. Totally dedicated, they literally sacrificed their lives to its conservation.

It is not, I trust, sentimental to say that before Uppark became a public resort, one left it after each visit wondering how such a magical house could survive in this rude age. Would it not one day vanish into thin air, leaving behind but the memory of a glorious anachronism?

Uppark's sad end calls to mind the forgotten minor classic, *The Last of Uptake*. Could Simon Harcourt-Smith in writing this enchanting fantasy, and Rex Whistler in illustrating it with exquisite vignettes at the height of the last war, have had Uppark in mind? And could they have had prescience of its ultimate fate?

Whistler's illustration shows a house in a very different style, yet one which has similar shape and certain superficial resemblances, such as the steps in the front and a portico in place of Uppark's pediment. The fictional Uptake was, we are told, situated just off the South Coast: perhaps in Wessex, or even in West Sussex, if the names in the neighbouring villages are anything to go by.

For it was 'where the Bearminster Road parted company with that which led to Dropping Camden, through Lesser Riddance, and Caudle-on-the-Marsh' that the ladies Tryphena and Deborah witnessed from their carriages the last of Uptake. 'Suddenly, a flame blossomed out of it, like a lovely flower, was joined by another, and yet more, till there was a bed of great petunias. They swayed in the moaning wind, these flowery flames; next there came a low rumble,

sparks like fireworks for a victory, and the whole of Uptake was
roaring and crackling.'

JAMES LEES-MILNE

September 4, 1989   Badminton, Glos

James Lees-Milne (1908–97) was a biographer and historian who played an important
part in setting up the National Trust's Country House scheme.

Unsuitable home for the Trust

SIR—How can the National Trust justify spending a five-figure sum
on purchasing a former council house, just three rooms up, three
down, in Allerton, Liverpool, just because it belonged to the family
of the Beatle Paul McCartney (report, Nov. 21)?

Without wishing to give offence, it must be said that this is a mean
and architecturally worthless terrace property, typical of hundreds
of others built in 1952 to the lowered specifications for public
building permitted by the then Housing Minister Harold Macmillan.

The founders of the National Trust 100 years ago were a pretty
bizarre group of people, but not so lacking in a scale of values as to
wish to waste money on a house too small to open to the public.
Their aim was 'to preserve places of historic interest or natural
beauty permanently for the benefit of the nation'. The Trust clearly
needs time to reflect on what values it wishes to uphold.

Other questions present themselves. Were there not other more
appropriate bodies who could have acquired this property, if it were
widely thought worthy of preservation? Are the interiors to be
preserved as they are, or is it to become a lovingly created museum
of working-class taste in interior design in the early 1960s?

And what projects has the Trust had to put on hold as a result of
this misjudged acquisition?

Finally, there must be quite a lot of worthless houses associated
with pop singers: has the Trust now a policy of acquiring these on a
regular basis?

DAVID WATKIN

November 25, 1995   Cambridge

Dubious benefit of skyscrapers

SIR—I am surprised that the City of London planner Peter Rees suggested the demolition of the NatWest Tower and its replacement with the world's tallest building (report, May 5).

When Mr Rees refused planning permission for an office tower 108 metres high at London Wall in April 1989, he explained: 'The City does not need any more high landmark buildings.'

He had a point. The truth is that the moment somebody embarks on the highest building, somebody else will plan to build one that is, at least, three feet taller.

Sixty per cent of costs of high buildings are engineering services, such as lifts and air conditioning; and nobody has yet quantified the costs of absenteeism due to working in such an artificial environment.

From a commonsense point of view, tall city buildings, which are in effect glass boxes, are highly uneconomic from the point of view of energy since in the summer they heat up and have to be cooled; in the winter they leak heat and have to be warmed up. In slender towers like NatWest the usable floor space is also extremely awkward.

In fact, the office tower form, as it has been developed, is largely a product of restrictive planning requirements, high land values and fashion. The history of the planning codes reveals that the starting point of the plot-ratio concept, as developed by Lord Holford after the Second World War, was not concerned to limit building bulk as such. It was to prevent concentration of office workers attracted by large building complexes, which would otherwise overload the transport and traffic system.

Policy has been elaborated over the years by bolting on various other requirements, but it would be very difficult to argue that there is much science in this; if there were we would not have the repeated juvenile calls for architects to construct the tallest building in the world.

Another consideration is that if the world's tallest building replaced the NatWest Tower, presumably it would also be the world's lengthiest building (timewise) to evacuate in the event of explosion or fire. Can this be regarded as progress?

After the World Trade Centre blast in New York, it took

practically all day to evacuate the building as the lifts are immobilised in an emergency.

Many occupants were taken to hospital suffering from exhaustion through walking down to the ground.

H. C. S. FERGUSON

May 10, 1992 London SW3

STAGE CRAFT

Decline of the panto

SIR—Christopher Fry's 80th birthday last Friday (Dec. 19) reminded me that the traditional Christmas pantomime season was upon us. I remembered that the charming Christmas panto written for the Marylebone Children's Theatre in 1946 was based on an Italian *commedia dell' arte* plot. In it Harlequin, complete with slapstick and a string of sausages, at first obstructed and finally helped the love-match of Pierrot and Columbine.

Since then the tenor of our pantos seems to me to have taken a sorry turn. *The Oxford Companion to the Theatre* defines pantomime as 'A word which has drastically changed its meaning over the years.' It occurs to me that recent changes have been even more drastic.

The *Companion* explains how in Britain the word (derived from the Latin *pantomimus*, though it must be Greek in origin) was eventually applied to a nineteenth-century entertainment, starring elderly comics, the Dames, in which the leading actress, the Principal Boy, came to play the young hero in a breeches role; and how this Yuletide jollification was turned into a hotch-potch of music-hall acts of doubtful propriety. 'A proper pantomime,' the *Companion* tells us, used to be a colloquialism for 'a state of confusion'. In our electronic age, with the advent of TV humour, the 'confusion' has clearly got out of hand. Gone are the days when youngsters, of either sex, could be taken to the panto without embarrassment. Today's jokes are bluer than ever and the stage-business seems, in the words of a recent critic, to 'revolve around the pelvis'.

Unlike Christopher Fry, the authors of today's pantos avoid an appeal to the brain or the heart. The 'middle of Fortune's favours', to borrow a phrase from *Hamlet*, seems to be their main target. Raucous, charmless, amplified music deafens the ears, the dialogue is banal, and the intellectual and aesthetic level of the gags is often plainly insulting. In olden days, to quote *Hamlet* once more, 'There was no offense in it.'

I wonder what Fry would make of today's pantos if he chanced to see any of them. There can be no denying that the mindless trash borrowed from television is largely to blame. Here I must except Danny La Rue, who believes that good, clean fun is far superior to the smut his rivals in show business are peddling today.

WILLIAM JAGGARD
August 24, 1987   London WI

~

Directors' power as employers

SIR—I find it reprehensible that *The Daily Telegraph* should lower itself to the level of the tabloid press to report with snide frivolity (Nov. 7) the splendid Gulbenkian-financed inquiry into the training of theatre, film and television directors.

Your correspondent refers to the theatre as 'a notably temperamental profession'. I have seen temperament in the cathedral close, in athletics stadia and the groves of academe, but never, in 48 years, in the theatre.

No one—not even a drama critic—can tell from seeing a theatrical performance whether a certain effect was the idea of the director, the actor or the aunt of either. It is a sad truth that young actors now leaving drama schools will find that 85 per cent of their future work is in television, and they are taught that the director is omnipotent.

This is, indeed, a sad change from the days when Lynn Fontanne said: 'I have always done everything a director asked me to do—unless I disagreed with him.' And Ralph Richardson declared: 'Directors? I always say "Good Morning" to them, and "Did you have a good breakfast?"'

The report shows that the basic problem is that directors now run theatres, and are thus the employers. They have power beyond their craft. If an actor wants to work again he must shut up and do as he is told.

DONALD SINDEN

November 13, 1989　　　　　　　　　　　　　London SW1

Value of catcalls from the gods

SIR—To boo, or not to boo (article, June 21)? To a gallery first-nighter in the Forties it was a nice question.

Why should the actors always bear the brunt of our disapproval when the author or director was usually the target? On the other hand, a flop is a flop, and why not say so then and there?

We galleryites were still a threat in the Fifties and sometimes in the Sixties (by which time I had moved down to the stalls). By then the managers, suspecting plots, decided to counter the risk of ill will from aloft by either closing 'the gods' on opening nights, or putting up the prices grotesquely—they are now about a third of the cost of a front stall, whereas in my day a seat in the gallery was only an eighth of the top price.

So 'the gods' no longer exercise their old sway, but a voice from that quarter was not always mischievous. The gallery was often the first to cheer, and to check inaudibility, with a bold cry from the darkness of 'Speak up, please!' It might be disruptive, but in the era before our players lost the art of making themselves heard without a microphone, it could be effective.

Now that nobody knows when a first night is, because of the preview system, and the overpriced gallery is generally empty, it is left to the nobs in the stalls to have their say; and, as Mr Farrell reminds us, they won't.

ERIC SHORTER

June 28, 1990　　　　　　　　　　　　　Bidborough, Kent

Critical gestures

SIR—Eric Shorter is right in saying that it is not appropriate nowadays for critics to lead the booing (letter, June 28).

Such self-denying ordinance was established as far back as 1930 when the impresario Sir Charles Cochran described the etiquette, 'which does not allow critics to express by applause their approval of performances witnessed by them in their official capacity, does not forbid them to convey to their colleagues or lay neighbours by agonised countenance, crude gestures of disdain, hoarsely murmured comments, deep or fitful sleep, the pain or weariness which they suffer so heroically in the cause of duty'. This was written long before Mr Shorter became a galleryite or critic.

PETER COTES
July 2, 1990   Chipping Sodbury, Oxon

~

Who hurt most?

SIR—Further to Stephen Fry's estimate of critics and criticism (Commentary, Nov. 22), a couple of years ago I was severely criticised by a theatrical critic—not so much for anything I had done in my performance, but merely for my being present in the production concerned.

While the critic caused me a somewhat uneasy breakfast, I contented myself with the knowledge that I had given him a perfectly ghastly evening.

JEREMY SINDEN
November 28, 1991   London NW10

Jeremy Sinden (1950–96) was the son of Sir Donald Sinden and one of the most promising farceurs of his generation.

~

All tosh about talking posh

SIR—Robert Gore-Langton complains that practically nobody in the theatre nowadays can do an upper-class accent convincingly (article, June 3). The truth is, they never could.

It has always been the hardest accent of all to pin down, because the upper classes are forever changing it, just to keep it exclusive. What actors used to be taught was something called the King's

English. (We never got round to calling it the Queen's English, perhaps because she never spoke it.)

In the days when actors were still the glass of fashion and the mould of form they were expected to be the repository of an ideal English that avoided both the braying mispronunciations of the aristocrat and the glottal stops of the cockney. It was an accent often aspired to by both ends of the social scale.

Noël Coward's famous clipped delivery, which he developed simply through compensating for lack of lung power (he had TB in his youth), was widely adopted by his middle and upper-class contemporaries.

In the Sixties the long overdue social revolution in the theatre also managed to produce some ninnies who decided that the King's English was no longer acceptable in any circumstances. All manner of spurious regional and urban accents were suddenly to be heard in green-rooms throughout the land. One celebrated actress is said to have flattened her a's overnight.

It wasn't until *Brideshead Revisited* and the films of the E. M. Forster novels that upper-class accents began to be in demand again.

But by this time Standard English was dead. It was abandoned even by the BBC, its final act being the shedding of Tony Scotland and Peter Barker from the last bastion of the spoken word, Radio 3.

So, the upper-class accent is now just as much a 'character' accent as Mummersetshire used to be. The only really watertight accent is the one you use all day—the one you're really not conscious of.

I was once in a play with an elderly actor who had made a successful career playing military men and country squires by dint of a fine natural moustache and never pronouncing his final g's.

The director suggested that as he was now playing a general of the Habsburg Empire, it might be more plausible if he gave up dropping his g's. 'Droppin' me g's?' he said in astonishment. 'What are you talkin' about?'

PAUL DANEMAN
June 5, 1993   London SW15

~

Groat for the Globe

SIR—In your stately columns (article, Nov. 16), a scurvy knave, one Robert Gore-Langton, doth ask, if William Shakespeare had not been born, who then would be the first playwright of this scepter'd isle? He doth elect Sir Noël Coward, Ben Jonson and Christopher Marlowe, but that way madness lies.

When we have matched our rackets to these balls, cry, out vile jelly! For he doth still others name: Bennett and Ayckbourn, Wycherley and Wilde, Massinger and Dickens (how he earns a place i' the story puzzles the will). All these are in his flowing cups freshly remember'd. Doth this varlet deny that, if the Bard had not been born, all these are nothing, the world and all that's in't is nothing, nor nothing have these nothings if Will be nothing?

But pardon, gentles all, for yet methinks this hempen home-spun hath a point. 'Tis not that Will was born that frights us so. What offends unto heaven is those who do perform his matchless works, and profit from him to such excess that, surfeiting, the appetite may sicken and so die.

Yet prithee hold! I have a device to make all well. Suppose that, for evr'y play of Master Shakespeare that sundry players strut out, a charge is levied by some Exchequer of the Drama—a royalty, a half per cent, no more, exacted by an Act of Parliament. O my masters, there would be such funds as to make our National Lottery seem a raffle in a Sunday school. And with the revenue so amassed, the theatre would profit mightily—and most mightily, forsooth, the writers and producers of new plays, more than may be dreamt of in your philosophy. Think on't.

RONALD HARWOOD
November 20, 1993   London SW10

Creative fear

SIR—I was concerned to read of three-year-old Morris Mitchener's terror at a recent production of *Peter Pan* (report, March 4). As someone working on children's fears, I know how deeply children experience fear and how angry parents may be when some image or event, among the mass of potentially frightening stimuli, triggers a long-lasting reaction in their children.

Morris's response, however, reminded me of an event recently described in a seminar given by David Edgar, whose play *Pentecost* earned the praise of *Daily Telegraph* critics. When Edgar was about three years old, his parents took him to a production of *Beauty and the Beast*. When the Beast came on stage, the young David screamed in terror.

His parents, hoping to ease his fear by proving to him that the Beast was really a very nice man, took him backstage during the interval, whereupon he calmly shook hands with the actor playing the Beast.

All seemed well for a calmer second half, and he bravely took his seat, now well schooled in the difference between illusion and reality. When the Beast appeared again, however, the wiser child let out another scream of terror.

This trauma, for David Edgar, gave birth to the determination that whatever he would do in life, he would be involved in making that magic, with the magicians.

A powerful response to illusion and drama may be far from damaging.

Dr TERRI APTER
Clare Hall, Cambridge

SIR— Our five-year-old daughter thoroughly enjoyed the production, which was excellently portrayed. The use of a semi-circular stage and the special effects were exceptional, and the production deserves only praise.

Our daughter thought the crocodile very well represented, and at no time showed any distress. Her only confusion arose from the fact that Mr Darling and Captain Hook were played by the same actor.

She was so prone to nightmares after such programmes as *Power Rangers* and *VR Troopers* that we had to stop her seeing them. We had no such problems after *Peter Pan*.

(Mrs) ANGELA BROWN
Clacton-on-Sea, Essex

SIR—I have clear, and still troubled, memories of my parents taking me to the Gaumont Cinema in Epsom to see Walt Disney's *Peter Pan*, around 1954.

As I spent most of the film on the floor, peeking over the back of the chair, particularly whenever Captain Hook appeared, I am today instructing my solicitors to prepare my case.

My only question is whom to sue: Walt Disney, J. M. Barrie or the Gaumont?

MARTIN HIGHMAN
Grayshott, Surrey

SIR—While reading about the family who are seeking compensation for their son's distress at *Peter Pan*, I suffered nausea, apoplexy and news rage. I am thinking of suing them.

MICHAEL ROTHWELL
March 6, 1996   Woking, Surrey

~

Dry wit

SIR—With reference to your correspondence about the dry martini:

Many years ago I appeared in an American comedy at Her Majesty's Theatre in the Haymarket. During the course of the action I had to mix two dry martinis. Acting on the instructions of my director—the late Robert Morley—I carried out the accepted routine regarding gin and ice.

I then produced the vermouth bottle, to which a scent and spray bulb had been attached. One brief puff over the top of the mixture produced one of the best laughs of the evening.

IAN CARMICHAEL
April 2, 1996   Whitby, North Yorks

STYLE CHANGES

Mod origins of the white sock

SIR—The assertion made in your continuing correspondence on the outbreak of white socks among Sandhurst cadets attributes their origins to suedeheads—'a smart Seventies version of skinheads'. This does not go far enough.

White socks were championed much earlier by the fastidious Mods of the Sixties who, as white-collar workers, favoured a tailored Italian suit in contrast to the rebel uniforms of greasers and teddy boys. Worn with slip-on shoes beneath 14 in. trouser bottoms, which were cut deliberately short to reveal the ankle, the white sock aimed to highlight the intricate footwork of dancing feet, this being a supreme activity through which Mods scored peer points.

All Britain's postwar sub-cultures have been unique products of our enduring class system, led by the young for whom politics has seldom provided the outlet it does in Europe and beyond. Their codes are strictly defined by class, dress and music.

For Mods, originally self-styled Modernists, their reaction to the disintegration of working-class traditions in the upwardly mobile Sixties was to adopt the black music of transatlantic immigrants—Motown, ska and jazz—and clothes from both North America and the Continent more sharply cut than any available in Britain.

Imports included the Ivy League jacket, Italian box suit, Perry Como and French crew haircuts; in addition to fashion from France came the innovative *discothèque*. Overseas student haunts such as *La Discothèque* and *Le Kilt* offered Londoners opportunities to dance nonstop and, in attracting Mods into Soho from the East End and counties along the Thames estuary, gave birth directly to the obsession for living for the long weekend.

During the Seventies the white sock dived underground with the black soul-music scene, to resurface—sported no less totemically by fashion-conscious dance tribes known as soul-boys—along with squeaky clean wedge haircuts, peg trousers and loafers.

By 1982, when the elite new night-clubbing scene went mainstream, Marks & Spencer was reporting significant sales of its white towelling sock.

Even after the emphatically working-class Dr Martens black leather lace-up had changed footwear fashion among all classes of British youth during the so-called 'style decade', the white sock thrived to emphasise the essential change which had overtaken popular music: from guitar-led rock to drum-led dance music.

What seems remarkable for a garment so naff is that for 30 years white socks have remained the acme of style among the acne set from 'Ackney.

DAVID JOHNSON
September 10, 1990   London W8

Lure of the right cardigan

SIR—I was delighted to read Claudia FitzHerbert's Commentary (Nov. 27). But she is wrong to suggest that the clothes women most enjoy wearing are not those which make them most attractive to men.

It is true that my first intention is to make the woman herself feel happy, and to give her clothes in which she can move freely, relax and be at ease.

However, I also believe that it is only by allowing women the pleasures of good fabrics and comfortable styling that their true sexuality can be seen.

For too long women have allowed themselves to be victims of the idea that they need to be trussed up like chickens in order to be attractive to men. The men you attract by using clothes as a barricade are not actually worth attracting.

To a woman with any nous, dressing for yourself turns out to be the same thing as dressing for the opposite sex. The right cardigan, worn in the right way, can drive men mad.

NICOLE FARHI

December 4, 1992 London W1

Case for a gentlemanly calf

SIR—As Stanley Harris points out (letter, Dec. 7), a finely turned leg was a masculine attribute much admired and sought after by gentlemen of style and virility in the past. However, it is wrong to imagine that the obsession ended with the eighteenth-century.

A good leg continued to be a sociological indicator for most of the nineteenth-century, when male sex appeal was to do with power and wealth—and the impeccable tailoring they could command. For a gentlemen, the erogenous zone was the calf.

In *The Whole Art of Dress* (1830), the anonymous writer wrote that tight pantaloons were 'certainly the most proper and becoming in every point of view'. However, if their legs were disappointing, he advised 'recourse to art to supply the defects . . . in which case a slight degree of stuffing is absolutely requisite, but the greatest care and circumspection should be used'.

As late as 1879, in Meredith's *The Egoist*, Sir Willoughby Patterne was the cynosure of all eyes because, as that shrewd commentator Mrs Mountstuart Jenkinson pointed out, 'you see, he has a leg'. The comment made clear that Sir Willoughby was more than a cut above his fellows in social aplomb as much as sex appeal.

In late Victorian times, a prominent calf was considered one of the signs of a gentleman and a good tailor could work wonders with the shanks of even the least well-blessed. No wonder the Pooters of this world were so envious of the well-tailored gentleman—an expression which in those days was almost a tautology—for the instant sex appeal his expensive tailor could give him.

Envy takes its revenge and the twentieth century has seen male fashion reduced to such a level that the man whose calves are dressed in Savile Row has no sartorial advantage over Groucho Club man in his ill-shaped suit from a top Italian designer. Now the only developed calves seen on the streets belong to cyclist messengers, whose appearance would not have pleased Mrs Mountstuart Jenkinson. For her, male anatomy could be highlighted, but never exposed.

Surely what is now required is not a rash of hairy legs in Sloane Street but a return to tailoring that will bring the male leg back into sexual prominence, not only for the young but also for those who parade the pantheons of power. Perhaps *Mrs* Conrad Black should take a page in your newspaper to berate the fashion gurus who, by ignoring the male leg, deprive us all of the doubtless pleasing sight of her husband's well-turned calves.

COLIN McDOWELL
London W9

January 9, 1993

Uniform of the gentleman

SIR—Nigel Reynolds is disturbed by the men's clothes which he saw at the recent shows in Paris (article, July 8) because he cannot dismiss them as unattractive. He is right. He is worried, though, because he does not know where and when he can wear them. It is clear that the man's suit—an English invention, I must add—is still worn by men at all times when respect for tradition and hope for an ordered future prevail.

The design of the suit contains many features which respect its history. The fastening over to the right gave a man access to his sword on the left. The button hole on the right lapel was not put there to take a flower, but for a button fastening at the neck. The fronts of a jacket are curved as they were when the coat was a riding jacket.

If these rules are not obeyed, the suit loses its power and becomes 'casual gear'. Of course the suit was once casual gear: hence its official name 'lounge suit'. The strength of its status was enlarged when Edward VIII decreed immediately after his accession that it could replace the frock coat, demanded sternly by his father for visits to the Palace.

The suit is the uniform of the gentleman. Casual gear, which is increasingly popular, represents freedom from the restraints of tradition in the design and the manner that dictate the appropriateness of the occasion. It allows colour and comfort to be used liberally.

Mr Reynolds says he might wear some of it to the office. I venture to suggest that he would be happy in a really modern suit—having the comfort of Armani's lightness and suppleness of manufacture with the tradition of English taste.

The suit is not a piece of stuffy uniform. It is a living thing, constantly changing. Remember that the modern commercially made and marketed garment is only a substitute for the bespoke job. Any development in the shaping and styling of a suit which is not acceptable by our famous traditional tailors will not last.

Sir HARDY AMIES
July 15, 1993   London SW1

~

Black hats make good company

SIR—Mr Stanley Reynolds uses the farcical goings-on at Aintree as an excuse for what can only be described as a disgraceful attack on the Homburg hat (letter, April 5).

He claims that this distinguished headgear disappeared overnight in 1956 after the Suez débâcle. By this he infers that all of us who wore or possessed Homburg hats at that time were in some way responsible for this disaster. Piffle.

I have a black Homburg (not to be confused with grey ones, worn only by cads) which is in perfect condition, having been delivered by its makers in 1934. It is a most useful headpiece, the wide brim shielding the eyes from the sun and the curl of the brim trapping the rain water.

Pushed back slightly indicates a certain raffishness, worn dead square reveals intellectual gravitas, tipped forward slightly a questing mind. It should be observed that none of these attributes was evident at Aintree last Saturday, but then there was not a Homburg in sight.

Perhaps you should seek the views of that well-known Homburg wearer, Mr Enoch Powell.

MICHAEL BLACKBURNE-DANIELL
April 8, 1993   Andover, Hants

~

Fashion leading . . . into trouble

SIR—Hilary Alexander claims that English designers have taken Paris by storm, and that we are all going to be swept away by 'a tide of glamour and elegance' (report, Oct. 17).

Precisely *who* is going to be so swept away? I may not be a typical customer (there are only 18 Conservative MEPs, and only two of us are women), but I must be typical of the many professional women who desperately search the shops for something attractive to wear.

What I am offered by 'the shapes of things to come' (your headline) is hopeless. I cannot turn up in my constituency wearing 'Montana's sequinned glam shorts'. Helmut Lang's plastic dress would probably be taken as some sort of statement about the EU packaging directive, and if I wore Issey Miyake's 'polished separates' I would attract the attention of the Wiltshire police.

The sad thing about all this is that I *can* find what I want in England. It is attractive, it is colourful (not in the tyranny of dusty blacks and beiges which dominate the shops) and it has probably been made in Germany. So our designers cannot be getting it right.

CAROLINE JACKSON, MEP (Con)

October 18, 1994   Swindon, Wilts

~

Keep on 'the woolly pully'

SIR—I was dismayed to read of the demise of the Army's 'woolly pully', which is about the most successful piece of tactical kit acquired by our armed forces in recent years (article, Dec 8). Unlike other items of military clothing, this flatteringly ribbed jersey with epaulettes did its job and was more, a psychological as well as physical comforter in times of stress and danger.

I speak with feeling on the matter. In the Falklands campaign and the Gulf, I was issued with the pully as standard war correspondent's kit. From the moment I landed in San Carlos, through two battles at Goose Green and Two Sisters, I was hardly ever parted from the garment.

It proved durable and warm, and at night served as pillow and blanket. It is the only piece of Falklands attire that I continued to wear years later. It has been worn by my children on numerous outdoor holidays and expeditions ever since. It has even been considered a fashion item in the wardrobe of the sartorially aware teenager.

In more recent conflicts, the main disadvantage for the itinerant correspondent is its colour. The distinctive Army green could suggest the wrong allegiance to a slivovitz-crazed Bosnian sniper. The only other disadvantage in a combat zone is the problem of washing. If the woolly-pully got soaked—as it did almost daily in the Falklands—it needed washing carefully with lanoline to restore body to the wool.

Rather than take the risk of serious shrinkage, the Falklands garment remained unwashed, and emerged a camouflage brown by the time I arrived back at Brize Norton at the end of June 1982.

As recent television modellings of the pully in Bosnia by the likes of Gen Sir Michael Rose and Gen Rupert Smith have shown, it is both flattering and combat-efficient. The decision to replace it with a distinctly baggy-looking 'blouson' seems an act of barminess by the Ministry of Defence in its promotion of the unisex Army.

The woolly-pully worked and looked good. It was a success, unlike the succession of less than satisfactory boots that soldiers have had to put up with these past 20 years.

The MOD should ask itself why, if an item ain't broke—or worn out—it should go through the hideously expensive rigmarole of procuring a replacement.

ROBERT FOX
December 8, 1995   London N1

Suitable insult
SIR—I wear an anorak. To some people this means I can be described as an anorak: a nerd or creep.

My anorak keeps off the rain and wind, and it has useful pockets. To my mind, a yuppie is someone so conned by the fashion industry that he pays several hundred pounds for a sack-like suit two sizes too large. I would rather call him a berk.

BRIAN CLIFTON
June 30, 1996   Wilmslow, Ches

Steed's bowlers

SIR—May I set the record straight about my attire as John Steed in *The Avengers* from 1960 to 1969 (article, July 10)? My bowler hats were flat-ironed, curled and fashioned by Herbert Johnson of Old Bond Street.

My suits were tailored by Bailey & Weatherall of Regent Street, where they were cut and fitted by Mr James, their senior cutter. The jackets were shaped to the body, as on an eighteenth-century man, full chested and low waisted, sporting collars of matching lady's velvet. The trousers were pencil-thin and settled neatly on a pair of elastic-sided 'Chelsea' boots, and my shirts were readymade from Turnbull and Asser.

The umbrellas, which were *never* opened, had knobbly bamboo (whangee) handles and were snugly encased in a matching sheath, like a banana in its skin.

PATRICK MACNEE
July 24, 1997　　　　　　　　Rancho Mirage, California

~

Why slash skirts?

SIR—It appears to be the fashion for some women to wear long dresses with an elongated slash in front from the hem to the upper thigh. As they walk, some of them pinch the separate pieces of material together with finger and thumb.

If these women wish to titillate, why do they do this? If they wish to retain their modesty why do they not adopt less revealing attire?

I ask only because I want to know.

R. M. B. BIRGELEN
August 13, 1997　　　　　　　　Newton Abbot, Devon

MUSICAL FOLK

Campaign against Furtwängler

SIR—I must defend the late Wilhelm Furtwängler (article, April 20). His reputation has been traduced for far too long.

Towards the end of the Second World War several Jewish musicians, whom the great conductor had spirited away from the Berlin Philharmonic, tried to persuade the American authorities to grant him a 'purification trial'—the process by which the Allies could clear him publicly of serving the Nazi cause.

But certain musicians in New York were determined to block this process. This was not due entirely to Toscanini's detestation of Furtwängler. In 1944, the violinist Jascha Heifetz made an (unsuccessful) attempt to persuade me to join his new union of soloists, AGMA, in order to protect us from the influx of European artists who would arrive with peace.

There was a shaming cabal against not only Furtwängler but also the Norwegian soprano Kirsten Flagstad and the great Spanish cellist Gaspar Cassado, which was only gradually defeated. This, I trust, answers Norman Lebrecht's query about why 'the Americans were tougher than the other nations on Furtwängler'.

The dilemma of whether to stay in one's country or leave can never be satisfactorily resolved: to leave can also be to abandon, to stay to use what means one has to help. Furtwängler chose the latter until the night he had to flee to Switzerland for several acts of defiance against the Nazi regime. The last of these—refusing to accompany the Berlin Philharmonic on their annual Paris visit—had proved the final 'sin'.

As for the niggling arguments with regard to 'modern music', Furtwängler incurred Goebbels's fury by conducting Hindemith (a Jew and a 'modern') in Germany. There was also the silly question of *tempi*; it is now forgotten that it was the mercurial Italian Toscanini who whipped them up in New York, thereby laying the foundations of the present criteria of speed and volume which destroyed the approach of style and respect.

Lastly, Furtwängler may have shaken Hitler's proffered hands, but I myself shook various hands which I would have preferred to avoid—and was photographed doing so. I wonder how many Americans today would resist shaking the extreme Right-wing hands of some of our more popular fascist thugs?

Lord MENUHIN
May 9, 1995   London SW1

Loony tunes

SIR—Your report (Jan. 5) about a study by psychologists at the University of East London on string players (moody and grumpy) versus brass wind players (jovial and beer-swilling) confirms my own keen amateur observations as a music-loving taxi driver over the past eight years.

I used to engage violin- and cello-carrying passengers in eager conversations—at first. After several years I learned, sadly, that all violinists were impatient of my conversational efforts, and showed signs of all the traits described in your report. They were ill-tempered, introverted, and never happy to continue a conversation.

What a contrast were the singers and cellists. All were delighted to find a musical cabbie and showed enthusiasm and interest, a notable example being Mr Julian Lloyd-Webber.

Brass players could be described as boisterous. Trumpeters, trombonists and French horn players showed up as loud, cheerful and optimistic.

I'm sure that an in-depth study is needed on violinists. Or could it be that something in their training conditions an aversion to taxi drivers?

DAVID BARNES
January 9, 1996   Bury, Lancs

Composer test

SIR—The test of a composer's work is not whether it founds a musical succession, but whether it continues to communicate and to be performed. More importantly, the Englishness of Vaughan Williams's vision is not an artificial construct, an escape to an idealised past, as Prof Vernon Bogdanor implies (article, Oct. 30).

It is the spontaneous expression of a way of feeling—gentle, lyrical, occasionally mystical and inspired, above all, by the English countryside—that is common not only to English folk music but also to a host of writers and artists. There is an obvious affinity, for example, with Blake and Constable. It reaches back even to the Anglo-Saxon poets, and can be regarded as universal to the English imagination.

An equally distinct individual identity can, of course, be recognised in French, German and other national cultures. The 'Europe' cited by Prof Bogdanor is in truth a propaganda creation, no more existing as a collective entity culturally than it does by nature politically or economically, though there will be plenty of Euro-voices during the coming months trying to tell us the opposite.

ALAN KIPPS
November 8, 1997   Hadleigh, Essex

Beatles were Thatcherite, too

SIR—I cannot understand all the fuss about the Spice Girls' endorsement of the Conservatives (report, Dec. 12). Their Thatcherite sympathies, evinced in the claim that 'Margaret Thatcher was the first Spice Girl', will come as no surprise to readers who have listened attentively to the lyrics of their songs.

Furthermore what is new about pop groups espousing Thatcherite ideology? The Beatles' hit 'Taxman' denounced both Harold Wilson and Edward Heath by name for their tax-and-spend policies. It specifically attacked the penal top rates of income tax:

> *Let me tell you how it will be*
> *There's one for you, 19 for me.*
> *'Cause I'm the Taxman.*

At the time the song was in the charts Mrs Thatcher was bound by the collective responsibility of Mr Heath's shadow cabinet. But when she became Prime Minister she took its message to heart, reducing top-rate income tax from 83 per cent to 40 per cent.

The song also took a swipe at Inheritance Tax, or Death Duty as it was then known:

> *And my advice to those who die*:
> *Declare the pennies on your eyes.*

Unfortunately Mrs Thatcher did not abolish this tax, although John Major has pledged to complete this piece of unfinished business.

But perhaps of still greater political significance was another Beatles number, 'Revolution'. Amid the student unrest of 1968 that song offered the timely warning:

> *If you go carrying pictures of*
> *Chairman Mao*:
> *You ain't gonna make it with*
> *anyone anyhow.*

In a rebuke for those students raising money for foreign terrorist groups, it added:

> *If you want money for people with*
> *minds that hate?*
> *All I can tell you is brother you'll*
> *have to wait.*

If Mr Blair does not want to earn the undying hatred of the Spice Girls he should agree to say no now to a single currency. They have made clear that is what they 'really, really want'. As for Mr Major he should resolve to follow his own Eurosceptic instincts. He might lose his Europhile Chancellor, Kenneth Clarke, but would delight this influential new group of supporters.

WILLIAM NEIL
December 14, 1996   London E3

Pipes and rock

SIR—Rock star Phil Collins's attempt to learn the bagpipes (Peterborough, March 8) may prompt some ill-suppressed rage among a few crusty purists, but this is nothing new. Two decades ago, Collins's former Genesis colleague Peter Gabriel credited bagpipes in the LP sleeve notes to his fine song 'Biko', although the resulting background strains could as easily have come from a synthesiser.

Learning the Highland pipes late in life can be hard going, as I have discovered. But if the bold Phil opts for electronic pipes, he will be able to concentrate on fingering without hyperventilating over the tricky balance between blowing and bag-squeezing—for the novice a torture straight out of a Hieronymus Bosch scenario.

In Scotland, where there has been a revival in the almost forgotten bellows-blown pipes, once favoured in the Lowlands and Border areas, an increasing number are learning to play both mouth and bellows-blown instruments.

The tartan-clad piper has often been a source of musical-hall jokes and White Heather kitsch. Beyond the hackneyed image, however, the Highland pipes have attained worldwide ubiquity on the back of British imperialism and Scottish emigration—as well as a phenomenally high standard of playing, among both bands and soloists.

In recent years a formerly rather hide-bound piping scene has broadened out vastly in its exploration of technique and repertoire. Highland and other pipes can now be heard playing within folk groups, rock bands, jazz ensembles and chamber orchestras, not only up here in Scotland but right across Europe, where indigenous bagpipes are being revived.

Phil Collins taking up the pipes may just be another music biz ploy—but it can also be viewed as part of this burgeoning 'piping consciousness'. If he just wants a gimmicky riff for his next single, the Collins dalliance with bagpipes will soon be forgotten. If he wants to make real music with them—fair play to him.

JIM GILCHRIST

March 9, 1994   Lowland and Border Pipers' Society, Edinburgh

Sinking again

SIR—Once again the pitch of the Greenwich time signal pips has dropped to B flat from the 'normal' slightly sharp B natural. As this is disturbing to musicians, I would like to suggest that a more logical pitch would be A-440, by which musicians could check their instruments.

I first drew attention to this matter in December 1990 and pips were restored to 'pitch'. Will the present lapse too be only temporary?

Dr CARL DOLMETSCH
July 2, 1993   Haslemere, Surrey

Carl Dolmetsch (1911–97) was a virtuoso and champion of the recorder.

Advancing noise

SIR—Barbara Reid asked whether establishments which think it essential to regale their customers with music have any research showing that they really like it (letter, Aug. 15). The answer is yes.

Last May, Leicester University psychologists reported having found that certain types of music not only swayed people's purchasing decisions, but could also affect how much money they spent in shops, supermarkets and pubs. What they did not say was what percentage of those interviewed were driven out of stores by music.

Many people are appalled at how many public institutions they regarded as impregnable bastions are falling daily to piped music salesmen. The RAF Club in Piccadilly now plays the *RAF March* while you wait for a phone connection.

DEREK DEMPSTER
August 23, 1997   Sandwich, Kent

OUT IN THE OPEN

Failure to predict Great Storm

SIR—As I sit typing this letter at 11 a.m. on Saturday, I am still chuckling over the forecast in your newspaper: 'Sunny spells, isolated showers dying out later'.

It is now almost an hour and a half since I could clearly discern the trees opposite through the torrential rain. It is also only 32 hours since our property was damaged in the hurricane-force winds of the unpredicted storm which 'tore the South apart' with such ferocity.

As an interested reader of meteorological books, I learned early how to detect the approaching fury of deep low pressure systems. When, on Thursday night I told my wife that the pressure on my 40-year-old barometer had dropped to below 28½in, or 960 millibars, I suggested that she removed any 'beloved' plants from the green-house. We have spent much of today sweeping the greenhouse off the lawn!

In 1944, Group Captain Stagg was given the supreme responsibility of forecasting the weather for a proposed invasion of Nazi-occupied Europe. So bad was the weather in early June that the Germans relaxed their state of readiness and a proportion of their defence forces were withdrawn for inland exercises. Field Marshal Rommel even went on leave to Germany.

But Group Captain Stagg spotted the brief respite in the lowest atmospheric pressure that had been recorded in any June this century anywhere in the British Isles. The respite was on June 6. The rest is history.

Group Captain Stagg had the good grace to write, in the post-script to his book *Forecast for Overlord*: 'In the years that have intervened since Overlord the science of meteorology and the practice of weather forecasting have been transformed out of recognition.'

His book was published 16 years ago, but it should be read by those responsible for forecasting our weather if for no other reason than to shame them into making better forecasts with equipment far below the enormous costs of the computers which they blamed for the recent, most disastrous 'non-forecast' of all.

ALAN J. RITCHIE
Littlehampton, W. Sussex.

SIR—Message to the weathermen: 'The wind bloweth where it listeth, and thou hearest the sound thereof, but canst not tell whence it cometh and whither it goeth.' (St John's Gospel, ch.3 v.8).

(Mrs) CAMILLA WAY
Isleworth, Middlesex

SIR—The most important factor in forecasting for the areas threatened by storm-force winds is knowledge of the precise track to be taken by the centre of the storm. Another important factor is the gradual change of air pressure. The magnitude of the pressure change indicates the likelihood of gale or storm-force winds and furthermore, isallobars (lines of constant barometric tendency) can be plotted and used as an aid to forecasting the movement and intensification of extratropical depressions, such as the one which produced the trail of death and destruction last week.

It is common knowledge that the computer forecast indicated a track which was well to the south of that actually followed by the storm's centre, hence the forecast for southern England did not warn of the violent storm-force winds, associated with the intense pressure-gradient in the southern quadrants of the cyclone.

How can the risk of this occurring again be minimised? An answer could be a change in operational procedure, with a special mandatory set of actions by the 'intervention' forecaster who is charged with spotting anomalous data and computer output at the Central Forecast Office, Bracknell. The intervention forecaster is well-experienced in the 'fine-tuning' of computer products. At the time of potential threat from a deep depression, he should compare a plot of the precise track of the centre and the central pressure readings with those taken from the computer's forecast charts for the corresponding period.

He can then assess the computer forecast's deviation from truth, up to that time. He should continue tracking the centre with the aid of current synoptic charts, and also add isallobars to his plotting chart or VDU (Visual Display Unit), as an aid to forecasting future movement and development. After further comparison with computer forecast charts, the intervention and senior forecasters at Bracknell can agree on any necessary modifications to the computer forecasts for the critical period, before these forecasts and supplementary advice are transmitted to the Regional Weather Centres.

Finally, I should point out that staffing in the Meterological Office is extremely tight, following a series of cuts over the last decade.

PETER G. RACKLIFF
Ex-Meterological Office, 6
Defence Services Branch
Workingham, Berks

SIR—We have recently been reminded of the Great Storm in November 1703, which devastated many parts of the country.

This storm was so severe that one Joseph Taylor, a Paternoster Row bookseller, left a bequest so that a commemorative service of thanksgiving for deliverance should be held annually in the Baptist Chapel, Little Wild Street, Lincoln's Inn Fields. An ancestor of mine, the Rev. Christopher Woollacott, preached this sermon in the 1850s which was published by the Baptist Tract Society (price one penny, or 25 for two shillings).

His sermon gives details of the damage done in many towns in the South of England as well as in London, part of which reads:

'Part of Her Majesty's palace (Queen Anne) was blown down and fell with a terrible noise. The roof of the guard house in Whitehall was quite blown off. The lead on the tops of churches and other buildings was, in many places, rolled up like so much parchment and blown to a considerable distance, as at Westminster Abbey, St Andrew's Holborn and Christchurch Hospital.

'The spires and pinnacles of many of the churches were also blown down. Upwards of 70 trees, many of them of considerable size, in Moorfields, were torn up by the roots, and a much larger number in St James's Park, and many other places.

'Some idea may be formed of the damage to the roofs of the houses in London by the fact that the demand for tiles was so great that the price was raised from one guinea per 1,000 to £6; and such was the difficulty in obtaining them, even at that price, that many persons covered their houses with deal boards; and to this day (12 months after the storm) we see whole ranks of buildings with no other covering.'

The Little Wild Street Church, where the sermon was preached, was demolished in the 1930s and the Great Storm Sermon was preached until recent years under the auspices of the Baptist Union. It would be interesting to know if this is still done. Perhaps the 1987 storm should be included.

CHRISTOPHER R. WOOLLACOTT
Winscombe, Avon

SIR—On your report of the escaped snow leopard (Oct. 19), I see a spokesman said 'So far the animal has not been spotted'. I beg to differ. Leopards are always spotted.

SPIKE MILLIGAN

October 21, 1987   Homeless under a Sussex tree

~

Cold baths and jungle fever

SIR—Returning from the wettest place on earth yesterday and having endured cold baths, mostly involuntarily, for more than 40 years, I read with great interest of the Thrombosis Research Institute's study on the effect of cold water on the production of sex hormones (report, April 22).

There may indeed be certain benefits, but I must utter a word of caution. It all depends on the temperature and location of the treatment. A dip in the Northwest Passage is more likely to cause chronic hypothermia or cardiac arrest than to overcome extreme fatigue. And bathing in the crocodile-infested Congo, where the water temperature is rarely below 80°F, can be detrimental to one's sex life.

In January 1962 I participated in a series of experiments at the Ullswater Outward Bound School. Hordes of naked schoolboys were driven into the freezing waters of the lake at dawn. The idea was to quell their natural instincts and thus protect the village maidens who lived near this beauty spot. Strangely it had the reverse effect. The colder the little blighters got, the more inclined they were to scale the walls!

However, on sailing expeditions I have found that the ardour of even the most lusty can be cooled with a good washing down from the ship's fire hose—though this could be due to the pressure of the water jet.

Recently, while leading a group of professional people on the glacier-fed Karnali River in west Nepal, I observed that frequent immersions gave them a great zest for life. They kept healthy, and worked with the energy of teenagers, bubbling over with enthusiasm, facing giant elephants and fierce tigers without turning a hair. The long-term effect of this on their libido is still under study.

Clearly this is an important subject, which requires further research. This August—spurred on by Professor Kakkars's initiative—I will carry out a series of experiments in the Guyana rainforest while searching for electric eels.

Col JOHN BLASHFORD-SNELL

April 24, 1993   Chairman, British Chapter Explorers Club,

Motcombe, Dorset

Remember Hilda the hippo

SIR—Your story (Jan. 16) about Hilda the Hippopotamus who was involved in a traffic accident on her way to an assignation with her lover (an arranged marriage organised by humans without her consent) and died of shock had an upsetting effect on me.

Perhaps this is not surprising, since I have long been singing a song about a hippopotamus having no difficulty in finding his mate.

Now when I sing this song, it will always bring back a mental picture of Hilda trotting gently across the central reservation of the A303 after the accident—not trying to escape, you understand, just noticing that there was good grazing over there.

Maybe it was for the best. She might have hated the virile pachyderm awaiting her at the end of her journey.

Perhaps having to re-enter the trailer that had shown itself capable of such alarming behaviour agitated this sleepy maiden's heart too much. We shall never know. I can only try to provide, with apologies to Flanders and Swann, this epitaph:

> *A young hippopotama was grazing one day*
> *On the verge of the A303.*
> *A jack-knifing trailer bar had quite given way.*
> *In a bound our dear Hilda was free!*
> *But breeding, alas, was the name of the game,*
> *Once again to her lover she sped.*
> *Said the vet, 'She's much calmer,*
> *No, ring the embalmer,*
> *I fear that poor Hilda is dead!'*
> *Dust, dust, all turns to dust.*
> *Hilda's mate's ardour will just have to rust.*
> *Let's hope she is lazing in pastures amazing,*
> *With happiness blazing yes, full fit to bust.*

IAN WALLACE
January 18, 1990   London N6

~

Unsolved mystery of the Surrey Puma

SIR—Twenty-five years ago there were reported sightings of a large cat-like animal which had similarities to the beast described by Mrs Di Francis (article, May 3).

The local paper on which I worked dubbed it 'The Surrey Puma', prompting us to suggest that a reporter, who was an aspiring novelist, should write a book about it entitled '*Paws*'.

Over the years there have been regular sightings in our area of unusually large cat-like animals, but none has ever been shot or filmed. They seemed to us the hunter's equivalent of the fisherman's tale.

Then late one afternoon about four years ago, my son-in-law, an ex-paratrooper, was driving his heavy vehicle-recovery vehicle on a Hampshire country road with forest on both sides when a large animal bounded out of the undergrowth.

He thought his vehicle had been hit by a deer, but when he halted to investigate he saw a large cat lying in the road.

Just as he was about to bend over it for a closer look the animal, obviously only stunned, got to its feet, looked at him, and then loped off into the undergrowth. My son-in-law said it was sandy coloured and looked like a puma.

He reported the incident to the local police who said several other people had also seen the creature that winter.

MAUREEN COVEY

May 11, 1993 Farnham, Surrey

~

Bigfoot lives on

SIR—I have considerable respect for Prof Loren Coleman's achievements in investigating unusual phenomena, but your report 'Why the legend of Bigfoot fails to stand up' (April 24) indicates that he needs to do some more research.

Reports of huge hair-covered bipedal primates circulated in North America long before Jerry Crew took a plaster cast of a 16-inch footprint to a newspaper office in Eureka, California, in 1958. They date back more than 100 years in British Columbia, where the creatures are known by the Indian name 'Sasquatches'.

The appearance of huge, human-like footprints in the loose dirt of Bluff Creek Road construction near Klamath, California, did indeed open a significant chapter in the story. Footprints in that area continued for many years, and one animal was captured on 16mm film there nine years later.

Of course, there have been fake footprints and false reports. Some samples of hair or faeces have turned out to be from other animals. But thousands of undeniably real giant footprints have been found throughout a million forested square miles of western North America; thousands of apparently responsible people have reported seeing huge, hairy bipeds; and there is, of course, the evidence contained in the movie.

These things require an explanation. To suggest that they can all be dismissed on the grounds that one set of footprints were faked in one place, at one time, makes no sense at all.

The events at Bluff Creek were examined up, down and sideways at the time by a lot of sceptical people. No one was ever able to explain how huge prints, an inch deep, could be faked in hard, wet sand in a creek bed inaccessible to machines, where human boots left almost no mark.

I must also dispute Prof Coleman's assertion that the respected zoologist Ivan Sanderson expressed doubts about the authenticity of the prints in private letters. I knew him well—he was adviser to organised investigations in which I took part both in California and in British Columbia, and I corresponded with him until his death.

No doubt he did occasionally express doubts—we all had doubts about various things from time to time—but Ivan was as convinced as anyone that the bulk of the evidence could be satisfactorily explained only if the creatures were real.

JOHN GREEN
Harrison Hot Springs, British Columbia

Different tunes of the wagtails

SIR—As a birdsong recording specialist for more than 40 years, I was interested in Dr Lance Workman's claim that songbirds, especially the robin, may well have regional accents (report, April 24).

As far back as 1809, A. C. G. Tucker commented on local dialects among chaffinches. This has been confirmed since then by such authorities in the Fifties and Sixties as Prof W. H. Thorpe and Dr Peter Marler in England and Prof H. Poulsen in Denmark.

The young male chaffinch has to learn part of its song, and its characteristic terminal flourish can be acquired only during a period of raised learning ability in its first spring when it tries to compete with other chaffinches. This leads to an establishment in the wild of distinctive community patterns of song.

Separation of one community of birds from another through behaviour or geographical isolation is a vital factor in permitting diverging songs or dialects to arise.

Tape recordings that I have made of the calls of four races of the yellow wagtail, which breed in different parts of Europe, reveal differences underlining a bi-acoustic separation linked to a geographical one.

For example, the race of the yellow wagtail which breeds in Britain has a musical disyllabic *tsuuee-eep* call.

The blue-headed wagtail of central and northern Europe uses a clearly different *pseep*, emphasised at the end, while the ashy-headed wagtail of central Mediterranean Europe employs a higher-pitched *tree-weep-weep*.

The Spanish wagtail nests in south-west France, Iberia and north-west Africa and calls with a sharp rising *shrie* note.

The grey-headed wagtail of northern Europe and Siberia utters a slurred *rssli*. These differences show clearly when sound pictures, or sonagrams, are made up of the various calls.

All these races of the yellow wagtail display different head colours and patterns as well. Such distinctions in voice and appearance may well have arisen through segregation in the wagtail's wintering quarters in Africa.

ERIC SIMMS
April 28, 1993   Grantham, Lines

Roll on . . .

SIR—English sheep have apparently only just caught on from their more intelligent and enterprising Welsh brethren in devising ways to cross cattle grids. More than 25 years ago it was reported that the sheep of Blaenau Ffestiniog regularly rolled across the cattle grids to enter the town, where they helped themselves to greengrocers' wares. Some even entered supermarkets.

Derbyshire sheep tend to be opportunist and thuggish. Some years ago, parked high on the moors near Buxton, I had my driver's window open and was eating a sandwich from my right hand, which was resting on the sill. There was a sudden tug and a fat, old and incredibly dirty ewe ambled away with the sandwich in her mouth.

ELLIS GLOVER
March 24, 1997   Bridestowe, Devon

Myth of the killer wolf

SIR—Opponents of the proposal to release wolves in the Scottish Highlands (report, Oct. 14) are greatly misinformed. During the 41 years I have been studying wolves in Canada and the United States as a biologist, there has been only one attack on a human in North America that resulted in a person's death.

It is true that wolves in captivity have, now and then, bitten keepers or, more usually, visitors to the wolf compounds who have thrust a hand through the bars.

I have followed wolf packs, slept out among them and handled newborn cubs taken from the den; I have photographed them, then returned them to their underground burrows. All this while the wolf pack has been milling around outside. But in the course of studying 52 wild packs I have never been so much as threatened, although I have been followed many, many times because wolves are extremely curious animals.

The idea that wolves are vicious, nasty beasts that would like nothing more than to kill and eat a human is absolute nonsense, developed from age-old ignorance in Europe.

At present in North America, foolish people who would boast of owning a hybrid dog-wolf are creating problems for those of us who study wolves, because dog-wolf crosses can be most aggressive and unpredictable. When a hybrid animal bites a person or, worse, kills a human infant, the wolf is blamed.

In fact, if a hybrid has more wolf than dog, it is highly unlikely that it will bite a human; on the other hand, if the hybrid is more dog than wolf, it may bite.

I am at present caring for a large wolf-Malamute cross, Shasta, who weights 140 lb and is very aggressive. More dog than wolf, she is manageable by my wife and to a lesser extent by me, but she is extremely aggressive towards visitors, who are not allowed closer than 5ft from her enclosure.

However, I also care for a husky-wolf cross, Alberta, who weighs 80lb and is so gentle that she carefully takes food (raw meat) from my mouth.

I can safely say, therefore, that while wolves are not aggressive, dogs, rather like humans, are definitely aggressive. It would be interesting to determine the number of Scots who have been bitten by dogs over the past 12 months.

R. D. LAWRENCE

October 26, 1996   Goodherham, Ontario

JORROCKS & CO.

Dishing our noble sport

SIR—In view of the current uproar about foxhunting I wonder if I may forward to you a letter I have just received from my old acquaintance, Mr John Jorrocks, MFH:

'Dear Mr Simple—Here's a fine how d'ye do! I've never been fond of writing, as you know. Riding is my forte. But as a former Master of Foxhounds I feel impelled to take up my eloquent pen in defence of all I hold dear! Abolish hunting, the image of war without its guilt and only five and 20 per cent of its danger? Dash my wig, they might as well try to abolish Old England! And that, if I'm not mistaken, is what the horrible schemes of these horrible people amount to!

'I hold no brief, mind, for the fine gentlemen in Leicestershire who have gone floundering into that rare old muddy ditch of theirs. Some of my old members in the Surrey Hounds used to call them "the Swell Mob" and wonder if they'd got their heads screwed on the right way. No matter.

'Fair play is a precious jewel, as scripture says. And creeping up on a hunt and hiding in the bushes with one of those moving cameras, or whatever the dratted contraptions are called, is not fair play. Nor is saving up the evidence for the opening of the hunting season. The fact is that these anti-hunting folk don't care what they do—they're crafty as any fox—if only it will help to dish our noble sport.

'Why are they so set against it? For all their fine talk, I reckon, it's not the cruelty, as they call it, they're really bothered about. If it was, they'd be up in arms against far worse, in bang-up-to-date machine farms and hellish laboratories. No, they want to put a stop to hunting because, being the kind of people they are, they can't bide the kind of people *we* are.

'Having the idea of England that they have—a country all tidied up and regulated—they want to do away entirely with our kind of England, a country of live-and-let-live, with room to breath in, where old ways of doing things can go on alongside new ways, where we can follow our own pleasures and pastimes without jumped-up inspectors of this and that and canting do-gooders with heads stuffed with paper telling us we can't.

'I don't want to stop these miserable beggars carrying on with their own pleasures and pastimes—if they have any, which I doubt. So let them keep their nail-bitten hands off ours. Do you know what kind of England we shall have if these pestilent busybodies prevail? It will be a country ruled and regulated down to the last detail for what these high and mighty prigs call the general good. And mark my words, Sir, England without hunting will be England no more.'

MICHAEL WHARTON
November 4, 1991   High Wycombe, Bucks

~

When hunt came to the rescue

SIR—I am a dairy farmer in North Wiltshire. On Christmas morning I had a cow dying in considerable pain. During her life she had been a faithful and much respected servant and, although receiving treatment from the vet, she was not responding. It was decided in consultation with the vet that she should be destroyed.

After ringing five abattoirs, who either did not answer the telephone or replied that they were not working on Christmas Day (and whom, incidentally, I would have to pay), I rang the local hunt kennels. They responded immediately, painlessly destroyed the animal and made no charge.

If hunting were abolished, would the anti-hunting fraternity provide an alternative service?

J. W. F. COLLINGBORN
January 1, 1992   Chippenham, Wilts

~

Bloody truth about foxes

SIR—I am amazed by Dr Ryder's claim that foxes eat only slugs, rabbits and rats (letter, July 2).

I started keeping poultry again about five years ago and, determined not to repeat an earlier experience when a fox dug under the fence and massacred all 13 hens, my quarter-acre run was built like Fort Knox. An 8ft-high wire fence was dug six inches into the ground and an electrified wire run all the way round the outside to stop any burrowing predators.

Early one sunny Sunday morning last summer I went down with the corn. Something was very wrong. No quacking was to be heard. And then the carnage became apparent. Nine ducks were strewn all over the grass, their heads turned back on their long necks, all dead, and only one half eaten.

Foxes kill half a million lambs each year and, with full grown lambs worth between £35 and £60 each, a farmer cannot afford to lose many if he is to stay on the right side of bankruptcy.

A friend who farms near Thame in Oxfordshire had to call the police when he found he was losing around 150 free-range piglets a month to what he supposed must be rustlers.

Two policemen staked out the farm at night for a week—no sign of human miscreants. Then it hit them. They had seen five foxes every night. Sure enough one was seen leaving the scene of the crime with a piglet in his mouth. Eureka! Five foxes, one piglet a night each for a month equals 150 missing piglets. Another murder inquiry was satisfactorily brought to a close.

Down the ages, for good reason, the fox, as in the fables of Aesop and La Fontaine, has been perceived as a cunning, intelligent and handsome predator, craftily going about his murderous business. It is only in the past 20 or so years that he has come to be portrayed as a cuddly, adorable and harmless furry animal, pursued and hounded by heartless human beings.

This image has been ruthlessly hyped by the rich animal rights movement, cynically playing on the sentimental tendencies of the animal-loving British urban population. It's just the first vital step in a campaign which will eventually try to stop all 'exploitation', as they call it, of animals. They will try to stop us eating meat (no more bacon-flavoured crisps), riding horses and even keeping pets.

The fox is a handsome, intelligent and even admirable beast but, like many wild animals, it is a clever and ruthless killer.

PENNY MORTIMER

July 4, 1996   Henley-on-Thames, Oxon

Out hunting for trouble

SIR—It is perhaps reassuring to know that all politicians are the same in the end.

We read that New Labour is backing down from a ban on foxhunting (report, Dec. 23). The cause, as we all know, is purely related to votes. How nice of them to realise that an awful lot of people who hunt are not mere 'toffs'.

I have come across many hunt saboteurs over the years and only once, or maybe twice, have I seen genuine concern for animal welfare. Last year, during a particularly savage display of social disruption in Gloucestershire, my horse, together with several others, was beaten with very large sticks which caused bruising and lumps on his hind legs, much to his puzzlement.

What has this behaviour got to do with anything related to the stated aim of animal welfare? It is my, and many others' belief that the only conceivable agenda here is civil disturbance and class warfare in an easy and open forum—the 'unpoliced' countryside.

If politicians want to win votes in the rural community they should stop to look at what is important: roadbuilding, greenfield development, Europe and beef.

HARRY CURSHAM

December 26, 1996   Badminton, South Glos

Doubts about value of evidence

SIR—Professor Bateson's study (report, April 10) produces convincing evidence of stress in the hunted deer.

However, until a comparable one is performed on, say, wildebeest that are routinely ambushed and pursued over much shorter distances by a 'pack' of lions, it is difficult to be satisfied that the condition identified by his team is exclusive to deer hunted with hounds. For those that foil their pursuers, there is, in any case, a benefit in the sharpening of the instinct for evasion and the talent for escape, one that is transmitted from generation to generation. That is the way evolution works.

The biggest problem is that the red deer species, as opposed to the hunted individual, will now be at risk, and the reason is distressingly simple. The red deer of Exmoor are a numerous, widely distributed and geographically accessible cash crop that will be claimed by ruthless gangs with none of the concern for the maintenance of a virile, healthy species that has been the hallmark of the yeoman farmer and staghunter.

CHARLES DRURY
Sudbury, Suffolk

SIR—It is ironic that the National Trust, which was formed to protect and enhance our heritage, is now committing itself to being instrumental in the destruction of two essential facets of our national heritage on Exmoor.

The Trust's decision to ban stag hunting will not only lead to the eradication of an age-long tradition on the moor, but will also inevitably lead to the demise of one of the last remaining herds of truly wild red deer in the country.

Sir HUGH STUCLEY, Bt
Crediton, Devon

SIR—You report that Henry Williamson predicted that a ban on hunting the red deer would be the end of the deer of Exmoor as farmers would not tolerate them. Williamson also said, in a BBC interview, that *only* the hunts, in his experience, could really be trusted to conserve the species, whether deer or foxes.

The chairman of the National Trust may not believe this, but how will his organisation deal with the wild deer that will take refuge on the trust's land, with inevitable overgrazing of young trees and shrubs? Is the trust ready to take steps against deer poaching, which often results in a wounded deer being left to die in slow agony?

Hunting is the preferable way of culling, as the deer has a fair

chance of escape and in fact around 50 per cent of all hunts end
without a kill.

MARGOT LAWRENCE
Edgware, Middx

SIR—Why has it come as such a surprise that hunting and taking of
deer with hounds is stressful to them? Only the most ignorant would
think otherwise. However, it is justifiably cruel. The only true
custodians of deer on Exmoor for the past 400 years have been
those who hunt them. Exmoor enjoys the finest herd of red deer
anywhere in Europe because the locals care about them.

The contradiction that those who care for an animal then go and
hunt it is hard to explain. But I am not ashamed to hunt deer.

ADAM TEDSTONE
Penkridge, Staffs

SIR—I have been hunted, and I will never forget the terror of
pursuit. It occurred in the late Sixties when a group of Portuguese
soldiers recognised me as a heckler of Ian Smith's at a meeting in
Rhodesia. They chased me in the dark across a golf course, three on
foot and three in a car, for three hours until I got away.

Fear gives strength and speed, but when this begins to give out,
legs shake, bowels tremble, every nerve screams fear. I doubt that
any stag hunters have had such experience.

PHILIP LOW
April 11, 1997   Newport, Lincs

Select compassion

SIR—Those who object to hunting on the grounds that it causes
suffering to animals (report, April 10) seem to be selective in their
compassion. Some years ago I was taken by my daughter and son-in-
law to a fox hunt in Nottinghamshire on New Year's Day. There
were about 20 anti-hunting protesters with placards, most of whom
looked like university students.

When the hunt had moved off, I asked one of them if he supported legal abortion. He said he did. Further questioning revealed the protesters to be, to a man (and woman), supporters of a woman's right to choose. Am I the only person to find this inconsistent?

Mrs VIOLET WHELAN
Richmond, Surrey

SIR—The only mystery about the Bateson report is: why has it taken so long to decide that stag hunting is unacceptably cruel? Every right-thinking person has known this for a very long time. And, of course, exactly the same applies to fox hunting, which must be banned by the next parliament.

Dr PATRICK MOORE
April 12, 1997 Selsey, W. Sussex

Selective pain

SIR—The anti-hunting angler Michael Foster, MP, claims that 'fish and mammals feel pain in very different ways' (report, June 17). Is the fish kind of pain a special kind that doesn't hurt? Weasel words, I think, from a slippery eel.

NIGEL BURKE
June 20, 1997 London SE13

Ripped to pieces

SIR—As a pathologist I know about pain and its causes. I think you may have missed the real issue driving the anti-hunting lobby—*how* foxes or deer are killed.

When a fox is caught in the open, more than one hound will attack, and the fox is literally ripped to pieces. The pain caused by stretching and tearing muscle is excruciating.

Dr ROBIN PAVILLARD
Riyadh, Saudi Arabia

SIR—Mr Foster's Bill has little to do with animal welfare but a great deal to do with class warfare.

GERALD HUMPHREYS
November 28, 1997 Berkhamsted, Herts

Too law-abiding

SIR—Until January, I had never attended a rally. Since then, I have attended three, the first two in defence of handgun shooting, the last on behalf of country sports. All three were good-natured and non-confrontational, and the speakers knew their subjects and put their cases eloquently and logically.

However, it occurs to me that we are doing it all wrong. We didn't set fire to earth movers, we didn't riot, we didn't leave tons of rubbish, we didn't resort to abuse or jeer at those who don't share our way of life. The result in each case has been pathetic news coverage on television. In a remarkable example of even-handedness, though, one news crew ignored 100,000 people with a proper reason to be in Hyde Park, cornered an anti up a tree and received the benefit of her opinion for viewers of the early evening news. Maybe we all should have scaled trees.

NIGEL PARRY-WILLIAMS
July 12, 1997   Market Harborough, Leics

MAN'S BEST FRIEND

When a rottweiler turned nasty

SIR—In 1983, I was living in Southern Africa when it had become fashionable among expatriates to have rottweilers as pets and guard dogs. I had a 10-month-old pup at the time which was excellent with children. He allowed them to climb all over him and was a very good dog generally.

My friends and I with our families, servants and dogs would regularly go into the bush at weekends, set up camp and do a little hunting. In the evening we would have a barbecue then stay overnight.

On one occasion all the men went hunting; we had about 10 rottweilers, a few alsatians and Rhodesian ridge-backs with us. One of us shot a *kudu* (small deer) which was intended to be our servants' supper. However we were flabbergasted when the rottweilers suddenly as a pack, attacked the carcass and tore it to pieces.

We returned to camp where the rottweilers stayed in a park. During the evening one of the alsatians ventured too near and was killed by the pack before any of us could move, even though we were only a few yards away.

The following morning we were told by the servants that the rottweilers had all left camp. We immediately grabbed our guns and went to look for them. Eventually we found them with four dead *kudus*. We had one hell of a job breaking them up and getting them back to the cars.

Following this incident, whenever we wanted to go out to the bush, our servant would only come if the rottweilers were excluded. And due to this incident I became uneasy about my dog. However, before I could find the dog a new home I caught my gardener beating him with a garden hose and I dismissed the man on the spot. A couple of months later I gave the dog to a farmer whose ranch was way out in the bush.

Some weeks later I was shocked to hear my ex-gardener had been killed by my rottweiler. It transpired that he had been employed by my farmer friend, unknown to me, and obviously the dog had remembered the hose beating and had his fearful revenge.

The reason I am relating these events is the awful thought that already negligent rottweiler owners will not have problem animals put down, but will start abandoning them on the streets or in public parks. I really must warn your readers and the responsible authorities that these dogs are a very real threat in a pack.

And I must say to all those people who will say 'my dog won't behave like that' that that is exactly what I would have said about my dog until I saw his behaviour in a pack with my own eyes. These dogs are a real menace in a pack, and heaven knows what they would be like if really hungry.

DAVID GALLIMORE

June 8, 1989   HM Prison, Wormwood Scrubs, London W1

Ear muffs for dogs

SIR—As a new shooting season opens, it is opportune to draw attention to what seems to me to be an unfair and unfeeling situation.

It is well established that any form of shooting is damaging to the ears and most game shots now wear ear defenders or earplugs to diminish the risk of this common sports injury. Many who have not done so have shot themselves quite deaf. Some of those who are not shooting but stand near the guns—wives, loaders and dog handlers, for example—are now wise enough to protect their hearing.

Although I understand that very little research has been carried out on the subject of the effect of gunfire on dogs' hearing and that there is no scientific evidence to support a view one way or the other, I am concerned that attention should be drawn to the possible harm being inflicted on gundogs.

It should not be beyond the wit of man to devise some means of protecting a dog's hearing, which we know to be more sensitive than a human's. Here, then, is a challenge for some inventor. It would need to be a device that would not irritate the dog while it sat waiting and could easily be removed before the dog was sent off to retrieve.

Sir JOSEPH NICKERSON
August 13, 1988 Rothwell, Lincs

Sir Joseph Nickerson (1914–90) was one of the finest shots who was accidentally peppered by the Deputy Prime Minister William Whitelaw when he slipped in the butts in 1984.

~

In their place
SIR—Being of Indian origin and culture I am neither a dog-lover nor a dog-hater. My dog gets fed, and looked after quite adequately, but kept in *its* place.

I am therefore constantly amazed at the attitude of some English people towards their dogs. For example, an Englishman writes (letter, Feb. 20): 'I have owned many dogs and must say that my rottweiler bitch is the only one *who* has ever let me remove a bone from *her* jaws.'

Should those words not read *which* and *its*? The fact that the gentleman has *owned* these animals shows that they cannot be spoken of as being human. Some people treat their dog as if it were a god—d-o-g read backwards. The English have many admirable traits, but this undue adoration of dogs is not one. It is probably due to this that so many dogs turn against humans. If human supremacy over animals is lost, woe betide us.

ROBERT SAXENA
February 23, 1990 Kettering, Northants

~

Barking mad
SIR—In all this debate about dog registration (report, April 11) is anyone considering the feelings of the dogs themselves?

If you're a dog of quality, of breeding, you're soon rushed off, alongside the royal corgis and the princely poodles, to the prestigious Kennel Club, to be registered in a kind of Dogs' Debrett among the great and the good. Hence that rather sniffy air?

But if you're just a run-of-the-kennel, undistinguished old pooch, not only has your licence been taken away but seemingly you're now to be denied your legitimacy by not being state registered. No wonder that hang-dog look.

It shouldn't surprise us to find, one day, our faithful friends exercising their doggy power by taking to the streets (and we all know what happens should they take to the footpaths too) in mass protest (shepherded no doubt by well behaved but unregistered police dogs) against being the canine underclass—'the lesser breeds without the law'.

Shouldn't we all be barking 'fair play for the dogs'?

Air Cdre HAROLD SHEPHARD

April 17, 1990   Tenterden, Kent

Tragic perceptiveness of royal Clumber

SIR—Even if Edward VII's dog Caesar was not Clumber (letter, Jan. 19), I would like to point out that George V had a large number of Clumbers. The Sandringham strain represented a major portion of the breed in Britain until it came to a sad end.

My gamekeeper grandfather was told by the Sandringham keeper in 1937 that they had all been destroyed because Edward VIII loathed them. This followed an incident when Edward unwillingly attended a shoot. One of them strolled up to the petulant prince and, with great dignity, lifted its hindleg to urinate over his trousers.

Everybody, apart from the Prince, considered this highly amusing. However, when the Prince became King one of his first actions was to telephone Sandringham and order the head keeper to shoot all the Clumbers immediately. The keeper related that it was the hardest thing he ever did.

Clumbers represent all that is best and noblest about the English character: intelligence, dignity, and rugged determination bordering on wooden-headedness.

HADRIAN JEFFS

January 26, 1991   Norwich

Hound of Blair?

SIR—W. F. Deedes makes the commendable suggestion that the image of Mr Tony Blair would be enhanced by the addition of a black and white spaniel as an aide-de-camp (Notebook, July 25).

I write to offer the services of my spaniel, Stormin' Norman, for this important public duty. Like Mr Blair, he is extremely photogenic (photo available on request). His friendly character would enable him to romp happily with the Blair children during the parliamentary recess.

Norman's large ears and the resultant ability to ignore anything said to him would equip him to survive long Shadow Cabinet meetings without a murmur. He has also proved himself to be an imaginative and forward-looking thinker.

Only yesterday, he suggested to me that Mr Blair should introduce a new policy of spaniel-only shortlists for all prospective Labour Party candidates. This brave move towards electoral reform, with its instant appeal to a nation of dog-lovers, would assure Labour's success at the next general election.

CAROL GRANT
July 27, 1994 Blewbury, Oxon

It's a dog's life

SIR—David Sapsted's report, 'Man's best friend is a dog—and not a wife' (March 8), comes as no surprise to me as co-editor of *Debrett's People of Today*. Using the CD-Rom. I have discovered that of the 34,000 entrants who feature, 127 list 'friends' and 159 'dogs' in their recreations.

By comparison, only 27 mention their wives, and not always in the most complimentary fashion. Dr Roger Wootton, Dean of the School of Engineering at City University, cites 'being a husband and father' as his most important pastime, with hot air ballooning a close second '(as means of escaping from former recreations)'.

And one City gent, who shall remain nameless, is quite happy to record 'being horrid to my wife'—an addition, after 'showering'.

As an unmarried woman, I'm heading for Crufts.

JESSICA HAILSTONE
March 15, 1996 London SW6

Bulldog belongs to England

SIR—How unfortunate that the Labour Party has used the word British in adopting the bulldog as an election symbol (report, April 16). As usual it has seized upon an idea without proper research.

The bulldog is not British; it is English. It can be called a bulldog or an Old English bulldog but never a British bulldog. Writing in 1792, William Augustus Osbaldeston described the bulldog as 'one of the most fierce and strong of the race, having their nose short, and their under jaw larger than the upper. The breed is in a manner peculiar to England.'

John Bull was an Englishman first and foremost, and proud of the totally English roots of the bulldog. The Scots, Welsh, Irish, Afro-Caribbean, Indian and Pakistani races are first and foremost their own nationality. They are British but not English. In effect, the Labour Party has decided to exclude all these people by adopting the English national dog.

CHRISTOPHER GRIEVSON

April 17, 1997   London SW19

PROVINCIAL PRIDE

Enjoying life in the rain

SIR—Mr Mark Diks does not want to give up the Ben Alder estate because his wife has threatened to leave him (report, Sept. 5); there is no doubt that a move to Scotland can put considerable pressure on a marriage.

I am Chinese, born in Malaysia, who married a Scot with a Scottish hill farm and sporting estate. Before I married I was used to temperatures of between 80 and 95 degrees all the year round, even during the short monsoon period.

My home is situated in one of the colder and wetter tracts North of the Border. After my first summer and winter here, I gave my husband the same ultimatum as Mrs Diks was said to have done, but with quite different results: I am still here 16 wet summers later!

Why? Well, we compromised. My husband did not sell up or kick me out. He kicked the animals out instead; out of the farmyard and on to the hills where they belong. He then converted the redundant farm buildings into areas where summer sporting activities can be safely engaged in summer or in winter—without getting unduly cold or wet.

My husband's intrepid sportsmen friends can still come and go in the wind and rain, leaving their timorous wives and children behind with me to enjoy their sporting life under cover. The indoor tennis court, barbeque and swimming pool help to make the time pass by for them agreeably enough.

If Mr Diks cannot sell his Scottish estate, I humbly suggest that he, and perhaps others in a similar predicament, might consider for the sake of their spouses, converting their redundant farm buildings into something all the family can enjoy. It might then be possible to neutralise the tensions of a wet August holiday, or even a freezing first week in September, and discover instead that Scotland is really a very worthwhile place to have a home—regardless of weather.

Lady TANLAW

September 7, 1992					Eskdalemair, Dumfriesshire

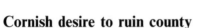

Cornish desire to ruin county

SIR—In comparing the quality of local planning in Edinburgh and Launceston, Mr Peters (letter, April 15) should realise that the Cornish have a masochistic desire to ruin what little unspoilt beauty is left in the county as quickly as possible.

If there is a pretty skyline, litter it with shoddy breeze-block bungalows; if there is an unspoilt valley, fill it with caravans, a 'piskie' shop, and—most important—a takeaway fish and chip shop to ensure plenty of litter.

If there is a plot large enough for five houses, build 10 and, in the process, chop down every tree in sight. To welcome visitors to beauty spots (such as St Ives) ensure there is a used car dump alongside the railway line.

Wherever possible, every house should have a lean-to shack tacked on to it made of corrugated iron or asbestos, and two derelict cars in the back garden. At weekends it is the local custom to go out and scatter old refrigerators, mattresses and household rubbish along the lanes.

Virtually all the really good quality building constructed in Cornwall over recent decades, using local stone and slate, has been the work of the much-maligned 'furriner' who has brought into the county a quality otherwise unknown.

Some 70 per cent of Cornwall's beautiful coastline has already been submerged in over-development. For example at Trebetherick, on the north coast, the plan was to have only a small number of high-quality houses carefully spaced so as not to spoil the beauty. Slowly, the green spaces have been filled-in so that now it is more akin to urban development.

Were it not for a few far-seeing private landowners and the National Trust (the latter now sadly littering its property with unnecessary signs) the remaining 30 per cent would vanish overnight.

The planners appear to assume that the more Cornwall is developed, the greater the wealth it will provide. Rustle a few notes, and talk optimistically about new jobs, and you can do what you like. Despite the fact that large areas of this county have already been irrevocably ruined by the mining and china clay industries, no one in authority seems to care or think much about the future.

JAMES RUSBRIDGER

April 24, 1991 Lanivet, Cornwall

James Rusbridger (1928–94) was an indefatigable letter-write to newspapers and an espionage historian with a weakness for conspiracy theories.

Paradise north of Watford

SIR—Those of us living in the barren wastes north of Watford Junction are accustomed to having our poverty-stricken existence compared unfavourably with the sunlit Elysium your scribes see from the windows of El Vino's (or wherever you adjourn since you went to the Dogs).

However, the eyebrows rose further than usual on reading (magazine, March 10) that the countryside within 50 miles of Birmingham is 'an Area of Outstanding Mediocrity' with 'derelict land and low-quality soil'.

Granted: the 12-mile journey from Birmingham to Wolverhampton is not high on tour operators' itineraries (although some Black Country towns such as Dudley are worth a visit). But well within 50 miles of Birmingham lie the fertile Vale of Evesham and Severn Valley, the dramatic Malvern Hills and the Cotswolds, and the woodlands of Cannock Chase and Wyre Forest. I suggest your scribe invest in a decent atlas of the British Isles.

For a little extra, British Rail will sell him a day return enabling him actually to see some of the places (and to get safely back home the same night). From the Stratford-upon-Avon to Birmingham line he would see wooded countryside recalling Shakespeare's Forest of Arden within 10 miles of the centre of Birmingham.

Such landscapes cannot be found within an equivalent distance of his metropolitan perch.

R. H. DARLASTON

March 16, 1990 Goostrey, Ches

Impractical oxen

SIR—I should hate to discourage Mr John Johnson and his oxen at Foston in Yorkshire, but that delightful photograph of them (June 27) rang faint bells. Happily, I have been able to trace the source.

'Was advised by neighbouring gentlemen to employ oxen; bought four—Tug and Lug, Haul and Crawl; but Tug and Lug took to fainting, and required buckets of sal volatile, and Haul and Crawl to lie & die in the mud. So I did as I ought to have done at first, took the advice of the farmer instead of the gentlemen; sold my oxen, bought a team of horses.'

The date is 1812; the author is the Rev Sydney Smith, at that time Rector of Foston in Yorkshire.

RAEF PAYNE
June 30, 1994   Oswestry, Shrops

SPORTSMANSHIP

No ball

SIR—You report (March 29) that with England chasing runs in their second innings in the third Test, the West Indies managed to bowl 17.5 overs in just under two hours after tea.

- Is this sporting?
- Is it gamesmanship?
- Or is it just plain cheating?

Whatever it is, it is certainly not cricket.

BRIAN JOHNSTON

March 30, 1990   London NW8

Brian Johnston (1912–94) was a cricket commentator and genial raconteur who wore co-respondents' shoes.

Burning Samoans

SIR—I do not wish to alarm the Scottish team before this after-noon's international, but your readers might be interested in a report of a match in the more seemly game of cricket involving two Samoan teams. It resulted in the destruction of the village of Matautu.

According to the *Samoa Weekly Herald* of March 25, 1893, a series between the villagers of Matautu and their neighbours of Salealua concluded in a Matautite victory:

'As is the custom, their triumph entitled them to the flag of their opponents, and they proposed to hoist it with their own in celebra-tion of so great an event. To this proceeding the Salealua braves decidedly objected, and the result was an extremely lively shindy.

'One of the natives had his head smashed with a cricket club, and although the injury is not likely to prove fatal, still the man was knocked senseless at the time and very severely injured. Early in the strife one of the stones, which were being freely hurled about, struck the well known chief Salima on the back—an incident which increased the trouble, since Salima, irate and vengeful, at once called out to his Salealua men to fight on.

'The mandate was promptly and vigorously obeyed, and the battle waxed hot and strong. After a time, during which no serious damage had been done, the belligerent parties separated, and it seemed as if the thing was all over.

'But to let the little difference drop without more ado would not have been in accordance with the Salealuan idea of the fitness of things, so they determined to burn down the village of Matautu. With the courtesy usual on such occasions they gave timely notice of their intention, and the Matautites were duly warned of the proposed descent upon their homes. They therefore removed all their moveable goods to places of safety, and betook themselves to their boats, leaving the houses at the mercy of the incendiaries.

'A white resident of the place asked why the men did not make some effort to prevent the proposed destruction, and in reply was told that such a thing would be contrary to Samoan custom. Sure enough a party arrived in Matautu from Salealua on Sunday night, and shortly afterwards the whole village was ablaze.

'Fifteen houses were completely destroyed, but no other property was damaged. The natives who departed in their boats before the conflagration—and they went away singing their most lively songs—are expected to return to their village and immediately begin the work of erecting new places of residence.

'In all probability nothing more will be heard of the dispute and doubtless the friendship between the parties will not be materially affected by their slight misunderstanding.'

My only concern is that, in the event of a disagreement after today's match, the Scots fans may prove less willing to let bygones be bygones.

J. H. MANNERS
October 19, 1991   Oxford

Scores of centuries for Hollywood XI

SIR—How nice it is to learn that the Hollywood Cricket Club, under Lord Alexander Rufus Isaacs, scored more than 100 runs in an innings, but this was not a first as you reported (Peterborough, Aug. 9).

The club was started by Sir Aubrey Smith (1863–1948). P. G. Wodehouse took the minutes at the inaugural meeting and the XI produced many innings of more than 100 runs. I do not have the complete figures but in a match against Pasadena 'Gubby' Allen and C. B. Fry played for the Hollywood team. Allen, then captain of England, scored 77 and Fry, a former England captain, 12, and David Niven 13.

In another match Sir Aubrey, who was the great C.A. 'Round the Corner' Smith of Cambridge, Sussex and England, was 61 not out in a total of 106. Sir Aubrey was, of course, C. Aubrey Smith, the actor, notable in such films as *The Prisoner of Zenda*, *Little Lord Fauntleroy* and *Rebecca*. He played, with a runner, until the year of his death.

As well as Niven and Errol Flynn, H. B. Warner, Nigel Bruce, Boris Karloff, Herbert Marshall, Ronald Colman, George Arliss and (once only) Laurence Olivier turned out for the great man.

STANLEY REYNOLDS
August 10, 1991   West Monkton, Som

Class war at the stumps

SIR—Peterborough may well be right in describing the present dispute about who should play cricket on Broadhalfpenny Down as 'class warfare' (Jan. 9); but I wonder if it is not more complicated than that.

Of course there was a time when first-class cricketers were formally divided into Gentlemen and Players. Gents were amateurs, listed with their initials in front of their names and wore fancy hats. Players were paid professionals who had their initials after their names and wore Brylcreem. They stayed in separate hotels and entered the field of play by different gates.

That all changed, although you still get occasional reminders of the bad old days. One such was the bizarre document recently sent out to all MCC members about the special general meeting to debate a no-confidence motion in the England cricket selectors. The letter from the dissidents wrote of 'Keith Fletcher' and 'David Gower', whereas that from the committee referred to the same people as 'Mr K. W. R. Fletcher' and 'Mr Gower'. This is evidence, however incomprehensible, of class warfare in action.

The MCC affair, perhaps like the Broadhalfpenny Down matter, is a riveting study for class warfare analysts. Two of the signatories of the no-confidence letter are Balliol peers, which would normally cast the rebels as the Gents. However, two on the other side are the president of MCC and the secretary—D. R. W. Silk, the former Warden of Radley, and a retired colonel called John Stephenson. The two men played in the same eleven at Christ's Hospital.

On a playing level it looks easier because 'Mr Gower' is an obvious gent whereas most of those who dropped him ('Mr Gooch', 'Mr Fletcher' and 'Mr Stewart') are obvious players. Two are even Essex men.

But it is not as simple as that. 'E. R. Dexter', chairman of the selectors, is the ultimate Gent, having played for Radley (aha!), Cambridge and England. In his day he played cricket in a very similar style to that of Mr Gower. Now, however, he has become the Leonid Brezhnev of modern cricket, wherein there is a deep irony.

My own view is that the argument is not about Gentlemen and Players but Roundheads and Cavaliers. And furthermore that many of the best Cavaliers are Players and the worst Roundheads are Gents. But that's another story.

TIM HEALD
January 11, 1993 Richmond, Surrey

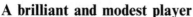

A brilliant and modest player

SIR—As somebody who partnered Peter May on the cricket field at Charterhouse, may I suggest that it would be a great pity if his achievements for England concealed the fact that he was the best schoolboy batsman of the century.

Peter had an ability to play brilliant, even beautiful strokes in the most difficult and unexpected circumstances. He was also gifted, for somebody with such extraordinary talent, with an extremely charitable disposition.

The headmaster, Robert Birley, refused to let him enter the First XI in his first year, the summer of 1943, on the grounds that he had to concentrate on his work for a junior scholarship, something he subsequently failed to achieve. After reading the results on the noticeboard I remarked that he had the head man to thank for this double disappointment.

But Peter replied that Birley must have been concerned that the double responsibilities might have led him to make a hash of his entrance in the First XI.

Peter's modest and embarrassed manner, which sometimes led him to be dismissed unfairly as a po-faced booby, reminded me of nothing so much as Horace's verse disclaiming any personal merit for having written his poetry but giving all credit to his Muse:

> *This is all thy gifts*
> *That I am pointed out by the fingers*
> *of those that pass*
> *As the minstrel of the Roman lyre.*

SIMON RAVEN

December 28, 1994   Deal, Kent

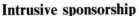

Intrusive sponsorship

SIR—There is a very simple answer to K. L. Haigh's letter asking why Mike Atherton was interviewed after the England Test defeat wearing what appears to be a meat porter's hat bearing the name of the England team's main sponsor (March 5): commercialism and sponsorship.

The England team are paid to wear the beer logo but they are not paid anything for wearing their England cap other than their tour or match fee.

When I captained the England women's team for 11 years, we wore only a white floppy hat or a headband. We never felt it necessary to appease sponsors by so vulgarly and unnecessarily displaying their logos in preference to the Rose of England. But then we were never paid to play for our country.

Apart from very occasional grant aid for travel, we paid our own fares and other travelling expenses for tours both at home and abroad. We also paid for our playing clothes—and even for our blazers and England badges.

Of course, I realise that sponsorship is an integral part of sport nowadays, yet it is surely a grating intrusion when such commercialism imposes on all that is good and traditional about our great English game of cricket.

This winter's tour of the Caribbean has been mercifully free of controversy, unlike England's scruffy designer stubble and prawn curry disasters in India last winter. But this overt display of a sponsor's logo at press conferences should be stamped out by the tour management.

Incidentally, I always understood that it was bad manners for a gentleman to wear a hat indoors.

RACHAEL HEYHOE FLINT
March 8, 1994   Wolverhampton, West Midlands

~

Running out

SIR—Surely the collective term for a group of England captains (letter, Dec. 13) is: 'a lack of principals'.

JOHN PINTEAU
December 14, 1996   Hartley Wintney, Hants

~

All blacks of the cricket field

SIR—Your report (May 23) on the Australian Aboriginal cricket team that beat a Scarborough XI in August 1868 might give the impression that it was the only match of their tour. In fact it was the 29th. The first was at the Oval on May 25 and 26, when a Surrey XI beat the slightly bewildered visitors by an innings; a total of 20,000 spectators attended.

They eventually won as many matches as they lost (14), their victories coming at venues as far afield as Halifax, Swansea, Norwich, Liverpool, North Shields, Southsea and Godalming, besides the match at Scarborough.

They played MCC at Lord's, where they were beaten but not

disgraced, their best player, the able all-rounder Johnny Mullagh, scoring 75 and taking eight wickets.

The team members were all from Victoria and were led by Charles Lawrence, who had stayed in Australia after the first tour by an England side (1861–62). They played under such nicknames as Dick-a-Dick, Red Cap, Bullocky and Tarpot because their real names, for example Jumgumjenanuke and Brimbunyah, were deemed too difficult for the press and public of the day. They wore coloured caps and sashes for ease of identification: hence 'Tiger Pink', who appears in the Scarborough scorebook, whose real name was Bonnibarngeet.

Some of the financial backing is said to have come from settlers who had taken tracts of tribal land and needed to salve their guilty conscience. *Wisden* almost ignored the venture, and *The Daily Telegraph*'s spring greeting was ambivalent: 'Nothing of interest comes from Australia, except gold nuggets and black cricketers.'

It was a profitable tour, but several of the players were debilitated by the cold and their exertions. One, King Cole, died at Guy's Hospital from a lung ailment. Back in Australia, most of his colleagues returned to the bush. Because of illness and alcoholism, few survived to any great age.

One hundred and twenty years were to pass before another Australian Aboriginal cricket team toured Britain.

DAVID FRITH
May 26, 1997   Guildford, Surrey

Football always a grubby business

SIR—Why all this fuss about the 'cult of dishonesty' in Association Football, and the pathetic plea that it is not endemic within the game (Sport, Sept. 20)? Throughout its modern history this has been regularly uncovered whenever those privy to its irregularities have been ready, for whatever reason, to disclose them.

It can be traced at least back to 1885 when the Corinthian founding fathers were obliged to recognise professionalism 25 years after the FA's foundation. This arose when Upton Park, a

London club, complained that Preston North End had used mercenaries for the then ostensibly amateur FA Cup competition. The North End chairman-manager, Major Sudell, openly admitted a common practice to challenge the near invincibility of Blackburn Rovers, and the barriers on professionals came down a year later.

In 1900, Burnley's goalkeeper, John Hillman, was suspended by the FA for offering a bribe to Nottingham Forest. Four years later, the entire FA Cup-winning Manchester City side was banned from ever playing for the club again after the immortal Billy Meredith admitted the existence of illegal payments.

In the 1920s, the entire Leeds City club and Arsenal's chairman were expelled from participating in the game ever again. After the Second World War, Swindon Town's chairman was found guilty of financial offences and so were Sunderland's players and directors (they were reinstated after High Court actions reversed an FA commission's finding on legal technicalities).

In contrast with the sanctimonious outcries against drugs in sport, which can at times be justified by *bona fide* medical treatment, the cult of violence in all contact sports—soccer, rugby and ice hockey— more often does not affect the offender or his club though his victim is permanently incapacitated.

There is no greater example than in the 1966 World Cup when Pele, the Brazilian, was brutally fouled on the pitch by Bulgarian and Portuguese opponents whom he later identified in his book, *My Life and the Beautiful Game* (1977). No sanction was applied against them by the game's authorities or the police.

Until the authorities are willing to prosecute or victims are willing to sue, violence will remain a shocking example to younger generations in all sporting disciplines.

EDWARD GRAYSON
September 24, 1997   London WC2

∼

Missing natives

SIR—Chelsea versus Bratislava (Sport, Oct. 3). Which was the English side? All but two of the names were alien and they could well have been playing for Bratislava.

Is it not time to accept that the naming of British clubs geographically is meaningless? I remember when only Yorkshiremen could play cricket for Yorkshire, but this convention has descended into lunacy.

Can nine Mexicans, a Swede and a Cockney truly represent the native population of West Bromwich? I exaggerate, of course. Should we take the Gladiators as an awful example, and find unpleasant titles for our teams? Slav Slaughterers, South American Assassins?

DAVID REES

October 4, 1997   Sunbury-on-Thames, Berks

Nibble quibble

SIR—As a former Welsh International rugby front row forward and having played against all the major rugby union countries of the world, I take exception to Mr Williams's comments (July 2).

The implication is that Welsh front row forwards are ignorant thugs. I cannot remember one such incident of ear biting. The only person to nibble my ear is my wife—and that not often enough!

BRYN MEREDITH

July 15, 1997   Usk, Monmouthshire

When a lady's place is at the tee

SIR—My sympathies go out to that band of golfers, mainly retired colonels and brigadiers living by the seaside, who refer to our ancient game as 'goff'; goff stands for everything they believe in: honesty, integrity, playing the game by the rules and accepting defeat graciously. Imagine their horror at the story of Mrs Goff (report, Feb. 27), the lady expelled from Shrewsbury club, who then asked for reinstatement and for the matter to be decided by a county court judge.

In golf, women know their place and enjoy a particular reputation. The case of Mrs Goff has, sadly, done us little good. One report suggested she wore skimpy shorts, when, of course, all women golfers are meant to wear tweeds, brogues and yellow ankle socks. Another suggested she cheated. How dare she! All women golfers are known to be obsessed by the rules. It is, after all, the prerogative of the men to drop a spare ball down those oh-so-baggy golf trousers.

Other stories suggested Mrs Goff to be a good player when, realistically, all men know that no such animal as a good woman golfer exists. Women golfers, one must remember, are tolerated in many golf clubs purely to give those elderly gentlemen retired from the game of goff some new challenge in life, something to grumble about to keep their wits alert.

Perhaps for the non-golfer, I can give an example: in 1969, when I joined the Professional Golfers Association, I discovered that 'lady members shall have the same rights and privileges as men, save they may not play in tournaments, attend meetings or vote.' The remaining right or privilege seemed to be that of wearing the Association's tie. It was a sad day for golf when the Sex Discrimination Act of 1975 forced a change in this traditional approach.

This year, in June, women golfers enjoy another piece of golfing tradition. The British Curtis Cup team defends the trophy against the Americans, the venue, once again, being one of those clubs where members usually acknowledge women golfers. At Royal St George's there are no lady members and no ladies' tees. If you are allowed out on the course, tradition has it that you let the men through and they, quite likely, respond by ignoring you and uttering, 'Isn't it nice to have the course to ourselves today?'

There, Mrs Goff can be treated equal to all other women golfers in the country. Perhaps if she does venture to Royal St George's to watch the Curtis Cup, she will begin to understand the traditions of the game we love and respect. Her name, after all, is synonymous with the game itself.

VIVIEN SAUNDERS
March 1, 1988   St Neots, Cambs

Off the track

SIR—It has been known for years that black runners and jumpers are better than whites (report, Dec. 11), but some balance should be drawn. World and Olympic medal tables confirm that whites, especially from Russia and east Europe, are the better weightlifters and swimmers. Afro-Americans are not supermen.

WILLIAM FORGE
London W6

SIR—Whites can't run? Hmm . . .

SEBASTIAN COE
December 13, 1997 London SW1

Sebastian Coe, the former Conservative MP, won the 1,500 metres track event at the 1980 and 1984 Olympics.

Advantages of global Games

SIR—After the appalling bomb explosion at the Atlanta Olympics, may I add my support to Philip Howells's idea (letter, July 25) to break up the Games into various events around the world.

As he rightly points out, by far the highest proportion of spectators of the Games are not those in the stands, but rather those who watch the events on television. Splitting up the events would reduce the Roman circus atmosphere of the Games and make them a less attractive target for terrorists and their ilk.

Many of the Olympic sports do not draw much public attention in the years between the Games, which means that much false enthusiasm is created in the weeks immediately preceding these events every four years. This generates crowds more interested in the spectacle and its competitive nationalism—raw jingoism in many cases—rather than in the sports and the sportsmanship which is supposed to be the point of it all.

What is also rarely mentioned is that the Games are not the joyous occasions so often depicted in the media—at least not for the athletes. When I was a junior publicist at the 1976 Montreal Games I was struck by the general gloom in the Olympic Village itself.

Before the event all were too keyed up to be cheerful; afterwards, while television cameras focused on winners, the majority were losers, and it was they who dictated the mood pervading the entire Village.

The sooner the International Olympic Committee sees the sense in proposals such as Mr Howells's, the safer and better the Games will be.

CHRISTY McCORMICK

July 29, 1996   Montreal

~

Fair rules of bullfighting

SIR—As the only English *matador de toros*, I cannot agree with the gored Vicki Moore's obsessive desire to ban bullfighting (report, June 27). But I have admired her commitment when we have met, and I share her dislike of some of the activities involving bulls.

I disagree, for example, with the habit of lighting rags on a bull's horns in order to make him charge around the streets with head held high: it sometimes results in the bull's head being singed.

I also dislike the practice of tying a fighting bull to a stake so that individuals from the safety of a balcony can use a blowpipe to aim darts at its hide. This activity is favoured by such villages as Coria, where Vicki was attacked; it is debased because participants incur no physical risk.

Such activities are not permitted in the bullring. Bullfighting is governed by an act of the Cortes. When in the ring I always knew that there were strict rules aimed at protecting the bull; he would be left completely free in his movements while I was totally unarmed.

Nevertheless, while I do not disguise my feelings about the unregulated practices in remote Spanish villages, I am conscious that my disapproval stems from my English background. I would hold back from attempting to impose my views on anyone from the cultural background of another country.

These feelings are just those at the heart of the present exasperation which so many British people feel about the ever encroaching European bureaucracy. The only way peoples can hope to get along is if they understand those cultural influences which cause others to behave in ways that can seem disagreeable.

If people do not like bullfighting they are quite free to attempt to get the law changed in a democratic way, by lobbying MPs in the Cortes.

FRANK EVANS

June 29, 1995   Eccles, Manchester

A bait to catch fishermen

SIR—There is an oft-told tale of an inveterate angler who, having died, believed that he was truly in Paradise when, on his first day's fishing there in a heavenly stream, he caught a fat trout with every cast. When this happened on three consecutive days he realised his true predicament—he was in Hell.

The essence of angling is expectation, which is rooted in the uncertainty that a fish may or may not oblige. Any innovation which pushes the balance too far in the angler's favour deprives the art not only of its fairness and the delicate skills needed for success, but of its charm.

Few anglers are likely to deprive themselves of a technological advance which increases the chance of success to a reasonable degree.

Recent examples now in standard use are strong nylon in replacement of weak silkworm gut, lightweight carbon rods instead of cane, and reels with slipping clutches reducing the risk of breakage. Sportsmen who are honest with themselves will admit, however, that such innovations have already tilted the odds so heavily against the fish that further artificial aids need careful watching—especially in the case of trout, which, being artificially bred on farms, are readier takers than their old wild counterparts. Now we face the marketing of an American concoction, Gotta Bite, said to send fish into such a frenzy of feeding that it would deprive fishing of all its uncertainty and magic (report, July 14).

Most sportsmen would be unlikely to descend to such an admission of defeat but some greedy anglers might, forcing fishing clubs and river authorities to ban it. Would overly successful anglers then find themselves facing riverside dope tests by water bailiffs? A dreadful prospect, but after a lifetime trying to understand what makes fish feed I doubt that our sport is at serious risk.

Gotta Bite seems to be on a par with the recent, equally 'scientific' theory that women are prone to catch large salmon because, unconsciously, they waft their sex hormones into the water inducing the fish to bite. What is not explained is how they manage to do this when encased up to the armpits in rubber waders. Similarly with Gotta Bite, a colourless, odourless and soluble liquid, how is it supposed to stay on the bait or fly in running water?

I suspect it is likely to catch more fishermen than fish and should not catch any true anglers at all.

CHAPMAN PINCHER
July 16, 1992   Kintbury, Berks

~

Evenings spent playing quoits in Eden

SIR—In answer to David Roberts's inquiry about the game of quoits (letter, Feb. 16), it is still played enthusiastically in this part of the Eden Valley, Cumbria.

On summer evenings the sounds come floating across village greens: the dull thump as a metal ring misses and settles in the sand bed, the sharp clank as a ring hits its target and falls over the metal peg set up in the centre of the bed, then a satisfied grunt from the successful team and perhaps a vexed sigh from the opposition.

The retired men are the chief players as they have more time, but later in the season, after the hay is safely brought in, the younger men and older boys have time to join in.

One of the main social events of the summer in this area is the Band of Hope Demonstration, on a Saturday in June at Appleby. Having dispensed with the nominally important business of a march with temperance banners and the presentation of Scripture Knowledge prizes to the children, and served out the picnic tea, the mothers and grandmothers slump gladly back in deck chairs to listen to the band, and keep an ear cocked for the progress of their menfolk at quoits.

(Mrs) CHRISTINE AKRIGG
February 26, 1991   Kirkby Stephen, Cumbria

~

True sportsman

SIR—Your correspondence on sporting behaviour recalled this definition of a sportsman that appeared in my local cricket club's fixture card in the Fifties and Sixties:

> *Plays the game for the game's sake*
> *Plays for his side and not himself*

Is a good winner and a good loser
Is modest in victory and generous in defeat
Accepts all decisions in a proper spirit
Is chivalrous towards a defeated opponent
Is unselfish and always ready to
help others to become proficient.

How times appear to have changed.

DEREK FORD
Tadworth, Surrey

April 8, 1997

THREATENED HOSTELRIES

Belloc's warning

SIR—Your sorry depiction of the English pub (article, March 11) brings to mind Hilaire Belloc's dread prophecy—'When you have lost your Inns, drown your empty selves, for you will have lost the last of England'—with chilling immediacy.

W. RAYMOND PARKES
March 16, 1996   Leatherhead, Surrey

Right to retain name

SIR—Your leading article (July 18) appears to have misunderstood my campaign and the Conservative principles upon which it is based.

The names of public houses frequently record important, if local, historical events, and give their names to small local areas. It is both wrong that centuries of community heritage can be erased at the stroke of a marketing-man's pen, and unfortunate that many local residents feel embarrassed or alienated by the contrived names adopted, particularly by theme pubs.

We should remember that the free market is our tool, not our master, and that society has every right to control that market to ensure that it conserves from the past that which is worth preserving, and changes that which needs improving. Contrary to the thrust of your argument, the trend towards theme pubs is equally the result of past changes in public policy and legislation as much as a response to spontaneous consumer demand.

What I have proposed is not a ban on changes or excessive regulation, merely a minor amendment to the existing regulatory regime—namely that the name of a public house should be part of the licence conditions and should be subject to change only with the approval of the local planning authority. It is otherwise a bizarre anomaly that the size, scale and luminosity of a sign come within the planning regime, but that the name which it displays, and which could cause greater offence, does not.

NICHOLAS WINTERTON, MP (Con)
Macclesfield, Ches

SIR—I strongly object to your criticism of Mr Winterton, who declared that it was an outrage that the Bull's Head, our town's 200-year-old pub, was to be renamed the Pig and Truffle. The issue has been raised twice at borough planning committee meetings, and all shades of political opinion opposed the idea.

The Bull's Head has a long tradition, being in the centre of Macclesfield, and was the start of the old coaching service to London. We have no desire whatsoever to have the name changed.

Cllr H. R. HARRISON
July 19, 1996   Mayor, Macclesfield, Ches

～

Ducal defeat

SIR—The coincidence of your articles (July 18) on the controversy over the re-naming of public houses and on the suggestion that Wellington's statue might be removed from Aldershot and placed in Trafalgar Square prompt me to the following.

In this locality lies a public house which has always borne the name Lord Wellington. Not long ago, when driving past, I saw to my outraged disbelief that the name had been changed to The Moody Cow.

I entered the pub in a state of high indignation to find it full of male drinkers, one of whom I soon ascertained was a local. I asked him why on earth the landlord (it is a free house) had changed the name from that of a national hero of such historical importance to something of such risible insignificance.

He looked at me steadily for a moment and replied: 'The Iron

Duke may have kept the Frogs out of England, but he'd never have succeeded so well in keeping women out of this pub.'

HUGH PIERSON
Hereford

July 22, 1996

Village symbols

SIR—Your leading article treating with contempt Mr Winterton's proposal to restrict the change of public house names (July 18) was disappointing.

The inn and the church have proved, for not entirely dissimilar reasons, to be the most enduring buildings of English towns and villages. They have a long history and frequently the name is part of that history. It is possible that, in a few cases, buildings serving the same purpose have stood on the same site since Roman times.

There were several Chequers taverns in Pompeii: the sign of the Cock has survived from the Roman empire, as may have other ancient signs such as the Bull, the Angel and the Crooked Billet. I doubt whether the Floozy and Firkin will last so well.

CHRISTOPHER EADIE
London N21

SIR—Nicholas Winterton (letter, July 19) perhaps has no need to worry about the change in the pub name. We have a pub that is now known locally as 'The Pheasant as it used to be'.

SUSAN MAXWELL
Tring, Herts

July 23, 1996

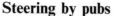

Steering by pubs

SIR—None of your correspondents has yet mentioned the importance of pub names as an essential aid to navigation.

I recently stopped in Frant Road, Tunbridge Wells, and was asked the way to Lamberhurst. Couldn't have been easier: left at the Bull;

over the crossroads; straight on past the Brecknock Arms; past the Elephant's Head; turn left at the Swan and you're there.

Change the names and a whole host of well-known and long-established landmarks disappear.

GODFREY BROWN
Southborough, Kent

July 30, 1996

SOME QUICK ONES

Step up, Sheikh Pir

SIR—It has been my pet joke for the past several years—and may have been overheard by Colonel Gaddafi (report, Aug. 4)—that Shakespeare was an Indian named Sheikh Pir.

India had and still has much closer relations with the English than have the Arabs. It is therefore more convincing that he was Sheikh Pir from India. We do have sheikhs in India, though it is likely that they may have originated in Arab areas and migrated to the sub-continent. When I was at school in India, I remember that our English teacher, born a Hindu, worshipped Shakespeare's picture and every morning offered a rose.

August 11, 1989

Y. S. NORAT
Nuneaton, Warwicks

~

Threat from East

SIR—Of course it was not 'Sheikh Speare' who wrote the plays, but the much more appropriately named 'Bey Con!'

August 18, 1989

GWEN MARTIN
Altea, Spain

~

French bard

SIR—Sheik Zubavr, Sheik Pir, Mah Lo, Bey Con, staff and nonsense. Has everyone forgotten the man whom Freud long thought responsible for my collateral ancestor's plays—namely the Frenchman, Jacques Pierre?

August 19, 1989

NICHOLAS SHAKESPEARE
London W10

~

Well translated bard

SIR—Sixty years ago while we sat on a lawn in Khartoum drinking tea and talking in Arabic, my brother proffered the opinion that, of course, Shakespeare was really Sheikh Zubeir, who was an erudite recluse from Taif.

My brother added (generously, I thought): 'But we must hand it to the British; they made a very good translation of it.'

G. KFOURI

August 23, 1989   Sudbury, Suflolk

The last Spike?

SIR—In response to a letter, I have received an acknowledgment card from your obituaries editor. I don't understand. Please tell me if I am dead; if I am not, let me know and I will take the shroud off.

SPIKE MILLIGAN

April 2, 1990   London W2

Changing station

SIR—There are two noticeboards at the entrance to Mortlake cemetery; one reads 'Crematorium' and the other 'Re-cycling Dept.'

HARRY LOVELOCK

January 20, 1990   London W4

Hellenic hit?

SIR—Far from being dark and voluptuous, claims Hadrian Jeffs (letter, Oct. 8), Cleopatra was 'flat-chested, broken-nosed and blonde'.

How does he know? Is it a case, to paraphrase a Forties song, of 'My mamma done Ptolemy'?

GILES WESTON

October 10, 1991   London SE22

Let dons delight . . .

SIR—The best-known story about Parson's Pleasure, the dons'
bathing pool at Oxford, must have been 50 years old when Maurice
Bowra was born (report, Jan. 31).

A punt full of ladies passed accidentally through Parson's Pleasure
when a party of Balliol dons were bathing there in a state of nature.

All the dons wrapped their towels round their middles but one,
Paravicini, who wrapped his round his head, hoping thus to avoid
recognition.

As the punt drifted away, one of the ladies is alleged to have
remarked: 'I think that must be Mr Paravicini—he is the only *red-
haired* don in Balliol.'

ANTHONY POWELL
February 5, 1992   Frome, Somerset

~

The wisdom of Paxman

SIR—Auberon Waugh's references to the Jewishness or otherwise of Jeremy Paxman (Way of the World, July 19) has confused
an already confusing issue, which I would therefore like to
clarify.

Once Jews came to believe that the God of Israel was himself an
Israelite they acquired a tendency—from which I suffer myself—to
presume that anyone of any eminence at all is Jewish, unless he or
she can show definitive proof to the contrary.

I don't know what steps Mr Paxman has taken in that direction,
but in a recent *Evening Standard* article he did not include a full
frontal exposure, or, indeed, an exposure of any sort. All he could
say was: 'I don't know.'

The evidence against or for him—depending on which way one
looks at it—is, on the other hand, fairly conclusive.

First, he is pushy, abrasive, assertive, even aggressive and, as Sir
Peregrine Worsthorne might have put it in *The Sunday Telegraph*
(July 18), he is as rude as a rabbi. Secondly, he confesses to a Church
of England upbringing.

Now who, these days, would claim to be brought up in a
church unless he had something to hide? The very fact that he is

not prepared to come clean on the matter and admit frankly and openly that he is a Jew may in itself be a proof that he is Jewish.

Thirdly, there is Paxman's long nose, black wavy hair and slightly semitic appearance.

Fourthly, he reads the *Jewish Chronicle*.

And finally there is the matter of his name. The first part is Latin, the second part Yiddish, and the Yiddish for *Pax* is *Sholem* so that his name could originally have been Sholeman or Solomon. On the other hand it could have been Suleyman, which is, of course, Arab. Therein may lie the solution to the mystery.

No wonder the poor chap is coy about his origins.

CHAIM BERMANT

July 23, 1993   London, NW5

~

How to cry for Greece, Dimitra

SIR—The Nineties certainly need a woman at the centre of power— to tell the men what to do with it. However, if Dimitra Papandreou ends up trying to emulate Evita Peron (report, Oct. 15), she will find that she has a hard act to follow.

I can offer her some guidelines. First, Mrs Papandreou has both the necessary sultry looks and the right name: three ringing syllables, which her followers can chant: 'Di-Mi-tra, Di-Mi-tra.' But she will have to learn to address the masses.

Evita, the second Mrs Peron, was a successful radio and film actress before she met the then Colonel Peron in 1944. So she entered government two years later well prepared. While Mrs Papandreou III has been an air hostess, experience of speaking on an in-flight address system to a trussed-up audience is not the same as addressing a crowd filling the square below.

It is important, therefore, that she sticks to Evita's example, not that of the third Mrs Peron, 'Isabelita', a dancer who met her husband in a Panama nightclub. On Peron's death Isabelita was President of Argentina for nearly two years before the army removed her.

She had the unfortunate habit, when trying to address a crowd like Evita, of shrieking as if she had stepped into something awful.

So while Mrs Papandreou III clearly has the talent for looking decorative in public places (besides her elderly husband), she should take elocution lessons.

Next, she must learn a list of short, sharp remarks about the wealth of the upper classes and the oppression of the poor. That should send the Establishment crawling up the curtains or running to open Swiss bank accounts and considerably enhance her popularity.

Finally, she must send talent scouts to the West End to recruit somebody who will write *Dimitra, the Opera*.

ANDREW GRAHAM-YOOLL
London NW11

First woman

SIR—Before there was a midwife (letter, Oct. 16) there was a mother. Surely, in this enlightened age you would not disagree that motherhood is the oldest profession.

MEGAN REID
October 18, 1993   London NW10

~

End of a name

SIR—I enjoyed an American newspaper advertisement: 'Tombstone for sale—cheap. Will suit somebody by the name of Robinson.'

C. B. EVANS
July 29, 1994   Bristol

~

Warning epitaph

SIR—J.V. Ayre (letter, July 27) reminds me of a memorable grave stone that tells it all with brevity:

> *Here lies the body of Albert Dunn*
> *He raced to the crossing,*
> *But the engine won.*

B. M. LOUGHLIN
August 3, 1994   Leicester

~

Blood up

SIR—Charles Laurence got my age wrong (Undead Alive and Well and Living in Manhattan, Nov. 7).

It is all right for vampires to be more than 2,000 years old but, as a woman, I object strongly to being given an extra decade and placed in my sixties. No way!

Otherwise, 'Fangs for the mammaries,' as they say in outer Transylvania.

INGRID PITT
November 9, 1994 Richmond, Surrey

Bad joke

SIR—I can identify the culprit who made off with Bob Monkhouse's collection of jokes (report, July 31).

It can only be the Thief of Badgags.

STEPHEN BAKER
August 1, 1995 Blackpool

Irish canon

SIR—Your selection of Irish jokes (May 10) was missing one old favourite, to be sure:

'Why are Irish jokes so simple?'

'Begorrah, it's so the English can understand them!'

CONOR PERRY
May 16, 1996 Dublin

Literary lapses

SIR—There is a different slant on the Irish joke in the tale about the foreman interviewing an Irishman for a labouring job on a building site:

'Do you know the difference between "joist" and "girder"?'

'Indeed I do. Joyce wrote *Ulysses*, and Goethe wrote *Faust*.'

PETER PETTS
May 21, 1996 Ely, Cambs

Sound logic

SIR—Could there be a happier illustration of 'Irish logic' (letter, May 22) than the tale to be found in *The History of English?*

The story is told of the railway station at Ballyhough. It had two clocks, which disagreed by some six minutes.

When an irate traveller asked a porter what was the use of having two clocks if they didn't tell the same time, the porter replied: 'And what would we be wanting with two clocks if they told the same time?'

Gen Sir IAN GOURLAY

May 23, 1996   London SE10

Pick of them all

SIR—Surely the quintessence of the Irish joke is as follows: Show three shovels to an Irish navvy and ask him to take his pick.

DAVID GOULD

May 25, 1996   Woodchester, Glos

INDEX

The names of letter-writers and the page references of their contributions, are in bold face.

372 *Index*